Tanzania Wildlif

MW00387788

Written and compiled by
Diane and Peter Swan

Diane & Peter Swan, 2021
Published by Meserani Publishing
www.meseraniproject.co.uk

A CIP catalogue record for this book is available from the British Library.
ISBN 978-0-9575134-1-9

Front cover image: A small herd of elephants walking straight towards us in Tarangire National Park.

Back cover image: Diane and Peter in the Ngorongoro Crater.

Dedicated to the memory of our dear friend Berry Bale, co-owner of Meserani Snakepark, Arusha, Tanzania, affectionately known to everyone as BJ.

We have travelled the world, and have been fortunate to have encountered so many wonderful people. Without doubt, BJ was the most amazing man we have ever met. He was a legend who touched on so many people's lives, always for the good. His memory lives on.

Rest in Peace dear friend.

Contents

FOREWORD

There is something about Tanzania. It has a magnetic allure to its exotic life and landscapes like nowhere else on Earth and for many of us this is epitomised by the notion of a *safari*. The word derives from Arabic and means "to travel overland on a hunting expedition" and up until recently it was perfectly applied, although thankfully now most of us are hunting with cameras and it is no longer a preserve of the privileged few. Thus if we are lucky we find ourselves holidaying in a foreign land in search of an unfamiliar fauna, and while there is no mistaking a giraffe or a zebra or a lion, there are many less known species to confound and confuse you, particularly the plethora of antelopes!

This guide provides the perfect introduction to the most frequently encountered creatures and supplements everything about their behaviour and ecologies that you have forgotten from your armchair TV safaris, with a useful overview of their biology, and a refreshing focus on the threats being faced by so many endangered species. It's accessible, easy to use, concise and has plenty of little nuggets of interest and importance. For instance, how do you tell a male from a female giraffe? Well, it's down to their *ossicones*, or horns, the males being bald on account of them being worn down when fighting. Imagine how good you would feel beating the guide to that little gem when one of your party asks the question!

But there is one frequently overlooked paradox when it comes to going on a safari, and that is that you will see and enjoy far more than most Tanzanians ever will. Only a tiny percentage of Tanzanian children ever see lions or giraffes, and worse, many live in a poverty we cannot imagine. The proceeds from the sale of this book will help address this by supporting the Meserani Project, based in a remote area of Tanzania. The charity has provided primary education for all pupils in the area, and sponsors many students through A' Levels and university. The target now is to build a secondary school, and the work will be overseen by trustees of The Meserani Project. I've witnessed the poverty of Africa myself, I've seen and smelled it, had a brief taste of utter desperation, and that's why I am so keen to support the project.

So take this book on safari, learn a lot about the exciting animals you find and be comforted by the fact that as well as taking great memories home from Tanzania you are putting a little back too, a little that will mean a lot to people with next to nothing.

Chris Packham
BBC Wildlife Presenter

6

Introduction

We are two experienced independent travellers who have developed a passion for Tanzania since our first visit in 2004, when we first fell in love with Africa. The wildlife, the landscapes and the people somehow get into your blood, and will not let you go. We have derived great pleasure from sharing our experiences with a wide audience, whether it be friends and family, or groups of students and adults that we have led on expeditions throughout Tanzania.

We have been privileged and fortunate to have spent so much of our time observing Tanzania's iconic wildlife at close quarters, we have been honoured to meet and share precious time with the local indigenous people and to observe the stunning, breathtaking landscapes, constantly changing throughout the seasons. Travelling through the Ngorongoro Conservation Area to the Serengeti you feel as though time has stood still. Much of what you see has probably not changed for hundreds of years. The peace, the tranquillity, being at one with nature, surrounded by all of the world's natural beauty is something you cannot put a price on. It is very surreal. Sitting quietly and motionless in your vehicle it is sheer magic, turn off the engine and observe what is going on around you. The stunningly beautiful blue skies, or the skies full of storm clouds, the wind rustling through the long grasses, the endless plains that seem to go on for ever, interrupted only by the iconic kopjes. The alarm call from a baboon, the braying of the zebra, the resonating male lion's call advertising his presence, the cackling of the hyena, and the barking of the male impala desperately rounding up the females are all familiar sounds. We would like to make it clear to you right at the outset that this is not a travel guide to Tanzania - there are plenty of these in existence, many of them are excellent, and we would not wish to compete with them. However, it would be remiss of us not to provide you with some 'insider tips' based on our own travelling experiences, and offering insights into opportunities available to travellers in Tanzania that may not be covered in the traditional travel guides - see the *Insider Tips* section near the end of the book.

The idea behind this book came to us one morning in Tarangire National Park. It was August 2008, and we were sat in our hired Landrover enjoying the peace and tranquility of the African bush, and sharing the lives of a small herd of elephants as they searched for water in the virtually dry river bed. It was an amazing experience just

listening to nothing else but the sounds they were making, and feeling extremely privileged to be the only people in the world who were sharing their personal time with them. As we watched their behaviour, and shared some of their peace and tranquillity, what suddenly hit us was the realisation that we did not actually understand the dynamics of elephant behaviour and the structure of the family unit. We felt that this experience we were sharing with them would have been so much more meaningful if we had some background knowledge on their diet, habitat and communication. In the days that followed, and as we began to share more and more quality time with the wildlife of Tanzania, the idea behind this book began to take shape.

This book provides us with the opportunity to reach an even wider audience. Moreover, what we hope our book provides you with is something that we have found missing throughout all our visits to the game parks and reserves of Tanzania, quite frustratingly so - and that is a guide that makes your animal sightings more meaningful and authentic, and makes your experiences more complete and wholesome rather than just a fleeting visual experience.

We have included what we believe to be the thirty-eight most popular animals to be found in Tanzania, nine birds, and eight interesting reptiles you may encounter. There is an entire chapter devoted to each, with an abundance of interesting and useful facts such as identification, behaviour, communication, predators and threats to survival. Physiology, habitat, location, diet and reproduction are also covered in a concise and easy-to-read style. Full colour photographs and illustrations are included in every chapter to help you with identification, and we believe it is worth mentioning that these are 'real' photographs, in that they were taken by us while on safari in Tanzania. As such they are typical of the kind of photograph that you yourself are capable of taking. Illustrations have been used where it helps identification, and where we were not able to take worthwhile pictures of certain rare species. All illustrations in this book have been drawn by co-author Diane.

Further chapters cover national parks and game reserves, landscapes, climate and migration, and there are anecdotal notes within many chapters giving more information to further enhance your safari experience. Our invaluable *Insider Tips* deserve a whole chapter to themselves, and we hope very much that you will find something here that will provide as much pleasure and inner satisfaction as we ourselves have experienced throughout our travels.

When researching material for the book what came to light is that a lot of the wildlife we have written about now faces extinction in the not too distant future. It is unbelievable how things have changed since we first visited Tanzania. Wildlife is threatened by loss of habitat, the effects of global warming and the illegal trade in wildlife, whether this be for their tusks and hides, for tribal medicine or simply to satisfy the trophy hunters. It has been quite heart wrenching writing the book and gradually realising that the future of these beautiful creatures is uncertain. They have as much right as us to exist on planet Earth.

As co-authors we both agreed from the very start that all money generated by sales of this book would be donated to The Meserani Project, a charity based in North Yorkshire and Teesside, U.K., run by a small group of volunteers, and with the sole aim of changing the lives of young people in the remote district of Meserani, Tanzania. The project has direct links with nine schools, and offers support and resources for these schools. Four primary schools have already been rebuilt, furnished and equipped, and almost 300 young people from Meserani have been funded to attend secondary school, further education and university. On behalf of all the young people who have benefited from the Meserani Project, we thank you for buying this book - your money has been well spent!

Africa

Africa is a continent not a country. Africa, the Garden of Eden, the cradle of mankind, is where the first human beings evolved and appeared on the Earth approximately 300,000 years ago. Remains dating back 300,000 years have been discovered at Jebel Irhoud, Morocco (June, 2017) and remains dating back 200,000 years have been discovered at Omo, Kibish, Ethiopia. The first modern humans began their migration out of Africa

approximately 70,000-100,000 years ago, and we are all connected in a 10,000-15,000 long chain to them.

Africa is the second largest continent on the planet covering 30.2 million square kilometres. Straddling the equator it stretches from the northern temperate zone (latitude 37.21N) to the southern temperate zone (latitude 34.51'15'S). It is the most tropical and hottest of all the continents and the second driest. The climatic zones in Africa are equatorial/tropical, mediterranean, desert, steppe and savannah.

Occupying six per cent of the earth's total surface area and twenty per cent of the land area, this is one enormous, diverse continent, environmentally, climatically, ecologically, archaeologically, historically and culturally.

It is home to 1.2 billion people (2016) and is the second most populous continent on the planet, accounting for 16% of the world's population. It is predicted that by 2030 the population of Africa will grow to 1.6 billion and will account for 19% of the world's population.

It is a continent that is rich in natural resources, yet it continues to remain as the world's poorest and most underdeveloped continent. Mineral resources include oil, gas, copper, coal, diamonds, gold, oil, platinum, uranium and aluminium, and agricultural resources include tea, coffee, fruit, timber, palm oil and wine. Poverty is widespread. It is the only continent where the average life expectancy is below 60. High levels of illiteracy (40% of all adults in Africa are illiterate), food insecurity, malnutrition, lack of investment in agriculture, climate change, ongoing regional conflicts, lack of access to health care facilities, high levels of communicable diseases, lack of access to clean water supplies, poor sanitation and infrastructure all contribute to the vicious, never ending cycle of poverty that traps the indigenous populations.

Tourism is a huge income generator, and tourists visit the African continent for many reasons. It is rich culturally, archeologically, historically and is steeped in tribal traditions. Its scenery, both inland and on the coast, is diverse and stunning. It is a place to go to if you seek adventure, and of course, it is the place to go to on safari to observe its iconic, majestic wildlife at close quarters.

Trivia

◆Prince Henry (1394-1460) a Portugese explorer and navigator was the first European to explore Africa.

◆Africa is the most vulnerable continent affected by global warming.

◆Africa is the continent with the shortest coastline.

◆Before Africa was colonised it was made up of 10,000 different states and groups. Each had their own language and customs.

◆Between 1000-2000 languages are spoken in Africa.

◆The driest place in Africa is the Sahara.

◆The largest country in Africa is Algeria.

♦The largest city in Africa is Lagos, Nigeria.

♦There are more pyramids in Sudan than in Egypt. There are 225 pyramids in the Sudan and between 118-138 pyramids in Egypt.

♦Timbuktu, Mali, is home to one of the world's oldest universities. Sokore University was established in the twelfth century by the erudite chief judge of Timbuktu. By the 12th century the university had a student population of 25,000.

♦Nigeria is the most populated country in Africa, with 206 million inhabitants.

♦Africa's biggest island is Madagascar.

♦Fish River Canyon in Namibia is the largest canyon in Africa and the second largest canyon in the world. It is 160km long, up to 27km wide and 550m deep.

♦The Serengeti, Tanzania, covers an area of 30,000 square kilometres and is where the world's largest migration of mammals takes place, involving 750,000 zebras and 1.2 million wildebeest. Cape buffalo do not migrate because of their dependency on water.

♦The Rift Valley was formed 20-30 million years ago when the earth's crust began to split. It is more than 6,000km long and extends from the Beqaa Valley in the Lebanon, Asia, to Mozambique in Africa.

♦The Nile is the longest river in the world, and is 6650km long. It has two main tributaries, the White Nile and the Blue Nile. The true source of the Nile is believed to be the Kagera River and its tributary the Ruvubu. The headwaters are located in Burundi.

♦The largest desert is the Sahara, and is almost the same size as the USA. It covers an area of 9,200,000 square kilometres.

♦Lake Victoria (bordered by Uganda, Tanzania and Kenya) is the world's second largest freshwater lake. It covers an area of 68,800 square kilometres and is 337km long.

♦Mount Kilimanjaro, Tanzania, is 5895m high and is the highest mountain in Africa.

♦The Ngorongoro Crater, Tanzania, is the world's largest unbroken caldera. The crater was formed two to three million years ago when a volcano erupted and subsequently collapsed in on itself. It is 19km in diameter and has walls that are 600m high, which actively discourages animals from migrating. It is home to 25,000-30,000 animals.

♦Victoria Falls in Zambia is one of the "seven wonders of the world" and is also the largest waterfall in the world. It is 1,708m wide and 108m high.

♦Hippopotamuses kill more people in Africa than lions and crocodiles.

♦94% of all cases of malaria occur in Africa (2019).

♦3,000 children a day die from malaria.

♦41% of children in Africa aged between 5-10 years old are involved in child labour.

♦The world's top 10 poorest countries are in Africa (2020).

♦It is projected that the world's global poor will become more concentrated in Africa.

National Parks, National Game Reserves, Forest Nature Reserves, Private Conservancies, Wildlife Sanctuaries in Tanzania.

National Parks

National parks are acknowledged as large areas of land of outstanding natural beauty, and usually contain a wide variety of wild animals and birds that are living in their natural habitat. Some are renowned specifically for their flora and geographical features, it is therefore worthwhile doing your homework beforehand if you think you are going on a safari to observe wildlife, otherwise you may be disappointed. National parks are  protected by the government, and the public are allowed to visit them for a fee, usually quoted and paid for in US dollars. Residents' park entry fees are usually at a lower rate and are paid in the local currency.

Human habitation is strictly forbidden in national parks. Boundaries of national parks are not normally fenced so the animals are free to come and go as they please. While in the park the animals are protected, but once they leave the park they are fair game for poachers or locals.

In Tanzania the national parks are maintained and administered by the Tanzanian National Park Authority (TANAPA) - www.tanzaniaparks.gov.tz The National Wildlife Game Reserves are a wildlife division of the Ministry of National Resources and Tourism. Nearly 25% of land in Tanzania is protected by national parks, game/hunting reserves and controlled zones.

National Game Reserves

National game reserves are usually found in close proximity to national parks. The land may be used for other purposes such as human habitation and grazing of domestic livestock.

Forest Nature Reserves

The forests of Tanzania are important for biodiversity conservation in Africa. Forest Nature Reserves are state owned and managed by the Tanzania Forest Service Agency, and were established to enhance the management and conservation of forests. No extraction of timber or animals is permitted in Forest Nature Reserves, and activities are restricted to research, education, and nature based tourism.

Private Conservancies

Private conservancies are privately owned and funded, and are able to invest and work intensively on wildlife conservation projects, which may involve local communities.

Wildlife Sanctuaries

Wildlife Sanctuaries are areas that have been set aside by the government or private bodies to protect wildlife. Hunting, shooting and fishing is forbidden.

Ngorongoro Conservation Area

The Ngorongoro Conservation Area is administered by the Ngorongoro Conservation Area Authority - www.ncaa.gov.tz

The Ngorongoro Crater is the world's largest unbroken and un-flooded caldera, and a UNESCO World Heritage Site. The crater was formed two to three million years ago when a volcano erupted and subsequently collapsed in on itself. It is 19km in diameter and has walls that are 600m high, which actively discourages animals from migrating. It is home to 25,000-30,000 animals.

The Maasai are allowed to graze their cattle within the crater, but must enter and leave each day.

Endangered Animals

Sub-Saharan Africa is recognised as a world-class destination for viewing a rich array of wildlife at close quarters, and Tanzania is one of the most popular countries in this respect. This is where the largest mammals on the planet can be found - but also the most endangered. Ninety-nine per cent of threatened species are at risk because of human activities. The principal causes of the reduction in number of wildlife species are: the effects of climate change, loss of and destruction of habitat, loss of food and water, pollution, loss of genetic diversity, disease, degradation, invasive species (plant and wildlife), deforestation, poaching, hunting and prey depletion.

Sudan

To go on safari and view these iconic, majestic animals in their natural surroundings is a privilege, it is an awesome experience, but at the same time it is tinged with the greatest of sadness as you are viewing animals at close quarters that are endangered and on the brink of extinction. For some species there is no going back - Sudan, the last male Northern White Rhino, died at Ol Pejeta Conservancy, Kenya, on 19 March 2018, and now only two elderly females remain. The northern white rhino has existed for millions of years and is now functionally extinct.

Habitat Loss and Environmental Destruction

Natural wildlife habitats are where the animals live. It is their home. It is where they find shelter, food and water, and where they raise their young. Habitat loss, alongside degradation, is the main threat to the vast majority of species living in Tanzania. Habitat destruction is defined as the process whereby the natural habitat is incapable of supporting its native species. Intense harvesting of timber, illegal logging, oil and gas drilling, mining, the expansion of agricultural land for food production, and overgrazing, along with the increased demand for land for homes and industrialisation, all play their part in habitat destruction. A myriad of complex infrastructures has to be put in place to support and sustain these developments, such as roads, railway lines and pipelines, and this results in the disappearance of natural wildlife habitats, (forests, swamps, lakes and plains).

Poaching

Poaching is the illegal hunting and capturing of a wild animal. More than 50% of the world's poaching takes place in Sub-Saharan Africa, and Tanzania is no exception. Serving a thriving international market, these professional, highly organised gangs of poachers use sophisticated technology, (GPS, night vision goggles and mobile 'phones), automatic weapons (AK-47s), and low flying helicopters to target and hunt down high value, defenceless wildlife. Alternatively poachers can lace the walking paths that rhinos regularly use with poisoned food, and poison the watering holes. All they have to do is wait until the animal dies, and there are no resonating gunshot sounds to be heard to give their presence away. The poachers go undetected and silently remove the body parts. Warning messages can be left on the carcass warning the rangers that if they attempt to follow them, they will be ambushed and killed. Hand grenades can be used to booby trap the carcass, and can also be thrown at the rangers. These heavily armed poachers are ruthless and extremely dangerous, and members of anti poaching teams risk their lives on a daily basis protecting wildlife.

The poachers remove the horns, hide, hair and body parts, (teeth, claws and bones), and these are trafficked out of Tanzania onto the illegal, international markets, usually Asia. The carcass is left to rot. Rhinoceros horns in particular are sold at lucrative prices, and in 2017 were making 65,000 U.S. dollars a kilo., which is more expensive than gold or diamonds. China, Thailand and Vietnam are the three major recipients of poached rhino horns. Animal body parts are used in traditional Chinese medicine, traditional magic, in ceremonial rituals, as an aphrodisiac, and for jewellery, figurines and trinkets. The list is endless, and whilst there is a market it will be extremely difficult, if not impossible, to eradicate poaching. The underlying issue is greed, and satisfying people's deep rooted beliefs.

The pangolin attracts a lot of publicity, as it is said to be the most widely trafficked mammal in the world. Its scales are in high demand and are used in traditional Chinese medicine, and its meat is a rare delicacy. Whilst extremely rare, they do occur in parts of Tanzania.

Hunting

Tanzania's indigenous poor, who have few livelihood alternatives, may get involved in hunting wildlife for a variety of reasons. Traditionally, people in Tanzania only hunted and killed what they needed, hides for clothing and shelter, bones for tools, sinews for bowstrings and the meat for food. They believed that animals were spiritual beings and were linked to deities. Currently animals are seen as a source of food, also known as bush meat, and they can provide income when traded for goods or cash. Loss of crops and livestock, and excessive droughts with a reduction in water, brings the animals into direct conflict with man. Man and animals are both competing for the same resource. Bridal price, prestige and tribal traditions are also other reasons why local people turn to hunting wildlife. Hunting usually takes place at night under the cover of darkness. Bows and arrows, wire snares, dogs, spot lighting and pit traps are used to trap and kill the animals.

Trophy Hunting

Trophy hunting is a multi million dollar industry and is legal in many countries. The trophy for the successful hunter is either the whole animal or part of the animal. The parts that are kept are the head, skin, horns and antlers. The carcass will be kept for food or given to the local community. The most expensive species to hunt down are the big five (Cape buffalo, elephant, leopard, lion and rhino.) Whilst Kenya for example has banned trophy hunting since 1977, Tanzania actually lifted their ban in November 2018.

Canned Hunting

Canned hunting is legal and is a form of trophy hunting that involves killing animals, (lions in particular), that are born and bred on a ranch specifically for hunting purposes. Captive animals are released into enclosures that are so small the animal stands no chance of escape. The animals are habituated and have a reduced fear of humans, this makes it easier for the hunter to shoot and kill the animal. This is an extreme, fast growing form of trophy hunting, where the appeal is the guarantee of a kill. The odds are heavily stacked against the animal, and they have little chance of avoiding death. In many people's opinion this is trophy hunting at its most indefensible.

Climate Change
Climate change, or climate crisis, is the result of global warming and is now considered by many as the biggest threat to the survival of Tanzanian wildlife, its wildernesses and its people.

The rise in global temperatures are now projected to be higher in Africa than any other continent, and yet the irony of this is that countries like Tanzania are the least responsible, hardly producing any of the polluting greenhouse gases. Changes in climate affects the delicately balanced eco systems which ultimately threatens people, animals and plants alike.

Global warming results in extreme weather conditions that disrupt and change the seasons. This brings with it droughts, crop failure, dying vegetation, famine, dried up river beds, receding water, melting glaciers, (Kilimanjaro), and flooding. Plant growth and production is also affected by the resultant spread of pests and diseases.

For the wildlife of Tanzania climate change results in the reduction and loss of habitat. They may be forced to migrate to different pastures in their search for the dwindling supply of food and water. Conflict with humans increases as a result, as they are all competing for food, water and other natural resources. Feeding patterns and behaviours change, reproduction rates change and slow down, and the prevalence of infectious diseases increases. Species that are already threatened, endangered or sensitive to changes in the environment are vulnerable. The future is undoubtedly, and alarmingly, bleak. Unless we change our behaviour and attitude towards global warming, and take the issue more seriously, many species face extinction in the not too distant future.

List of endangerment as defined by the international Union for the Conservation of Nature
Scientists measure birth and death rates so they can calculate if a species is threatened/endangered. It is a measurement. Where a species are small in number, they reach a critical point whereby there are not enough left alive to continue the species. Some species are rarely encountered in the wild and there is insufficient data available to state if they are threatened/endangered, therefore they are not listed.

Least Concern (LC)
A species which is not threatened, near threatened, or conservation dependent.

Banded mongoose, bat eared fox, black backed jackal, black & white colobus monkey, blue monkey, Cape buffalo, eland, hartebeest, gemsbok, greater flamingo, greater kudu, impala, Kirk's dikdik, maribou stork, monitor lizard, Nile crocodile, olive baboon, ostrich, reedbuck, roan antelope, spotted hyena, vervet monkey, warthog and water buck.

Near Threatened (NT)
A species that is closely threatened with extinction in the near future.

Brown hyena, caracal, East Africa oryx, gerenuk, lechwe, lesser flamingo, porcupine, puku, stripped hyena, Southern white rhino, and Thomson's gazelle.

Vulnerable (VU)

A species that will become endangered if the circumstances threatening their very survival and reproduction do not improve.

Cheetah, hippopotamus, leopard, lion and topi.

Endangered (EN)

A species that is very likely to become extinct.

African wild dogs (1990), chameleons (depends on species), chimpanzee (1996), crowned crane (2012), elephant (2021), Rothschild's giraffe (2010) and vulture (depends on species).

Critically Endangered (CR)

A species that possesses an extremely high risk of extinction in the wild.

Black rhino (1996), Grevvy's zebra (1986) and vulture (depends on species).

Extinct in the Wild (EW)

The only living members of a species now live in captivity, and are unable live in their normal habitat.

Functionally Extinct.

The species is no longer viable. Although not completely eradicated, the species is effectively extinct, whereby only a handful of individuals are left, and the odds of reproduction are slim.

Northern white rhino (2018).

Extinct (EX)

No living members of a species exist anywhere in the world. The species has died out.

Fatu and Najin, the only remaining northern white rhinos, are being protected at Ol Pejeta Conservancy, Kenya. Both are female.

Big Five

The "big five" is a term originally used by big game hunters who considered the elephant, rhinoceros (black & white), leopard, lion and Cape buffalo as the most difficult and dangerous of all Africa's animals to track and hunt. This meant that they were highly prized among dedicated trophy hunters, whereas in the present climate where wildlife is protected, the big five are now regarded by tourists as top of their "must-see" list purely for photographic purposes.

Big Nine

The "big nine" has evolved as a recognised extension of the "big five" and includes the hippopotamus, zebra, giraffe and cheetah.

Our "Big Ten"

African/Cape Buffalo
(*Syncerus caffer*)
Swahili: *Nyati/Mbogo*

Identification

The Cape buffalo is a large heavily built animal with a cow-like appearance, and is one of Africa's "big five".

The head is large, and it has a short, thick neck and broad chest. It has small eyes protected by the horns. The large, droopy, fringed ears are also underneath the horns. The muzzle is wide and hairless, with moist nostrils. A prehensile tongue and broad incisors enable it to feed on tall, coarse grasses.

The Cape buffalo's hide is extremely thick and protects it from thorny bushes and the penetrating claws of predators. The short, coarse, sparse coat is grey-black in colour; this thins with age along with the appearance of bald patches.

Its limbs are strong, powerful and muscular with black splayed hooves. The front hooves are bigger than the rear hooves.

Both sexes have two low, rigid horns that grow out of the sides of the head and curve upwards. The male's horns, which are larger and thicker than the females, are joined by a shield (boss) that covers the entire forehead. The boss protects the skull of the male from serious injury when engaged in fighting.

The tail is long and has a tuft of hair on the tip.

Cape buffaloes have poor eyesight and hearing, but have an excellent sense of smell.

Head & Body Length: 2-3.5m
Shoulder Height: 1.4-1.7m
Tail Length: 0.75-1m
Weight: 500-900kg
Horn Length: 1.25m

Life Span
Sixteen to eighteen years in the wild.

Habitat
Cape buffaloes need a large area to roam around in, and are usually found in savannahs, grasslands, forests and woodlands. They can live at sea level or at altitudes of up to 4,000m, and are always found near water.

Behaviour
Cape buffaloes are sociable, non-territorial animals that live in large, mixed, stable herds/obstinacies of up to 1,500 individuals. The majority of the herd is composed of females (cows) and their offspring, surrounding the main herd are sub herds of bachelor males, sub herds of dominant males (bulls) and sub herds of females. The older bulls are to be found on the periphery. The majority of Cape buffaloes are docile

and placid if left alone; serious fights are rare. When resting, they may lie down on the ground with their backs touching each other.

When threatened by predators, Cape buffaloes form a tightly knit group, with the calves protected in the centre. This makes it hard for a predator to select, identify and isolate a suitable victim. Their cumbersome appearance is deceiving - although they cannot accelerate quickly, once they have gained momentum they can run at speeds of 57km/h and can easily outrun a lion. A lion attacking a Cape buffalo risks a mob attack with the chance of been gored or trampled to death.

Old bulls usually live on their own, away from the safety and security of the herd. If disturbed, they can become unpredictable and highly dangerous. Solitary bulls are easy prey for lions.

During the dry season, when grass and water is in short supply, the herd disbands, regrouping again in the wet season. Undisturbed, they will graze continuously, but in the vicinity of humans and predators they prefer to feed in the early morning and evening. Making quick work of the food available, they are constantly on the move, searching for fresh food and water. Without a regular, plentiful supply of food and water, the Cape buffalo's physical condition rapidly deteriorates, more than any other animal on the African savannah.

Cape buffaloes are diurnal and nocturnal.

Diet

Cape buffaloes are herbivores and graze on tall, coarse grasses. They need to drink water daily. During the dry season when food is in short supply they will eat the leaves from trees, shrubs and bushes.

Communication

Cape buffaloes are quiet, communicating with each other during the mating season by grunting and bellowing, and gently mooing to each other while eating. A calf in danger will bellow for its mother. They also use sight, scent and bodily postures to communicate.

Reproduction

Cape buffaloes are polygamous and breed all year round. The peak season for giving birth is during the rainy seasons. The dominant males mate with, and are protective towards the females. During the mating season they will search for females in oestrus by smelling and tasting their urine.

The gestation period is between 330-346 days. The female gives birth to a single calf, which remains hidden in thick undergrowth until it is able to follow and keep up with the herd. The calf has a thick, dense coat of brown-black hair, and

is weaned by the time it is 12 months old. The bond between the female and the calf is strong and remains until the arrival of the next offspring, at which time the calf is chased away. Females remain with the maternal herd.

Cape buffaloes are sexually mature between three to five years old

Predators/Threats

Healthy Cape buffaloes do not have any natural predators, apart from lions. The young, old, injured and diseased are easy prey for crocodiles, hyenas, and leopards. They are hunted for their meat and for sport by the trophy hunters. They can come into conflict with humans if they break fences, raid crops and are suspected of carrying bovine diseases. They are susceptible to rinderpest, foot & mouth and bovine TB. Loss of habitat and competition for food from domestic livestock threaten the Cape buffalo's survival. The effects of climate change should not be underestimated. If the rains fail, the resulting drought conditions can decimate a water dependent animal population like the Cape buffalo dramatically and quickly.   Currently there are 398,000-401,000 mature Cape buffalo, 75% live in protected areas (national parks, game reserves). The Cape buffalo is listed as a *near threatened species* (2018).

Trivia

♦The nickname for an old Cape buffalo is "dagga boy".

♦Cape buffaloes are extremely dangerous and capable of killing any animal or human that stands in their way. If injured they will circle back and lie in wait for the perpetrator then strike when least expected.

♦Cape buffaloes suffer from heat stress and must drink twice a day.

♦Cape buffaloes have a strong musky smell.

♦Flies can lay their eggs in the horns of the Cape buffalo. When the larvae hatch, they bore holes into the horns, which can seriously weaken and fracture the structure.

♦The Cape buffalo's head and neck is extremely large, and it can take between 30 to 60 minutes for a lion to successfully suffocate or strangulate it. This is a long, slow and painful death.

♦Cape buffaloes have a weak immune system and are susceptible to bovine tuberculosis and foot and mouth disease. Tuberculosis is highly contagious and can rapidly decimate a herd of buffalo and their predators.

♦It is not advisable to domesticate the Cape buffalo as it is unpredictable and highly dangerous.

♦The Cape buffalo is immune to bovine sleeping sickness, which is carried by the tsetse fly.

African Elephant
(*Loxodonta africana*)
Swahili: *Tembo/Ndovo*

Identification

The African elephant is the world's largest land animal.

The rough, grey, sensitive, wrinkly skin is 2.5-cm thick and is almost hairless. There is a sparse covering of hair around the mouth, along the trunk and on the tip of the tail.

The head is large with a short neck and is supported by strong neck muscles. The eyes are small in comparison to its size. The head of the male African elephant is rounded whereas the female's head is square.

The long, flexible, prehensile trunk acts as an extra limb and serves many purposes. It is used to syphon water, which it then pours into its mouth and drinks. Mud or dust are also sucked up in a similar manner and then showered over the body to cool it down. It is also used to breathe, smell, communicate, gather food, dig for water, as well as lifting and gripping objects. In fact an elephant cannot survive without its trunk.

Two nostrils run the length of the trunk.

Two dextrous finger-like projections present on the tip of the trunk are used to grip small objects.

Both male and female elephants have two tusks made from ivory that continue to grow throughout their lives. The tusks differ in shape, size and angle and are used to identify individuals. The tusks serve many purposes: foraging for food, digging up tree roots, searching for water, stripping bark from trees, pushing trees over and fighting. African elephants have a preference for either the right or left tusk, consequently one tusk wears out first or is damaged more than the other.

The African elephant's teeth have evolved over time to cope with their coarse diet.

They have four molars that have large grinding surfaces made up of many adjoining ridges/sections called laminae. The molars start growing at the back of the mouth and gradually move forwards to replace the old teeth as they fall out. They are replaced six times during the elephant's life. The absence of teeth in later life results in the elephant suffering from the effects of malnutrition and eventually dying from starvation.

The large, fan shaped ears are covered by a network of fine blood vessels close to the surface of the skin which dissipate heat and help to keep the elephant cool. Flapping of the ears also cools the elephant down. The skin on the ears is thin and delicate and easily torn by sharp thorns when foraging for food in the bushes, or when engaged in combat. These tear marks are used to identify individuals. Males have more tears on their ears than females.

Four short, stocky legs sit directly beneath the large barrel-shaped body. Sponge-like cushions on the pads of the feet act as shock absorbers and allow the elephant to move silently through the bush. Toenails are present on the toes.

The tail is short and has a tassel of black hair on the tip.

African elephants have poor eyesight, excellent hearing and a keen sense of smell.

The male is larger than the female.

Head & Body Length: 5-7.5m
Shoulder Height: 3-4m
Trunk Length: 2m
Tail Length: 1-1.5m
Weight: 2,268-6,400kg
Weight of Tusks: 22-45kg

Life Span
Up to 70 years in the wild.

Habitat
African elephants are usually found in savannahs, grasslands, woodlands and forests, where there is a plentiful supply of food and water.

Behaviour
African elephants are intelligent, sociable animals that live together in a small family group called a herd. The herd, which has a complex, hierarchical social structure based on age, is made up of 10 to 20 closely related individuals and consists of the matriarch (leader), 3-4 adult females, their offspring, newborn calves and adolescent males and females. If the herd gets too large it will split into two, one group will be led by the older matriarch and the other will be led by a sister or cousin. It is extremely rare to find a female African elephant alone. Males tend to be solitary but may live together in an all-male group.

Herds will temporarily merge during the wet season when food and water is plentiful. The herds disband during the dry season when they need to concentrate their efforts on searching for the dwindling supply of food and water. Walking at 6km/h they can cover large distances in their search for food.

African elephants spend 16 hours a day feeding, drinking, socialising, dusting themselves with fine dry soil and wallowing in mud to cool down. A combination of dried-on mud and dry soil acts as a sunscreen to protect the delicate skin, as well as serving as an exfoliator for dislodging ticks, flies and other parasites.

African elephants are particularly affectionate towards each other, using their trunks to greet and touch each other, as well as reinforcing old relationships. They also tend to and look after the old, sick and injured members of the herd.

Although gentle and peaceful animals, they can be extremely dangerous if they are wounded, sick or injured, or are protecting their young. They are more than capable of seriously injuring or killing anything that gets in their way.

African elephants mourn their dead by remaining close to them for several days, by covering them with dirt, twigs, branches and leaves, and sensitively touching whatever remains with the tips of their trunks.

African elephants are diurnal and nocturnal. They rest at midday and sleep between 4-5 hours per night.

Diet

African elephants are herbivores and have a preference for fresh grass, but during the dry season when food is in short supply, they have to seek out alternatives. They are fortunate in that their size, strength and the presence of their trunk allows them to access sources of food that are normally inaccessible to other animals. They will uproot trees and shrubs, strip bark from the tree trunk, tear branches and twigs away from the tree, and reach up for fruit and seed pods. African elephants are destructive, and when present in large numbers they can put some plant species at risk of extinction. In order to manage this delicately balanced ecosystem elephants may be translocated or culled by humans. The majority of the vegetation that the

elephant eats is of poor nutritional value and they need to eat 200-300kg of food per day in order to survive. They produce 36kg of dung and 2,000 litres of methane per day. African elephants usually drink water daily, but when in short supply they can drink every second or third day. Water aids digestion and cools them down, and they can drink up to 189 litres a day.

Communication

African elephants use a variety of vocalisations, visual signals, bodily postures and their trunk to communicate with each other and their offspring. They are able to communicate through infrasonics over 9km at low frequencies not audible to the human ear. They usually use this form of communication early morning or in the evening when it is cool.

Reproduction

African elephants breed any time of year.

Males (bulls) come into musth in their mid to late twenties and begin to mate with the females when they are over thirty. Musth is a state of heightened sexual excitement and occurs at regular intervals, usually lasting from one week up to three to four months, with a nine-month rest break during which time the bull will live alone. Bulls in musth are domineering, aggressive and unpredictable, and should be avoided by humans. Older dominant bulls are able to remain in musth for longer periods.

When the bull enters musth the temporal glands above and behind the eyes increase in size causing the cheeks to swell, and a sticky fluid to continuously flow down either side of the face. A constant, strong smelling flow of dribbling urine is also present. The bull sends out low frequency calls to attract the attention of females. Following any female that responds to his calls, he will use his trunk to test if she is in oestrus. The male and female will then spend some time sniffing one another before proceeding to mate. The older, larger and stronger bulls are more likely to succeed in mating with the females. Females also have a preference for older bulls.

Females (cows) give birth to their first born between the ages of 10 and 20 years old, and thereafter every 4-6 years. When resources are scarce and unable to sustain a high elephant population, the females can either alter their reproductive status so that they reach sexual maturity when they are older, or give birth less frequently. This increases the survival rate for them and their offspring. During years of drought the mortality rate for the calves can be as high as 50%.

Females come into oestrus during and after the rainy season. They are in oestrus for between 4-6 days, during which time they secrete a sticky fluid from the temporal gland down either side of their face.

Ninety-nine per cent of females give birth surrounded and protected by other females during the night. The gestation period is 22 months, with the female giving birth to a single calf. At birth the male and female calves are the same size. The males grow more rapidly, especially during their teens, and this continues throughout their lives. Females grow slowly and their growth ceases by the time they are 25 years old.

The calves are able to walk within 2-3 hours of being born and will spend the first few weeks of their lives lying down, resting and sleeping. Within two weeks, the pinkness behind the ears will have disappeared. Relying solely on their mother's milk, they suckle with their mouths from the two breasts that are located between the two front legs, usually for the first four months of their lives. They then begin to supplement their diet with soft green succulent grasses, progressing to the coarser grasses after 12 months. The calves continue to drink their mother's milk until they are 4-6 years old or until the next offspring arrives. For a short period of time the calves eat their parents' dung to establish essential micro organisms in their gut that aid digestion. Their tusks appear externally when they are 30 months old. Weaning is completed by the time the calf is five years old.

The calf is unable to control the two finger-like projections on the end of its trunk, necessary for grasping and manipulating objects, until it is six months old.

Playful and full of mischief, the calf has to learn basic motor coordination, behavioural and life skills from its mother in order to survive.

Females are fiercely protective and band together to protect their own and other females' calves. Juvenile females between two and eleven years old are attracted to, and will tend and care for small calves. This is known as "allo mothering" and increases the calves' chances of survival. Orphaned calves are looked after by lactating females. When threatened, the adults form a protective circle around the youngsters.

The female's reproductive life ceases between the ages of 45-50 years old. She will then spend the remainder of her life tending and caring for the young.

As the males begin to mature they will start to spend time away from the natal herd and will make the final break when they have reached sexual maturity at around 14 years old. This prevents in-breeding. During their teens they need the leadership of a matriarch and may latch onto a herd of females, but in their twenties they seek out the companionship of either younger or older males. They may also live a solitary life in isolation as an independent bull.

Females remain with the natal herd.

Predators/Threats

The major threat to the African elephant's survival is poaching, and this market is escalating out of all proportions. African elephants are illegally hunted by poachers for their tusks. The booming Chinese economy and the rise of their middle class has seen an increase in demand for ivory. Ivory is a status symbol - a sign of wealth. Loss of, and fragmentation of habitat, the effects of climate change and the increase in conflict with humans who are all competing with them for the same diminishing resources (food and water), are also a threat to the African elephant's survival. They are illegally hunted for their meat. The calves are natural prey for lions, hyenas, African wild dogs and crocodiles.

The African elephant is classified as an *endangered species* (2021)

Trivia

♦African elephants are larger than Asian elephants.

♦African elephants' ears are three times larger than Asian elephants and are shaped like the map of Africa! The African elephant's ears can grow up to 1.8m. Asian elephants' ears are small and rounded.

♦Asian elephants only have one finger-like projection on the tip of their trunk, and can only scoop objects up.

♦The African elephant has two finger like projections at the tip of their trunk that allows it to pick up small objects.

♦It is difficult to sex elephants as the male testes are internal.

♦*Musth* is an Urdu word that means "intoxicated".

♦Elephants are excellent swimmers.

♦Unlike Asian elephants, African elephants are not easily domesticated.

♦Male African elephants continue to grow throughout their lives and can reach more than 7,000kg in weight.

♦Female elephants can run faster than males.

Ivory

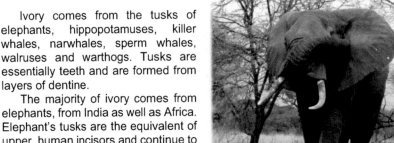

Ivory comes from the tusks of elephants, hippopotamuses, killer whales, narwhales, sperm whales, walruses and warthogs. Tusks are essentially teeth and are formed from layers of dentine.

The majority of ivory comes from elephants, from India as well as Africa. Elephant's tusks are the equivalent of upper, human incisors and continue to grow throughout their life. Subject to wear and tear and damage from fights, elephants can often be identified by the condition of their tusks alone. Despite the 1989 worldwide ban on the trade in ivory, the black market is alive and thriving. Poachers are willing to risk all to satisfy their client's insatiable desire and greed for ivory. The only way poachers are able to retrieve ivory from an elephant is by killing them, usually with a bullet, but occasionally by poisoning. The head has to be cut open, as 25% of the tusk is usually deeply embedded inside it. Once the tusk is removed, what remains is left to the scavengers.

Ivory has multiple uses: jewellery, cutlery, piano keys, furniture inlays, handles, billiard balls, religious objects, daggers, decorative boxes and works of art.

Trivia

♦The ivory from the tusks of the hippopotamus is of a different texture to that of the elephant, being denser and harder. It is usually used to make buttons, but has also been used to make false teeth.

♦The recent surge in the demand for ivory has seen the tusks of the stuffed heads of elephants and hippopotamuses being removed, usually as they go to auction. What was initially worth tens of thousands of pounds is suddenly worthless.

Black Rhinoceros
(Diceros bicornis)
Swahili: *Faru/Kifaru*

Identification

The black rhino is an odd-toed ungulate and has the reputation of being unpredictable, bad-tempered and aggressive.

It's thick, smooth, hairless skin is grey, but can be varying shades of brown if it has been wallowing in mud. The thick skin protects it from the thorns on the trees and bushes that it feeds on. The skin harbours parasites such as ticks, flies and crabs. It has no sweat glands. Hair is present on the fringes of the ears, on the tip of the short tail and as eyelashes.

The body is large and rotund, with a broad chest. Its legs are short and stumpy. It has three toes on hooved feet, and its footprint resembles the ace of spades.

The head is large with a long neck and an elongated face. It has a broad snout, large nostrils and a triangular, pointed, upper lip. Incisors and canine teeth are absent, and it is heavily dependent on its prehensile muscular lips to grasp the twigs and leaves on the trees and bushes upon which it feeds. Two horns made of keratin sit centrally behind the nose. The horns have no bony skeletal attachment but actually grow from the skin and continue to grow throughout life. The anterior horn is longer than the posterior horn. Occasionally a third horn is present.

A keen sense of smell and hearing compensate for its poor eyesight. The eyes are very small and are placed on either side of the head. In order to look straight ahead the rhino has to turn its head sideways. The black rhino is short sighted and cannot detect an immobile object at 30m. It can detect a moving object at 30-50m. The large, prominent, funnel-shaped ears are mobile and move independently of each other.

Males are slightly larger and heavier than females.

Head & Body Length:	3-4m
Shoulder Height:	1.4-1.7m
Tail Length:	50-70cm
Weight:	800-1,350kg
Horn:	Anterior: 50cm-1.3m
	Posterior: 0.02-55cm
Combined Horn Weight:	6kg

Life Span

Forty years in the wild.

Habitat

Black rhinos are found in wooded areas such as woodlands, forests, shrub land and tropical bushlands. They can also be found in savannahs, grasslands and deserts. They like to be near water holes and mud wallows.

Behaviour

Black rhinos are not very territorial and may have home ranges that overlap. The perimeter is scent marked at regular intervals with urine and communal dung heaps or middens. Urine is sprayed backwards at great force in the direction of bushes and trees.

Black rhinos have a solitary existence except when mating and raising offspring. They display little or no aggression towards each other. Despite their cumbersome appearance black rhinos are surprisingly agile and can run at speeds of up to 50km/h.

They are more nocturnal than diurnal, browsing on food early morning and evening and during the night. During the day they like to rest and wallow in mud, which serves to cool them down. Dried mud acts as a sun screen and exfoliator as well as helping to deter ticks, flies and other parasites.

Diet
Black rhinos are herbivores and heavy browsers, feeding on branches, twigs, leaves, fruit, buds of woody plants and bushes, as well as small seedlings and herbs. They are capable of uprooting small bushes and shrubs and digesting thorns.

They prefer to drink daily but can live up to five days without water.

Communication
A range of vocalisations are used to communicate with their offspring, with other rhinos and when threatened. They may grunt, growl, scream, squeal, snort or trumpet. Bodily postures and scent markings are also used.

Reproduction
Black rhinos are polygamous and breed throughout the year. The majority of births take place at the end of the rainy season. The gestation period is between 419 and 478 days. The courtship can be complex and prolonged. To attract the female (cow), the male (bull) snorts, swings his head from side to side and then sweeps his horn across the ground. The mating pair may stay together for several weeks and mate several times a day. The female gives birth to a single calf. Weaning begins at two months and is complete by twelve months. The calf always walks behind its mother, and will remain with its mother for two to four years or until another calf is born. It is then chased away by its mother, to lead an independent life in solitude.

Females reach sexual maturity between five and seven years old and males between seven and nine years old.

Predators/Threats
Black rhinos have no natural predators apart from poachers who illegally hunt them for their horns. They are easy prey as they are creatures of habit living in a clearly defined home range. Their poor eyesight will not detect the presence of poachers until it is too late. Their horns are worth thousands of US dollars and are used in traditional Chinese medicine and as ceremonial daggers. They are a symbol of wealth, success and are an aphrodisiac in Chinese and Vietnamese societies. The demand for rhino horn is rising unabated and cannot be sustained. Loss of habitat for agricultural purposes and the effects of climate change are also a threat to the black rhino's survival. The black rhino is classified as a *critically endangered species* (2020).

Black & White Rhino Trivia
♦Black rhinos are nicknamed the hooked-lipped rhinoceros. White rhinos are nicknamed the square-lipped rhinoceros.

♦Rhinos are able to eat plants that are highly toxic to other animals, such as euphorbia.

♦Rhinos belong to the same family as the horse.

♦If the horns are removed to deter poachers, the rhinos are able to get along well without them, but the long term effect is unknown. The horns grow back at the rate of several inches a year.

♦Even when asleep the rhino is able to move its ears around to detect any noise.

Cheetah
(Acinonyxjubatus)
Swahili: *Duma/Chita*

Identification
The cheetah is renowned as the world's fastest land animal. Its super light, flexible, streamlined body is lean and muscular in appearance. Its legs are long and thin.

The short, coarse fur is tan in colour and is covered with small round/oval black spots, which act as camouflage. The throat and underside are white.

The tail has spots, four to six dark rings and a white, bushy tuft at the tip.

The blunt, semi-retractable claws of the cheetah are visible and exert a traction effect when running at speed. The dew claw is short and sharp and is used to pull prey to the ground.

The brown eyes are set high, on a small head. Black teardrop-like marks, which absorb bright light and reduce the glare from the sun, run from the inner corner of each eye to the corner of the mouth. The backs of the ears, lips and nose are black.

The cheetah has excellent eyesight and sense of smell.

The male cheetah is slightly bigger than the female.

Head & Body Length: 1.2-1.4m
Tail Length: 0.6-0.8m
Shoulder Height: 70-90cm
Weight: 35-65kg

Life Span
Twelve years in the wild.

Habitat
Cheetahs require a large home range in order to survive, they are usually found in the savannahs, grasslands, deserts and open woodlands, in the vicinity of abundant plain grazers. They are highly visible on the savannahs and need bushes and tall grasses to hide from the ever-present, marauding predators who stalk them.

Behaviour
Cheetahs are shy, solitary elusive animals.

Females remain solitary for life, unless they are raising cubs or there is a temporary mother-daughter allegiance.

Males either live alone, which is rare, or in small groups known as a *coalition* of up to four males, which can last a lifetime. Males living in a coalition are very territorial and will kill intruders if necessary. They all contribute to marking their territory, by urinating, spraying urine, defecating and sharpening their claws on trees.

Cheetahs usually hunt on their own, and they prey on small antelopes. They have remarkable vision and can spot prey 5km away. When a coalition hunts together, they are able to target larger prey such as wildebeest and zebra.

In order to be successful when stalking prey, cheetahs need to get within 30-60m, before giving chase. They can achieve and maintain a top speed of 100km/h for 300m, if they are not successful within one minute they have to quit the chase, because of the sharp rise in body temperature and ensuing exhaustion. The increase in body temperature, if it is maintained, can lead to dehydration and brain damage. The tail is used as a rudder when in pursuit, allowing them to manoeuvre sharply in response to their prey's constant change in direction. They use its forefeet to trip their prey up, then locks their jaws firmly onto the throat. The victim's death is by strangulation and is usually prolonged. The success rate when hunting prey is only about 50%.

Cheetahs have to consume their prey quickly as the ever-present scavengers (lions, hyenas, jackals, leopards, and vultures) will move in quickly and relieve them of their catch. They only eat live prey, and do not cache food or return to a kill. Cheetahs are diurnal and hunt either early morning or late afternoon, resting at midday.

Diet

Cheetahs are carnivorous, and hunt and kill small to medium sized antelopes (oribi, springbok, gazelles), small mammals (hares) and game birds. They will hunt and kill larger antelopes (zebras, wildebeest) when hunting as a group.

Cheetahs can go up to ten days without water.

Communication

Scent marking is the primary form of communication. Cheetahs use a wide variety of vocalisations to communicate with their offspring (chirping), with other cheetahs, or when threatened (growling). Visual signals, bodily postures, tactile/sociable greetings (sniffing, face licking and face/cheek rubbing) and antagonistic, aggressive behaviours are also used.

Reproduction

There is no distinct breeding season. Males are only found in the presence of females when mating. The gestation period is up to 98 days. The female can give birth to up to nine cubs, and she raises them on her own. Newborn cubs are blind and helpless, and their eyes open between 4-10 days. The cubs initially have blue-grey fur with a black underside that quickly fades and takes on the colouration and markings of the adult. A fluffy grey mantle of hair runs from the neck down to the mid back. This begins to disappear at three months.

The cubs are hidden in dense vegetation and rocks for the first month. They move from den to den every few days. Cubs are prey to hyenas, leopards, eagles and lions, and the mortality rate is as high as 90%. Lions are four times the size of a cheetah and once the cubs have been discovered the female is unable to protect them.

Cubs venture out with their mother at five to six weeks to join her for a kill, and they are weaned by three months.

The cubs have a long period of dependency, and this can be up to 24 months. Instinctively cheetahs do not know how to hunt, catch and kill prey and avoid predators, this must be taught by their mother. Before they are six months old the mother will bring home small, disabled, live prey for the cubs to practise chasing and killing under her supervision. They are unable to successfully kill on their own until they are 15 months old.

Cheetahs reach sexual maturity at two years old.

Predators/Threats

Loss of habitat, loss of prey, low reproduction rates, the effects of climate change and hunting by humans are all threats to the cheetah's survival. They are hunted for their fur, body parts and are a source of bush meat. Cheetahs are currently perceived to be a luxury pet and status symbol, and many cheetah cubs are illegally poached and transported to foreign destinations in the Middle East. Very few survive.

Cheetahs continue to be classified as a *vulnerable species* (2020). Scientists are demanding that the cheetah's status be uplisted to the *endangered/critically endangered species* category. Many believe that the cheetah is perilously close to extinction.

Trivia

♦Cheetah is a Hindu word that means "spotted one".

♦Cheetahs in the wild are prone to corneal injuries as they hunt with their eyes open and injure themselves by running into sharp thorns.

♦Cheetah flies, which are unique to cheetahs, are a nuisance and cause them tremendous irritation when present in large numbers.

♦Cheetahs are less aggressive than the other big cats, and can be tamed.

♦Cheetahs can purr but cannot roar like a lion.

♦Cheetah cubs that are brought up in captivity with only human contact are difficult or impossible to integrate back into the wild, as they have not been taught the art of hunting or survival by their mother.

♦Cheetahs in captivity are prone to gastritis and this is believed to be stress related.

Common Plains Zebra/Burchell's Zebra
(Equus quagga formerly *Equus burchelli)*
Swahili: *Punda milia*

Identification
Although generally recognised as being similar in appearance to a horse, the zebra has a short, stocky body and short legs.

Its most distinguishing feature is the coat, with the

broad, black and white stripes which are as individual as a human finger print.

The stripes are vertical over the head, neck, forequarters and body, but become horizontal towards the hindquarters. The stripes on the

legs are narrow and horizontal and extend as far as the odd-toed black hooves.

The black and white striped, bristly mane is short and upright.

The tail is long, with a straggly dark tuft at the tip.

The zebra has large eyes on the side of the head, and has excellent peripheral vision. The ears are large and turn in all directions. The muzzle is black.

The zebra has excellent eyesight, hearing, sense of smell and taste.

Head & Body Length: 2-2.5m
Shoulder Height: 1-1.5m
Tail Length: 47-56cm
Weight: 175-385kg

Life Span
Twelve years in the wild.

Habitat
Zebras are found in the savannahs, grasslands and woodlands, up to altitudes of 4,500m.

Behaviour
Zebras are sociable animals, and live together in a harem. The harem is a stable, family group that is led and defended by one male (stallion), and has up to six females (mares) and their offspring. Occasionally, harems may come together, as in migration, to form a large herd.

A dominance hierarchy exists amongst the females. The dominant female who is the alpha female, leads the group and is the first one to mate with the male. The most recently acquired female is ranked the lowest.

A harem is created by a male abducting the fillies as they approach their first oestrus. If the male is successful, the filly will remain with him for the rest of her natural life. The male defends the harem vigorously from other predatory males and can hold a harem for up to 15 years.

Males leave the harem between the ages of one and four years old as a result of the arrival of new offspring and the continuing, deteriorating relationships that it has with its mother. Males may choose to live alone or with other males until they are able to have their own harem, which occurs at the age of six years old. Up until that age they do not have the necessary skills to manage and defend a harem.

Zebras are nomadic by nature and migrate with other species (wildebeest, gazelles) following the rains. They are the first grazer to enter the newly replenished grasslands. They graze on and trample the long grasses, leaving in their wake the succulent short grasses for the wildebeest and gazelles to feed on.

When threatened by predators, zebras unite in a tightly knit group that is virtually impregnable. For that reason alone, hyenas have a preference for hunting zebras in a pack. Zebras are able to run in short bursts at speeds of 65km/h to escape from predators.

Zebras sleep standing up and retreat to the plains at night time where there is good visibility. There are usually one or more lookouts throughout the night, spotting predators ,and their night vision is excellent.

Zebras are diurnal and nocturnal.

Diet

Zebras are nomadic herbivores, spending the majority of their time grazing on long and short grasses. They will also browse on young shoots, herbs, leaves, shrubs, twigs and leaves. The digestive system has developed to allow the zebra to rapidly extract protein from food of poor nutritional value.

Because zebras are able to eat short coarse grass, they cannot survive for long without water and are usually found in close proximity to water sources.

Communication

The primary form of communication with each other is barking and whinnying. The position their ears assume is also a form of communication and is an indication of their mood, whether they are calm, frightened or angry. Zebras will use their lips and teeth to groom each other.

Reproduction

There is no distinct breeding season, but the peak season for giving birth is in the short dry season between December and January. Zebras are polygamous.

The gestation period is up to 365 days. The female gives birth to a single foal which is striped brown and white. Within 15 minutes of being born the foal is able to suckle, stand upright and walk. For a period of three days after the birth, until the foal is able to recognise its mother's voice, smell and sight, it is kept away from the harem. The foal is suckled for six months.

Fifty per cent of foals born are lost to predation. If threatened, the harem physically closes ranks, with the foal protected in the centre. The harem is aggressively defended by the male.

Zebras reach sexual maturity at three years old.

Predators/Threats

Zebras are natural prey for African wild dogs, cheetahs, hyenas, leopards and lions. They are hunted for their meat and hide. Loss of habitat for agricultural purposes and livestock grazing and the effects of climate change are a threat to the zebra's survival. Zebras cannot survive without access to readily available water. The common plains zebra is classified as a *near threatened species* (2016).

Trivia

♦Burchell's zebras are named after the famous British explorer, William John Burchell.

♦Zebra is a Portuguese word that means "wild ass".

♦Zebras are closely related to donkeys and horses, and can walk, trot, canter and gallop.

♦An upright mane is clear indication of good health in a zebra. A flagging mane is an indication of bad health. This is a result of loss of fat in the neck which supports the mane.

♦Burchell's zebras can mate with donkeys to produce a zebdonk, zonkey, zebrass or zorse.

♦Zebras are unpredictable by nature and this makes it difficult to domesticate them.

♦It is believed that the zebra's stripes act as camouflage when they are near long grasses, and that the stripes make it difficult for predators to differentiate one from the other when they are grouped together, especially in fading light.

Giraffe
(Giraffa camelopardalis)
Swahili: *Twiga*

Identification
The giraffe is a peaceful, cloven-hoofed ungulate and is the tallest mammal and largest ruminant in the world.

The background colour of the short fur is cream to tan, and is covered with an array of spots (polygons) in varying shades of brown that cover the entire body, apart from the underside. The spots darken with age.

The head of the giraffe is relatively small. It has large eyes with long lashes and medium-sized ears. The bump between the eyes (central swelling) is larger in the male. The muzzle is long and narrow. The prehensile, black tongue is up to 45cm long. It is toughened to enable the giraffe to eat the foliage of the acacia tree, including the thorns that are pulverised by the molars. The tongue is very effective at removing any insects on the face.

Both sexes have two horns (ossicones), which are up to 13cm long. The female horns are smaller, and have tufts of black hair on them. The male horns tend to be bald due to the tufts of hair being removed with time as a result of regular necking and combat fights with other males. The male giraffe may develop an additional three horns that are formed from calcium deposits as a result of combat fights.

The neck is long, and consists of seven cervical vertebrae. The brown mane, which runs the length of the cervical spine, is short and upright. The back slopes sharply from the shoulders to the hind quarters.

The legs are long and thin, with the forelegs approximately 10% longer than the hind legs. When strolling along, the foreleg and hind leg of one side move forward together, and alternate with the opposite side. This results in a peculiar, ungainly gait which is not particularly noticeable when walking slowly. When running, both of the hind legs move forwards together and cross over on the outside of the forelegs. The giraffe can run at speeds of 56km/h over short distances.

The tail has a tassel of long black hair at the tip.

The giraffe has good eyesight.

Height: Male 4.7-6.2m
Female 3.9-5m
Tail Length: 0.8-1m
Weight: Male 1,100-1,900kg
Female 700-1,200kg
(These figures are dependent upon species).

Life Span
Twenty-five years in the wild.

Physiology
The sheer height and size of the giraffe requires a large heart that is capable of maintaining adequate blood pressure to the brain. A combination of a series of one-way valves situated in the neck, and a network of finely meshed, elasticated veins and arteries at the base of the brain, prevents pooling of blood in the brain when the giraffe

lowers its head to drink, and reduces the pressure when it lifts its head up quickly. The body weight places additional pressure on the blood vessels in the lower legs. Toughened skin and an extra-tight sheath encapsulate the legs and maintain adequate pressure and circulation.

Habitat
Giraffes are found in the savannahs, open plains, grasslands, woodlands, and dense forests, particularly in the vicinity of the acacia tree.

Behaviour
Giraffes are non territorial, sociable animals, living in a leaderless, disorganised group, called a herd, of up to 20 individuals. They do not establish long-term relationships, therefore membership of the herd is fluid and constantly changes.

The herd includes females (cows), their offspring and younger males. Females usually stay with a herd. Dominance among the males (bulls) in the herd is established by necking. Males may live together in bachelor herds, while older males live a solitary life in isolation.

Giraffes sleep standing up, for a period of up two hours per day. They may occasionally rest on the ground with their legs folded beneath them, this makes them vulnerable to their predators as they have difficulty rising from the ground quickly.

Giraffes are diurnal and nocturnal

Diet
Giraffes are herbivores and browsers and spend up to 20 hours a day eating. They browse on bark, twigs, leaves, fruit, flowers, seed pods, climbers, vines and herbs. They have a particular liking for the foliage of the mimosa and acacia tree.

They are able to survive on very little water. When water is available they drink copious amounts, and in order to do so they have to splay their forelegs wide apart so they can lower their head and neck. In doing so they put themselves at risk from their predators.

Communication
Giraffes are quiet animals. They communicate through infrasonics, but will use a variety of sounds to communicate with each other when required - grunting, snorting, hissing, whistling and coughing.

Reproduction
Giraffes are polygamous and breed throughout the year. The majority of births take place in the dry months.

Males are constantly searching for females that are in oestrus, and detect this by smelling and tasting the female's urine.

The gestation period is up to 465 days. The female gives birth to a single calf while standing up. The calf, which is usually 1.8m tall, is able to run around shortly after being born. For the first two weeks of its life the calf spends a lot of its time lying down and resting. It is particularly vulnerable to predators such as lions, hyenas, leopards and wild dogs. Only 25-50% of calves reach adulthood.

While being fed by its mother the calf will be placed in a crèche alongside other calves, allowing its mother to go in search of food. The females take it in turn to look after the young calves. The calves grow at the rate of 2.5cm per day.

By the time the calf is six months old, it is relatively independent of its mother. Full independence is achieved between the ages of one and three years old.

Females reach sexual maturity between the ages of three to four years old. Males reach sexual maturity between the ages of four to five years old, but do not breed until they are eight years old.

Predators/Threats

Although lions are the only predator to threaten the adult giraffe, they are illegally hunted by poachers for their meat, hide, bones and hair. The tail hair is used to make jewellery and the hide is used to make rugs. Giraffe bones are now replacing elephant bones to make gun and knife handles and ornate earrings. This is a new booming, lucrative market. It is widely believed in Tanzania that giraffe bone marrow and brains cure HIV and AIDS. Hunting giraffes is illegal in Tanzania.

Loss of habitat for human settlements, agricultural use, pastoralism and timber logging is on the increase. Woodland environments are rapidly disappearing as the demand for charcoal increases. Consequently the giraffe's main source of food is diminishing and the home range is shrinking. There is nowhere to go. The erratic, prolonged droughts associated with climate change seriously affect the giraffe's long term survival. The Masai giraffe and reticulated giraffe are both classified as an *endangered species* (2019).

Trivia

♦Giraffe is an Arabic word that means "one that walks very fast". It can cover 4.5m with a single stride.

♦Giraffes were nicknamed "camelopards" by the ancient Romans, who believed that they resembled a cross between a camel and a leopard.

♦Necking is used in combat but can also be a sign of affection.

♦Giraffes are plagued by ticks, which are effectively removed by the oxpecker bird.

♦Giraffes are not a threat to humans or their livestock because they are a browser, eating foliage at a high level.

♦The female giraffe can delay the birth of the calf by up to two months until climatic and environmental conditions are more favourable.

♦The giraffe is the only animal to be born with horns (ossicones).

♦When threatened, the giraffe can deliver a single powerful blow with its legs that is capable of killing a man or lion instantly.

♦Some African tribes treat nose bleeds by using smoke from the burning hide of a giraffe.

♦The meat of a giraffe is edible and tastes like camel.

♦Local inhabitants openly try to sell tourists bracelets made from the tail hair of the giraffe.

♦Adult male giraffes develop glands underneath the skin that release an offensive rancid odour. Bull giraffes are nicknamed stink bulls.

Red-Billed Oxpecker Bird
(*Buphagus erythrorhynchus*)
Swahili: *Askari wa kiaru*

The red billed oxpecker bird or "tick bird" has a symbiotic relationship with its host and is regularly spotted riding round on the backs of antelope, eland, rhinos, hippos, giraffes, impala, zebras, warthogs and buffaloes, to name but a few.

They are semi-parasitic, living on a diet of dead skin, scabs, crabs, open wounds, ticks, larvae, fleas and flies from their host. They have a shrill, raucous alarm call that alerts their host and those nearby to the presence of predators.

Oxpecker birds are usually found in savannahs, bushlands, grasslands and wooded forest areas, being particularly common in national parks and game reserves.

Ruminants

Ruminants have a three-to-four-chambered stomach that allows them to process indigestible plant material into food of nutritional value. The half-chewed food is swallowed and enters the *rumen*, which is the first chamber of the stomach. This partly digested food is later regurgitated for further chewing and is known as *cud*. This process is repeated many times before the food continues through and exits the digestive system.

Trivia
♦Ruminants produce copious amounts of gas.
♦Ruminants' dung is fine ground.

Ticks
Swahili: *Kupe*

Ticks are small, blood-sucking, parasitic mites that live on mammals (including humans), birds and reptiles. They are capable of passing on dangerous, life-threatening diseases.

They bite their host, and insert a probe into the skin. Having attached themselves firmly, they slowly begin sucking blood. They are very difficult for the host to remove, and this is usually done by an oxpecker bird or by the host wallowing in mud. When submerged in clear water an air bubble forms around the tick's mouth, providing it with oxygen, but if thick mud is present, the small air bubbles cannot form, so the tick is deprived of oxygen and dies. Afterwards the host rubs itself against a tree or rock to remove the mud and the tick.

Hippopotamus
(*Hippopotamus amphibius*)
Swahili: *Kiboko*

Identification
The hippopotamus is the third largest mammal in the world.

The thick, smooth, sensitive skin is brown to greyish purple in colour, but the creases and the underside are pink. It has no sweat glands, but the pores secrete a colourless, oily substance, (blood sweat), which turns red and eventually brown. This acts as a moisturiser, sunscreen and anti-bacterial agent. Hair is present as bristles around the nose, mouth, ears and on the tip of the short, paddle-like tail. There is a sparse covering of fine hair over the whole body.

The body is large and barrel-shaped, and the legs are short and stumpy. There are four webbed toes on each foot that help to support and distribute its weight when it is on land.

The hippo has a large, broad head. The mouth is enormous with long, sharp, tusk-like canine teeth that may be up to 72cm long. The mouth opens to an angle of 150°.

The eyes and ears are small and are placed high on the head, allowing it to almost completely submerge. They have excellent eyesight and hearing, and a keen sense of smell.

Head & Body Length: 3.3-4.6m
Shoulder Height: 1.5-1.6m
Tail Length: 35-50cm
Weight: 1,800-3,600kg

Life Span
Forty-five years in the wild.

Habitat
Hippos are found resting and wallowing in wetlands, freshwater lakes, dams, slow-flowing rivers and swamps during the day, and at night they forage in the surrounding grasslands.

Behaviour
Hippos either live on their own, or in a family group called a pod. The average pod size is 15 but can be as big as 30. The pod includes the dominant territorial male (bull), females (cow), their offspring and inferior, submissive males. The only social bond is between the female and the calf.

Hippos have a sedentary lifestyle, resting, sleeping and wallowing in mud or water for up to 16 hours a day. The water keeps them cool, and prevents the skin from cracking, drying out and getting sunburnt. The eyes, ears and nostrils close when the hippo dives underwater. The hippo is able to submerge and resurface by inflating or deflating the lungs, and is able to remain under water for six minutes. They defecate in large quantities while in the water.

Male hippos are fiercely aggressive and territorial in water and will not tolerate the presence of another male. Only submissive males that have no mating rights are tolerated in the pod. Territories cover up to 250m along the bank of the river. They mark their territory by urinating backwards and spreading dung, as they defecate, with their swirling, short, paddle-like tail.

Hippos are not territorial on land, and emerge from the water on an evening to forage on their own. Travelling a well worn path of up to 10km, they spend four to five hours searching for food, consuming up to 45kg of grass. They return to the water before dawn.

Despite their cumbersome appearance hippos are surprisingly graceful in water, and on land they are able to run at speeds of 40km/h over a short distance.

Hippos are diurnal and nocturnal.

Diet
Hippos are herbivores and grazers, feeding on aquatic plants during the day, emerging from the water in the evening to feed on grass, crops, leaves, roots, tubers and wood bark in the surrounding grasslands. They are reputed to have carnivorous tendencies and may eat carrion or small mammals if the opportunity arises.

Communication
Hippos use a variety of vocalisations to communicate with each other in and out of the water - honking, wheezing, grunting and bellowing. Constant yawning is a warning sign.

Reproduction
Hippos are polygamous and breed throughout the year. The majority of births take place in the rainy season, when food is plentiful. The gestation period is up to 240 days. The female withdraws from the pod for a period of 14 days and gives birth to a single calf, this can occur either on land or in the water. The female is highly protective of its young calf. The calf is able to suckle under water. Weaning occurs between six and eight months. The calf remains with its mother until the next calf is born.

Females reach sexual maturity between five and six years old. Males reach sexual maturity between seven and eight years old.

Predators/Threats
Hippos have no natural predators, apart from poachers who illegally hunt them for their meat, hide and ivory canine teeth. The ban on the trade in elephant ivory has made poachers look further afield for another alternative, and hippos have been the perfect answer. Their teeth are easily carved into ornate objects. They are killed by locals for their meat and hippo fat, and if they raid crops in human settlements. Lions, crocodiles and hyenas are the main threat to the calf. Loss of habitat and the effects of climate change are a threat to their survival. The hippo is classified as a *vulnerable species* (2016).

Trivia
♦The word hippopotamus comes from a Greek word meaning "river horse".

♦Male hippos are easy to sex, as they are covered in scars as a result of combat fights with other males.

♦It is a myth that hippos can swim, they propel their bodies along the bottom of the river/pool bed with their legs.

Leopard

(*Panthera pardus*)
Swahili: *Chui*

Identification

The leopard is the smallest of the four big cats (tiger, lion, jaguar and leopard).

It has a long body and tail, with short, powerful legs. The broad paws have long, hooked, retractable claws that enable the leopard to climb trees.

The soft, dense, tawny-tan fur is covered with black circular rosettes. The underside is lighter with black spots. Single black spots are present on the head, throat, chest, and lower limbs. White spots are found behind the ears and on the tip of the tail.

The head is large in comparison with the rest of its body. The jaws are strong and powerful. It has small, rounded ears and yellow eyes with circular pupils.

The leopard has good eyesight, excellent hearing and a keen sense of smell.

Head & Body Length: 90cm-1.7m
Shoulder Height: 45-80cm
Tail Length: 60cm-1m
Weight: 30-90kg

Life Span

Fifteen years in the wild.

Habitat

Leopards are adaptable and are the most widely distributed of the big cats. They are found in savannahs, grasslands, desert plains, woodlands, forests and mountainous regions.

Behaviour

Secretive, solitary and elusive, leopards are extremely difficult to spot in the wild, spending the daylight hours resting high in the trees. They hunt alone, during the hours of darkness between dusk and dawn. By nature, leopards are extremely dangerous, aggressive and unpredictable.

Leopards are highly territorial and regularly patrol and defend their home range. They mark the boundaries of their territory with urine, faeces and claw marks on trees.

They are highly skilled and accomplished predators, using stealth and cunning to get close to the prey. They are extremely quick and agile, can run at speeds of 60km/h and are capable of bringing down prey three times their size. Giving chase over a short distance they pounce on their prey, and deliver a swift, powerful bite to the throat that kills instantly. They are known to kill prey when they are not hungry and will cache it away, either up a tree or in dense vegetation, away from other predators and scavengers such as hyenas and lions. They can return several days later to feed on the decomposing flesh.

Leopards are nocturnal.

Diet

Leopards are carnivorous and a highly efficient killer. They hunts and kill small to medium ungulates (antelope, gazelles), small mammals, primates, rodents, birds, fish and reptiles. They also prey on cheetah cubs.

Leopards can survive long periods without water.

Communication

Leopards are solitary animals and use scent marking and claw marking to make their presence known. A variety of vocalisations - growling, roaring, hissing, grunting and meowing, are utilised to communicate their mood and presence.

Reproduction

Leopards are polygamous and breed throughout the year. Solitary males are found in the company of a female (leopardess) for a period of one week, when they are in oestrous. There may on occasions be a fight for reproductive rights if another male is present. Courtship is a tense and noisy affair, with the female presenting herself in a crouched position. They mate continuously.

The gestation period is up to 105 days. The female gives birth to two to four cubs in a secluded spot, surrounded by dense vegetation and boulders. The cubs are hidden for up to eight weeks. They open their eyes after ten days. Their coat is a smoky grey colour, and has faded, poorly defined rosettes.

The female has a strong maternal bond with her cubs and raises them on her own. The cubs are suckled for three months and begin to eat meat at six to seven weeks. Instinctively leopards do not know how to hunt, catch and kill prey and survive as a predator, this must taught by their mother. The cubs accompany their mother on hunts at three months old. Small, disabled, live prey is used by the mother to teach the cubs the art of hunting, chasing and finally killing. By 12 months old the cubs are able to fend for themselves but may remain with their mother for up to 18-24 months.

Leopards are sexually mature between two to three years old.

Predators/Threats

Leopards are illegally hunted by poachers for their beautiful soft fur, teeth, whiskers, claws and tail. Their hide is used to make ceremonial robes, and body parts are used in traditional medicine in Asia. Trophy hunters will pay vast sums of money for the privilege of hunting and killing a leopard. Locals will shoot, poison and trap leopards in snares if they threaten their livestock. Loss of habitat, especially trees, competition from other predators for the diminishing prey and the effects of climate change are a threat to the leopard's survival. The leopard is classified as a *vulnerable species* (2015).

Trivia

♦Leopards are the largest spotted cat.

♦Leopards are the most elusive of the big cats, due partly to the fact that they are nocturnal and spend the daylight hours resting high up in a tree.

♦If a leopard is habituated it loses its natural fear and respect for humans, and can never be returned to the wild because of the danger it poses to tourists and local inhabitants.

♦Leopards are the most adept of all the big cats at climbing trees.

Lion
(*Pantheraleo*)
Swahili: *Simba*

Identification
Lions have large, powerful, muscular bodies and are the second largest member of the cat family, after tigers.

The short, coarse fur is a uniformly coloured golden yellow. The underside is lighter in colour.

The head is rounded, and the jaw strong, with long, powerful canine teeth. The amber eyes are spread wide. Excellent eyesight, good hearing and a keen sense of smell make lions a formidable predator.

Quick reflexes, combined with strong hind legs, enable the lion to pounce on its prey. The forelegs are more suited to grasping and knocking down prey, and are assisted by claws that are retractable and razor sharp.

The male's thick, shaggy mane covers the ears, neck and shoulders. The colour of the mane ranges from blonde to black, and darkens with age. The mane makes the male lion more attractive to females and offers some degree of protection to vital structures around the head and neck when fighting.

Both male and female lions have a distinctive black tuft of hair on the tip of the tail. This develops at five months onwards.

Males are up to 50% heavier than females.

Head & Body Length:	Male	1.7-2.5m
	Female	1.4-1.75m
Shoulder Height:	Male	1.2m
	Female	1m
Tail Length:		0.7-1m
Weight:	Male	150-240kg
	Female	120-180kg

Life Span
Sixteen years in the wild. Females live longer and are more numerous than male lions. The majority of males do not live beyond ten years, and usually die a violent death. Their risky lifestyle involves them engaging in frequent bouts of fighting with other males for dominance of the pride.

Habitat
Lions are usually found in savannahs, grasslands, bushlands, woodlands and semi-deserts.

Behaviour
Lions are sociable animals, living and hunting together in a permanent group called a pride. The average size of a pride is 15 but they can be as big as 30.

The pride consists of 4-12 related females (lionesses) who remain with the pride for life, as well as offspring, and a small number of unrelated adult males known as a coalition, who mate with and defend the females.

Male lions can lead a pride for up to three years, but the average length of time is 18 months.

Lions are territorial and regularly patrol their boundaries at night, marking the territory with urine, faeces or scent from their paws.

They tend to hunt under the cover of darkness, but are particularly active at dusk and at sunrise. Males do not usually participate in hunting, unless they are nomadic.

The lionesses work together as a highly organised, coordinated and successful team, in difficult, open terrain. Females are more suited to hunting than males, as they are smaller, more agile and less conspicuous. When hunting, they outmanoeuvre the prey by identifying, isolating and encircling the victim, usually getting to within 30m before launching a swift strike. They are able to run at speeds of 48-59 km/h for only a few seconds. The endurance of their prey tends to be much better - zebras and gazelles can accelerate and outrun a lion in less than six seconds. The victim is either strangled with a crushing bite to the windpipe, or is suffocated by the jaws completely encasing its muzzle. This 'kiss of death' is usually quick and clean. On very rare occasions the victim may be eaten alive.

After a kill the male eats first, followed by the lionesses and then the cubs. The feasting goes on for hours. The remains of the kill are left to scavengers.

Where adult male lions are present at a kill it is rare for the pride to be bothered by hyenas. Where there are fewer than five females present, hyenas are usually successful at stealing the kill.

Lions are nocturnal.

Diet

Lions are carnivorous and are highly efficient killers. Being at the top of the food chain, they have little to fear. Their skill, speed and strength allow them to successfully hunt and kill animals three times their size.

They hunt and kill medium to large ungulates (wildebeest, zebras), other predators and their cubs (leopards and cheetahs in particular), small mammals, rodents, birds and reptiles. It is not unknown for lions to scavenge from other predators, hyenas in particular.

It is extremely rare for lions to attack a buffalo or giraffe because of the risk of serious injury to themselves.

Lions can survive long periods without water.

Communication

Lions are unusual among the cats as they are sociable and live together in a commune. They spend up to 20 hours a day resting and sleeping in the shade. They display affection towards each other with facial and bodily postures and tactile behaviours that involve touching, rubbing and licking the head and neck. They use a variety of vocalisations to communicate with each other, purring to display pleasure, and roaring as a means to locate each other, to establish territory and to advertise their presence.

Reproduction

There is no distinct breeding season. The male members of the pride do not have established mating rights. The first male to encounter a female in oestrus has the rights.

It is usual for the females to give birth at approximately the same time as each other. This increases the cubs' chances of survival as they all develop at the same rate. The females share the responsibility of rearing the cubs together.

The gestation period is up to 120 days. The female gives birth to up to six cubs in a secluded spot away from the pride. New born cubs are blind, with their eyes opening after one week. They have lightly coloured brown spots on their bodies that fade away with time. The cubs are introduced to the pride after a period of six to eight weeks. Weaning occurs between six to seven months. They begin to participate in hunting at one year old and are able to hunt effectively by two, at which stage they usually leave their mother.

When young males reach maturity, they either leave the pride voluntarily or are forced to leave. Remaining is not an option, as they are systematically killed. They then lead a nomadic life, either on their own or with another male, until they are five years old and are able to challenge and take over their own pride. They have fully developed manes by the age of four years old. Young lions have pink noses until they are about four years old, after that black pigment begins to cover the nose.

The mortality rate for cubs is high, at about 80%. They are easy prey for jackals, hyenas, leopards, vultures, snakes and the occasional nomadic male lion. Death by starvation is common among cubs. They are last in the pecking order at a kill, and by the time their turn comes round, there is very little meat left. New males that challenge and take over a pride will kill all of the cubs that they encounter. This brings the females into oestrus, so that he can then father the next set of cubs in the pride.

Females reach sexual maturity at four years old. Males reach sexual maturity between three and five years old.

Predators/Threats

There are only 20,000 lions left in Africa. In the last decade the lion population has declined between 20 to 50%. The biggest threat to the lion's survival is loss of habitat due to agricultural expansion and urbanisation. Lions now occupy only 8% of their historical range. They are killed by locals for bush meat, and also when their livestock is threatened. Lions are killed in tribal rituals as a symbol of bravery, and are illegally hunted by poachers for their hide and body parts. It is believed that their body parts, bones in particular, possess medicinal and magical properties. Due to the decline in the number of tigers, poachers are now substituting tiger bones with lion bones in the Far East. Trophy hunters pay large sums of money to have the pleasure of hunting and killing a lion. This is unsustainable as the number of lions is rapidly declining. Competition from other predators for a declining number of prey, inbreeding and exposure to viruses are also threats to the lion's survival. Disease spreads easily amongst lions because they are sociable and a pride can soon be decimated. The effects of climate change should not be underestimated, the resulting drought and floods provide perfect conditions for the spread of epidemic diseases.

The lion is classified overall as a *vulnerable species* (2014), but is *extinct* in 26 African countries, and is classified as *critically endangered* in West Africa.

Trivia

♦The lion's mane is a strong indicator of its health and fitness: the darker and the thicker the mane, the healthier the lion. A lion with a black mane is superior, has more testosterone, will live longer and is more likely to survive from being wounded.

♦A lion's roar can be heard up to 8km away.

♦If a lion is habituated it loses its natural fear and respect of humans, and can never return to the wild because of the danger it poses to tourists and local inhabitants.

♦When stalking prey, the lion may wait up to nine hours before launching an attack.

♦Lions are not very efficient at losing heat, and this causes them to be quite lethargic during the day.

♦Lions' tongues are extremely abrasive - a triangular pattern of barbs that point backwards towards the throat help to strip skin and flesh from the bones of their prey.

♦A lion's night time vision is six times more powerful than a human's.

♦Small antelopes, such as the dik dik or impala, are captured alive by adult lions and are used as bait to teach the cubs the art of successful hunting.

♦Lone, male lions are particularly dangerous. They have usually been cast out of the pride by younger males who are competing for dominance. Being old, weak and injured and having no females to hunt for them, they turn to hunting for the weakest of prey, and that may include humans.

Spotted Hyena
(Crocuta crocuta)
Swahili: *Fisi*

Identification

The spotted hyena has a dog-like appearance.

Its most recognisable feature is a sloping back - this is due to the forelegs being longer and more muscular than the hind legs. There are four claws on each foot that are non-retractable and blunt.

The short, rough fur is tan to light brown in colour with irregular black/brown spots that fade with age. The underside is lighter in colour.

The mane is coarse and has reversed fur (fur that lies in an upward direction towards the head).

The tail is short and bushy with a black tuft at the end, and hangs down when standing or walking.

The head is small in comparison to the size of its body. It has large rounded ears, a dark muzzle and a black nose.

The genitals of the female resemble those of the male, which makes it very difficult to distinguish between the sexes.

Body Length:		0.95-1.5m
Shoulder Height:		75-85cm
Tail Length:		25-35cm
Weight:	Male	56-63kg
	Female	67-75kg

Life Span
Twelve years in the wild.

Habitat
Spotted hyenas are usually found in savannahs and grasslands, although they can be found in woodlands, tropical rain forests, forest edges, outskirts of a desert and in mountains up to 4,000m. They are able to survive near human habitations.

Behaviour
Spotted hyenas live together in a clan, which is a permanent social group. The clans are hierarchical, complex and sociable. The average clan size is up to 12, but can be as big as 90.

A single alpha female, the matriarch, dominates clan life. Male spotted hyenas are subservient and dominated by the females, and in the spotted hyena social hierarchy they are ranked the lowest. Males leave the clan when they reach sexual maturity and go in search of a new clan. Females remain with the clan for life.

Individually hyenas are not territorial, but once a group has been formed they will defend their territory aggressively. Clan life centres on the den, which is situated in the centre of the territory. The den has several entrances with numerous underground, interconnecting tunnels.

The hyenas mark the perimeter of their territory with a strong-smelling, yellow-coloured, oily substance that is excreted from the anal glands. Faeces deposited in latrines, and glands in their feet also allow them to scent-mark their territory.

Despite their reputation as opportunistic scavengers, spotted hyenas are actually bold, dangerous, highly skilled and organised hunters. They hunt on their own or in a small group. Hunting and tracking medium to larger ungulates is a team effort, initiated by one member of the pack. Their keen hearing, eyesight and sense of smell is essential for hunting, and their large heart gives them the ability to run long distances at 10km/h without tiring. They can achieve speeds of 60km/h over short distances when required.

Mainly nocturnal, spotted hyenas are particularly active at dusk. In game reserves they tend to be diurnal, sleeping from 10 a.m. until 4 p.m. to avoid the oppressive heat.

Diet

Spotted hyenas are Africa's most common carnivore, and their preference is for medium-sized ungulates. Their diet consists primarily of wildebeest, zebra and Thomson's gazelle, but they will eat birds, fish, tortoises, lizards, snakes, fruit, eggs, invertebrates, and other animals' excrement.

Spotted hyenas raid food stores and crops close to human habitation.

A combination of powerful jaws and teeth and highly acidic fluids within its digestive tract enables the hyena to digest its entire prey. Hair, horns and hooves are later regurgitated in the form of pellets. The faeces is white due to the high calcium content, as such it is easily recognisable.

Spotted hyenas can consume up to 18kg of meat at one time, almost one third of their body weight. This raises the body temperature, requiring rest afterwards to cool down.

Communication

Spotted hyenas are very vocal and use a wide range of vocalisations to communicate with each other - eleven in total. They also communicate by tactile phallic inspection, social grooming (mother and offspring only), scent-marking boundaries, and through body postures and courtship rituals.

Reproduction

There is no distinct breeding season. Spotted hyenas are polygamous and to prevent in-breeding the females mate with males from other clans. Courtship can last for up to a year.

The gestation period is up to 110 days. The female gives birth to two to four cubs and raises them on her own. The cubs are black at birth. Born with their eyes open and with fully developed teeth, it is not unknown for cubs of the same sex to either fight to the death or severely maim rival siblings until only one is able to survive. Cubs are introduced to the clan at two weeks old.

Cubs are suckled on milk for up to 18 months. The milk has an extremely high protein and fat content, which allows the female to go on long foraging trips leaving the cubs for periods of up to nine days without feeding them. Because of the speed at which spotted hyenas eat, they are unable to regurgitate their food to feed their young.

The cubs remain in the den until 12 months old, after which they accompany their mothers on foraging trips. Young hyenas are dependent on the clan system for their survival until they are two to three years old.

Spotted hyenas reach sexual maturity at about three years old.

Threats/Predators

Lions are the only predator to threaten the hyena. When livestock are threatened, humans actively hunt hyenas. They are usually killed by poisoning. Outside protected areas they are perceived to be a pest. The main threat to the hyena's survival is loss of habitat and the effects of climate change. The spotted hyena is classified as a *species of least concern* (2014).

Trivia

♦The hyena is closely related to the cat and mongoose, and is believed to be the evolutionary link between dogs and cats.

♦Female hyenas are 10% larger than the male and are more aggressive.

♦Male hyenas do not cock a leg to urinate.

♦Hyenas are very good swimmers.

♦Locals refer to the hyena as the dustbin man, as they rid the landscape of dead animal remains; they are also superstitious of hyenas and call them the dog of the devil.

♦In captivity hyenas can become very tame.

♦Hyenas are not on the trophy hunters' hit list because they are deemed ugly and unattractive.

♦Traditionally the Maasai leave their dead on the plains for the hyena to consume.

Antelopes
Swahili: *Swala*

Fifty species of antelope can be found in the continents of Africa and Asia, inhabiting a variety of environments ranging from tropical forests, mixed forests, marshlands, grasslands and savannahs to deserts and mountainous areas.

Antelopes are elegant, agile, cloven-hoofed ungulates that vary in size, shape and colour. Their short fur is light brown to grey. Antelopes that live on the plains are particularly vulnerable to predation and usually have an array of blotches or stripes on their head, body and legs to act as camouflage. Some species have white makings on their rumps that act as a warning signal to others when they are on the run from predators. Their legs are long, slender and powerful

Antelopes have large eyes with elongated horizontal pupils, and large ears. They have excellent eyesight, and a keen sense of smell and hearing

Their horns are hollow and lightweight and usually last a lifetime.

The males (buck) are usually larger than the females (doe)

Antelopes are herbivores and ruminants, and are either a grazer or a browser, or a combination of both. Antelopes that are pure grazers are water-dependent and need to drink every one to two days, whereas the browsers are able to extract sufficient moisture from the plants they feed on. All antelopes are diurnal, but have a preference for feeding early morning and late afternoon

Antelopes that live in or near woodlands and forests where there is a constant, plentiful supply of food and water, usually remain there throughout their natural lives. The antelopes on the plains are constantly on the move searching for food and water.

The majority of antelopes live in large herds on the open plains either in bachelor herds made up of young males, small herds of females, mixed herds or solitary bulls. Some species of antelope live on their own.

Most antelopes are polygamous, however a few species (such as the dik-dik) are monogamous. The African antelope only produce one offspring. The gestation period for the small to medium-sized antelope is 120-182 days, and for the larger antelope is 243-273 days

Antelopes reproduce when there is an abundance of food, and in some cases are able to reproduce all year round

Antelopes are prey for all the major predators, who seek out the young, sick, injured and old. They are one of the world's fastest land animals, and being extremely agile, their constant dodging, twisting, turning and change of direction enables them to confuse and outrun most predators. Some species go into hiding in the bush when threatened.

Antelopes use a variety of vocalisations to communicate with each other. Visual signals, scent marking, tactile behaviours and bodily postures are also used. When threatened, intimidated or required to assert their dominance they will utilise antagonistic, aggressive behaviours.

When alarmed or excited antelopes are able to jump up and down on extended, straight legs. All four legs leave the ground at once and the back is arched - this is known as pronking or stotting. This demonstrates to any watching predators that they are fit and would not be easy prey. Glands in the hoofs release scent that allows any antelopes that have lost their way to find their way back to the herd.

Bushbuck
Tragelaphus scriptus
Swahili:*Pongo /Mbawala*

Identification

The bushbuck is a graceful, medium sized antelope, and the smallest of the spiral horned antelopes.

The colour of the bushbuck's coat varies according to its geographical location. Bushbucks living in Eastern and Southern Africa are yellow in colour and have fewer white markings. Bushbucks living in Northern and Western Africa are reddish brown in colour and have an increase in number of stripes and spots present.

The male bushbuck's coat is a rich chestnut to dark brown colour. Narrow white stripes are present on the sides of the body alongside white spots. The fur around the knee is black. The female's coat is lighter in colour. Highly visible geometric white spots are present on the chin, ears, neck, tail and leg. A white band is present at the base of the neck. Ticks may be observed round the neck of the bushbuck as it will not tolerate the oxpecker bird removing them.

Both male and female coats darken with age making any white markings more conspicuous.

The ears and eyes are big. The muzzle is white.

Only the male bushbuck has horns. These start to grow when they are 10 months old and continue to grow throughout its life. The horns are long, sharp and straight, with one twist near the base.

Shoulder Height:		65cm-1m
Weight:	Males	40-80kg
	Females	25-60kg
Horns:		40cm
Tail:		20cm

Life Span
Twelve years in the wild.

Habitat
Bushbucks are adaptable living in a variety of environments, from sea level to mountain tops (3,000m), deserts, semi-arid areas, savannahs, bush lands, woodlands, rain forests and montane forests. They like to live near water in the bushy undergrowth or on the edge of forests in the shade.

Behaviour
Bushbucks are shy, elusive and live a solitary life. Males avoid each other. Females form temporary bonds with the young, and they only spend a few hours each day together. Bushbucks are not territorial. Males (ram) only defend their territory when the females are in oestrous. When confronted by a rival male, they both arch their backs and walk around each other in an intimidating manner with a high stepping gait. It is very rare for a bushbuck to engage in a fight. They are a slow, awkward runner, a good swimmer and can jump 1.8m. When they are alarmed or threatened they freeze and

lower themselves down to the ground, remaining motionless in the hope that they have not been detected, moving on once the danger has passed.

Bushbucks are active 24 hours a day. They are particularly active early morning but can in certain habitats become entirely nocturnal.

Diet

Bushbucks are adaptable herbivores and are grazers and browsers. They are primarily a browser feeding on tubers, herbs, shrubs, bark, twigs, leaves, acacia pods, fallen fruit and flowers, and grazing on selective grasses if there is no other alternative. They are usually found living in close proximity to water. They are able to survive on the early morning dew when there is a shortage of water.

Reproduction

The mating ritual of the bushbuck involves rubbing and spreading their scent on each other's bodies and resting their heads on each other. The gestation period is six to seven months. The female (ewe) gives birth to a single calf (lamb) in dense undergrowth, usually in the rainy season. After the birth she cleans the calf, and eats the placenta. Returning several times a day she will suckle the calf and eat its dung so that the predators cannot detect the calf's scent. The calf accompanies its mother when it is four months old.

Females reach sexually maturity at 14 months old. They are able to reproduce twice a year.

Males are sexually mature at 11 months old but do not mate until they are three years old.

Predators/Threats

Bushbucks are natural prey for African wild dogs, cheetahs, crocodiles, hyenas, leopards and lions. The young are natural prey for baboons, chimpanzees, golden cats, servals, eagles and pythons. Bushbucks are perceived to be a pest by the local farmers and are hunted for their meat and thin, supple hide. Loss of habitat and the effects of climate change are a threat to the bushbuck's survival.

The bushbuck is classified as a *least threatened species* (2016).

Trivia

♦Bushbucks are also known as imbabala.
♦Bushbucks are closely related to the kudu and nyala.
♦Bushbucks are widespread - approximately 1.3 million bushbucks live in 40 African countries.
♦Bushbucks have 32 teeth.
♦Bushbucks suffer from rinderpest.

Common Eland

(*Taurotragus oryx*)
Swahili: *Mpofu/Mbungu/Pofu*

Identification

The eland is the largest and slowest species of antelope.

It is a large, muscular antelope with a cow-like resemblance. It has a smooth, light tan-coloured coat, with a blue-grey hue over the neck and shoulders that darkens with age. Males are darker than females. Narrow, vertical white stripes may be present over the forequarters.

The neck is short and thickened and a hump straddles the shoulders. A large, loose fold of skin covered in black hair hangs down underneath the neck - this is known as the dewlap. The dewlap on the male is more prominent and increases in size with age.

A short, darkened upright mane runs down the neck. The ears are small and narrow and the mouth and muzzle are pointed. The eyes are on the side of the head and the pupils are elongated horizontally - this increases the eland's peripheral vision. A tuft of black hair is present on the male's forehead, which gets longer and thicker with age.

Black and white leg markings are present. The hooves are rounded and scent glands are found above the hooves on the hind legs - this allows the eland to leave a scent trail for any that have wandered away from the herd.

The tail is long with a tuft of long black hair on the tip.

Both sexes have long, black spiralled horns with a sharp point.

Elands have excellent hearing and a keen sense of smell.

Head & Body Length:	Male	2.4-3.4m
	Female	2-2.8m
Shoulder Height:	Male	1.5-1.8m
	Female	1.2-1.5m
Tail Length:		50 -90 cm
Length of Horns:		60-65cm
Weight:	Male	400-1000kg
	Female	300-600kg

Habitat

Elands are adaptable and is usually found in semi-deserts, savannahs, grasslands, miombo woodlands and mountainous regions up to 4,600m.

Behaviour

Elands are gregarious, non territorial, nomadic antelopes living in loosely formed herds of 30-80 individuals that roam over large areas, particularly during the dry season. Membership of the herd is fluid and constantly changes.

Females live together either in a small, all-female group, or with a group of females and their offspring. Males live together in small all-male groups of three to four individuals in which there is a dominance hierarchy based on size, strength and age. Older males are usually solitary. Elands are shy and docile and if disturbed they quietly disappear, but when threatened will make a very hasty retreat.

Elands are sedentary and despite their cumbersome appearance they can run at speeds of 40km/h. They also have sufficient stamina to maintain a steady trot indefinitely, and have the ability when required to jump 2-3m high in the air from a standing position.

Males are more sedentary than females.

Elands are diurnal and nocturnal.

Diet
Elands are adaptable herbivores and are browsers and grazers. They browse on leaves, branches, bark, berries, fruit and seed pods, and graze on grasses, tubers, bulbs and roots. If water is in short supply the eland is capable of extracting sufficient moisture from the plants it feeds on to meet its needs.

Communication
Elands use a variety of vocalisations, visual signals, bodily postures, movement and scent marking to communicate with each other.

Reproduction
Elands are polygamous and breed throughout the year. The majority of the births take place before the start of the rainy season. During the mating season the males (bucks) become increasingly possessive towards sexually receptive females (does), and will fend off potential rivals. The gestation period is 280 days. The female gives birth to a single calf, which is hidden in vegetation for up to two weeks before being introduced into a nursery where it joins the other calves. The calves spend a lot of time establishing bonds by grooming and licking each other. Adult females present in the nursery group protect and defend the calves.

The calf is weaned by the time it is six months old. It will remain in the nursery group until it is two years old, after which it will join a single sex group.

Females are sexually mature between 30-36 months old.

Males are sexually mature between 4-5 years old.

Predators/Threats
Elands are natural prey for African wild dogs, cheetahs, hyenas, leopards and lions. They are also hunted by humans for their hide and rich tasting meat. Loss of habitat and the effects of climate change are a threat to the eland's survival. The eland is classified as a *species of least concern* (2016).

Trivia
♦The eland is also known as the *southern eland*.

♦Elands are depicted in early East African rock art.

♦Attempts have been made to domesticate elands, but this has proved extremely difficult as they like to roam over large areas. With persistence they do adapt and are able to mate in captivity.

♦Their meat is considered to be rich and tasty, and their milk is highly nutritious due to the high fat and protein content.

♦Elands are able to conserve water through raising their body temperature by as much as 7°C.

♦Images used in this section were taken at Crater Lake Sanctuary, Naivasha, Kenya.

Coke's Hartebeest
(Alcelaphus buselaphus)
Swahili: *Kongoni*

Identification
The hartebeest is a large antelope, renowned for its speed and endurance when pursued.

It appears awkward, cumbersome and ungainly. It has a sloping back with humped up shoulders that are higher than the hindquarters. The legs are long and slender.

The coat is long and fine and is a light tan/fawn colour. The hair on the chest, underside, legs and rump is much lighter in colour.

Males are darker than females. The tail is relatively short with a tassel of long, black hair.

The hartebeest has a long head. The eyes are set high on the narrow face, with glands present beneath each one. The ears are long, narrow and pointed.

Both sexes have horns that arise from a pedicle on the forehead. The horns are short, ringed, curve upwards and backwards and have sharp tips.

The hartebeest has good eyesight and a keen sense of smell.

Body Length:	1.5-2.45m
Shoulder Height:	1.1-1.5m
Tail:	30-70cm
Weight:	120-220kg
Horns:	30-70cm

Life Span
Between 10-15 years in the wild.

Habitat
Hartebeest are usually found in savannahs, grasslands, open forests and woodlands up to an altitude of 2,000m.

Behaviour
Hartebeests are sociable, sedentary, peace-loving animals that live in mixed herds. These herds can on occasions contain up to 300 individuals and are comprised of:

♦Females and their offspring that have formed small to medium-sized herds of 5-20 individuals moving freely between territories. Females remain with their mother until they give birth to their own offspring.

♦Bachelor herds made up of young males who have left their mothers by the time they are 20 months old. They will attempt to take over and establish their own territory when they are three to four years old. Males defend their territory aggressively when challenged, and particularly during the breeding season. The boundary of the territory is marked with urine and dung heaps placed at regular intervals. Males lose their territory after seven to eight years and live in solitary isolation.

♦Non-territorial adult males.

♦Territorial males who may be solitary.

Because of their sedentary nature hartebeest are conspicuous and easy prey for predators and hunters. When feeding they have a lookout on duty who will warn of approaching danger by snorting loudly. When the need arises they are able to run at speeds of 70-80km/h, usually remaining in single file.

Hartebeest are diurnal. They are active early morning and late afternoon.

Diet
Hartebeests are herbivores and pure grazers that are able to feed on medium height grasses of poor quality. They are water-dependent and need to drink daily.

Communication
A variety of vocalisations, visual signals, scent marking, tactile and territorial behaviours are used to communicate with each other.

Reproduction
Hartebeests are polygamous and breed all year round. The peak season for giving birth is in the dry season. During the mating season the male is preoccupied sniffing females' genitals, checking to see if they are in oestrus before proceeding to mate.

The gestation period is 214-242 days. The female gives birth to a single calf in a secluded spot. The calf is hidden in dense undergrowth for two weeks, with the female returning several times a day to feed it. Females remain with the maternal herd until they give birth.

Hartebeests reach sexual maturity between 18-30 months old.

Predators/Threats
Hartebeests are natural prey for African wild dogs, hyenas, jackals, leopards and lions, and the young are preyed on by cheetahs. They are hunted by humans for their meat. Loss of habitat and competition for grass with domestic livestock, alongside the effects of climate change, are a threat to the hartebeest's survival. The hartebeest is classified as a *species of least concern* (2016).

Trivia
♦The hartebeest was used in sacrificial ceremonies by the ancient Egyptians.

♦The meat is apparently delicious and tastes like venison.

♦Hartebeests are rarely seen in zoos as they are difficult to breed and are a danger to each other and humans when in small confined places.

♦Despite the short length of its horns the hartebeest is capable of using them to kill.

Gerenuk

(Litocranius walleri)
Swahili:*Swala twiga*

Indentification
The gerenuk is an antelope with a giraffe-like appearance, that is related to the gazelle.

The smooth upper coat is a reddish brown/tawny colour, and the flanks are light fawn. The underside and inside of the legs are cream coloured. Scent glands are present on their knees and between their split hooves.

The gerenuk has an elegant, slender, elongated neck. The small narrow head is wedge shaped, with

a pointed mouth that has mobile lips which are surrounded by white fur. The ears are large. The large, round eyes are encircled by white fur. Preorbital glands are located in front of the eyes, which produce a tar like substance that is used to scent mark their territory. The long thin legs enable the gerenuk to run quickly, but are prone to breaking, making them easy prey for predators.

The tail is short with a tuft of black hair on the tip.

The male has strong, heavily ringed, lyre shaped (s shaped) horns. The female does not have horns.

The gerenuk has excellent hearing and eyesight.

The male is larger than the female.

Height/Tall:	Males	80cm-1.05m
	Females	80cm-1m
Head & Body Length:		1.4-1.6m
Tail Length:		25-35cm
Horns:		25-44cm
Weight:	Males	28-52 kg
	Females	28-45g

Life Span
Eight years in the wild. Thirteen years in captivity.

Habitat
Usually found in deserts, open plains, savannahs and woodlands. They are one of the most desert adapted antelopes, and can survive long periods without water.

Behaviour
Females live in same sex groups of up to ten individuals, and may include their offspring and juveniles. Young males live in bachelor herds, and older males are usually solitary and highly territorial, spending their time scent marking their territory with secretions from a preorbital gland. Gerenuks spend most of their time feeding.

They are able to run at speeds of 56km/h

Gerenuks are diurnal.

Diet
Gerenuks are adaptable herbivores that browse on the leaves, buds, flowers and fruit of bushes and trees. They also eat young shoots and herbs. The gerenuk's ability

to stand upright on its hind legs, along with its long neck, enables it to feed on foliage that other antelopes cannot access. Their ability to extract sufficient water from the plants they eat enables them to survive in deserts and scrublands.

Communication
Gerenuks are very vocal and use a variety of vocalisations to communicate with each other. They will whistle when annoyed, bleat when in danger and make a buzzing sound when alarmed.

Reproduction
Gerenuks breed all year round. The male usually mates once he has established a territory. Mating begins when a male encounters a female, he will display his neck and horns sideways, and if she is receptive he will mark her with the scent from his preorbital scent gland and taste her urine.

The gestation period is up to 212 days. The female leaves the herd to give birth to a single fawn (calf) that she licks clean. The fawn is able to stand up and walk within minutes of being born. For the first few weeks of its life the fawn remains hidden in long grass, and the mother returns two to three times a day to feed it. Before leaving the fawn she will lick it clean and eat its waste to remove any traces of its scent. The mother communicates with the fawn by gently bleating.

The mother cares for the fawn until it is one year old. Male gerenuks leave the maternal herd when they are 18 months old to establish their own territory.

Females reach sexual maturity at one year old. Males reach sexual maturity at 18 months old.

Predators/Threats
Gerenuks are natural prey for African wild dogs, caracals, cheetahs, lions, leopards, honey badgers, hyenas, jackals and servals. Loss of habitat and the effects of climate change are a threat to the gerenuk's survival. The gerenuk is conservation dependent and is classified as a *near threatened species* (2016).

Trivia
♦The Gerenuk is known as the giraffe gazelle and as the Wallers gazelle.
♦The name gerenuk means *giraffe necked* in the Somali language.
♦The gerenuk was first described by the naturalist Victor Brooke in 1878.
♦The images in this section were taken in Meru National Park, Kenya.

Grant's Gazelle
(Gazella granti)
Swahili: *Swala granti*

Identification

The Grant's gazelle is a medium-sized antelope, often found grazing alongside the Thomson's gazelle.

The upper coat is a pale fawn colour, while the inside of the legs, the rump and the underside of the body are white. The white markings present on the rump extend to above the tail. A fine black stripe encircling the white rump is sometimes present on the female. The skin on the female's teats is coloured black, and white hair is present on the udder. The legs are long and slender.

The eyes are large, and the ears are long and pointed. A white stripe with a black outer edge extends from the horn to the muzzle. There is a white patch under the throat.

Both sexes have long, black-ringed horns that curve backwards and then forwards in an S shape.

Grant's gazelles have excellent eyesight and hearing.

Males are larger than females.

Body Length:	1.4-1.6m
Shoulder Height:	75-90cm
Weight:	38-82kg
Tail Length:	20-28cm
Horns:	45-80cm

Life Span

Between 10-14 years in the wild.

Habitat

Usually found in savannahs, grasslands and semi-desert areas up to an altitude of 2,500m, they avoid areas where there is tall grass. They are extremely tolerant of dry habitats.

Behaviour

Grant's gazelles are sociable animals living either in small herds of females with their young (10-25 individuals), all-male bachelor herds or territorial males. Membership of the herds is fluid and is constantly changing. When food is plentiful the herds may merge and number several hundred, but as food becomes scarce the herds fragment.

Grant's gazelles are territorial. During the breeding season males mark their territories with secretions from glands located on their face, groin, knees and feet, as well as using urine and faeces. The territorial male defends its territory, and actively seeks to retain any females or groups of females that randomly stray into its territory.

Young males are tolerated in the herd as long as they ignore the females.

The Grant's gazelle's agility and ability to run at speeds of 76-80km/h help them to outrun their predators. While on the run they leap high in the air with all four legs leaving the ground, and this alerts other gazelles to the presence of predators.

The Grant's gazelle is diurnal and nocturnal.

Diet
Being migratory herbivores they graze on succulent, short green grasses and shoots, and browse on herbs, shrubs, leaves, fruit and berries. They are water independent and are able to get all of the necessary moisture from the plants that they feed on.

Communication
They are quiet animals and use bodily postures to communicate with each other, this can include squatting while defecating and passing urine that warns off other males, leaping high into the air with all four legs leaving the ground to alert other gazelles of predators, and scent marking for territory identification using urine and dung heaps. Young males engage in fighting, but with age they use ritualised postures (feet stamping, bucking and rearing up).

Reproduction
Grant's gazelles are polygamous. Births peak in the months of January and August. The gestation period is 196 days and the female gives birth to a single fawn in tall grass. The female returns several times a day to feed the fawn. The fawn remains hidden in the grass for two to six weeks before joining the herd. They are weaned by the time they are six months old. Males leave the maternal herd when they are 12 months old to join bachelor herds, this also prevents in-breeding.

Females are sexually mature between 9-12 months old.

Males are sexually mature between 18-24 months old.

Predators/Threats
Grant's gazelles are natural prey for African wild dogs, cheetahs, hyenas, leopards, lions and pythons. The young are preyed upon by jackals. They are hunted by humans for their meat, hide and horns. Loss of habitat and the effects of climate change are a threat to their survival. Grant's gazelles are classified as a *species of least concern* (2016).

Trivia
♦Grant's gazelles are tolerant of high temperatures and drought conditions.

♦If the bodily temperature rises above that of the brain, a combination of panting and air-cooled blood circulating through the nose will reduce the overall temperature.

♦It is thought that the white underside helps to deflect the heat radiated from the ground.

Impala

(Aepyceros melampus)
Swahili: *Swala pala*

Identification

The impala is a slender, elegant medium-sized antelope.

It has a short, smooth, glossy top coat that is a pale, chestnut brown colour and has tan-coloured flanks. The underside and buttocks are white. A narrow, vertical black stripe is present on both rumps. The tail is small and white with a single black stripe down the centre.

The neck is long and slender. The ears are very large with black marking on the tips and white hair inside. White hair is present on the eyebrow, the chin and upper throat. The large eyes are encircled by white hair.

The impala has long, slender legs with hoofed feet. The hind legs have a tuft of coarse black hair posteriorly above the hooves, which covers a scent gland.

The male impala has lyre-shaped, ridged, ringed horns that continue to grow throughout life. The tips of the horns become shiny with age. Females do not have horns.

The impala has a keen sense of sight, smell and hearing.

The female impala is slightly smaller than the male.

Body Length:	1.2-1.6m
Shoulder Height:	75-99cm
Tail Length:	30-45cm
Weight:	40-80kg
Horns:	45-92cm

Life Span

Up to 15 years in the wild.

Habitat

Impalas are usually found in savannahs, grasslands, open forests and woodlands with little undergrowth. They are always found near water and avoid areas with tall grasses.

Behaviour

Impalas live in single-sexed herds. Males live in herds of up to 30 individuals. Females and offspring are found in herds of between 10-50 individuals with one dominant male, but herds can be as large as 200. If females wander into another male's territory and attempt to join the new herd, the male will try to stop them but is rarely successful.

When food is plentiful, and during the rutting season, the dominant male becomes highly territorial and will round up any females that enter its territory. They mark their territory with urine, dung heaps (middens) and with a scent that is excreted from facial glands. The dominant male will defend his territory aggressively with bodily postures, threatening behaviour and loud vocalisations. Young males congregate in bachelor herds and are allowed to remain in the dominant male's territory as long as they ignore the females.

During dry periods the territories are abandoned and large herds of males and females form and go in search of food together.

Impala are prey to all major predators. They are extremely agile, and are able to leap 2.5m high in the air and jump distances of 9m. When frightened and alarmed the herd scatters in all directions, usually in the direction of dense vegetation. Their constant dodging, twisting, turning and change of direction, confuses the predators and enables the impala to outrun them. The impala can run at speeds of 64km/h.

Impala are primarily diurnal but are also considered to be nocturnal.

Diet
Impalas are adaptable herbivores, and are grazers and browsers. They graze on young succulent grasses during the rainy season, and browse on herbs, shrubs, seed pods, fruit, blossom and leaves during the dry season. During the dry season they need to drink daily.

Communication
Impalas are very vocal and use a variety of vocalisation to communicate with each other from grunting and roaring to snorting. Visual signals, scent marking and bodily postures (tail raising) are also used. When threatened, intimidated or required to assert their dominance, they will utilise antagonistic, aggressive (chasing, fighting, herding) behaviours.

Reproduction
Impala are polygamous. Mating (rutting) takes place between March and June and lasts for three weeks. Dominant males (bucks) are highly territorial during the rutting season. They will try to separate and keep any females (does) that are in oestrus and wander into their territory so that they can mate with them. The males are able to detect females that are in oestrus by smelling and tasting their urine.

The male expends an enormous amount of time and energy defending his territory from rival males, and rounding up and keeping the females together in the herd. The more females in the herd, the more time the male has to spend on keeping them together. The male is particularly vocal during this period. At the end of three months the male retires, exhausted, to recuperate in a bachelor group. After the mating season, other males are allowed to join the herd.

The gestation period is up to 200 days. The female gives birth to a single fawn in a secluded spot. The fawn is able to walk shortly after birth and is usually isolated from the herd for several days before being introduced into a nursery, where it joins the other fawns. The young fawns are vulnerable and are safer in a group, as it is more difficult for a predator to isolate and pick one out. Maternal bonds are weak and the only contact the fawn has with its mother is when it is suckled and when predators are present. The young are weaned between four to six months, after which any existing maternal bonds completely disappear. Young males are forced to leave the maternal herd between six and eight months old and join a bachelor group. They are unable to hold a territory until they are six years old. Females usually remain with the maternal herd.

Females reach sexual maturity at one year old. Males reach sexual maturity at 18 months old.

Predators/Threats

Impalas are natural prey for African wild dogs, caracals, cheetahs, hyenas, jackals, leopards, lions, crocodiles and pythons. The young are preyed on by baboons and martial eagles. They are one of the most commonly hunted antelopes, and are hunted for their meat and hide. Loss of habitat and the effects of climate change, particularly drought conditions, are a threat to the impala's survival. The impala is classified as a *species of least concern* (2016)

Trivia

♦The female impala can delay the birth of the fawn between two to four weeks until climatic and environmental conditions are more favourable.

♦Impala use designated areas to excrete in.

♦When it rains, impalas stop feeding and stand close together, with their backs to the wind.

♦Hunters use impala as bait when hunting leopards.

♦When the impala leaps into the air, scent is released from a special scent gland above the hoof which enables other impala in flight to pick up and follow its trail.

♦The meat of the impala is tender and sweet. It can be tenderised in pineapple juice for 30 minutes covered with papaya leaves.

Kirk's Dik-Dik
(*Madoqua kirkii*)
Swahili: *Digidigi funo/Dikidiki/Digidigi/Dika mbwa/Dik dik*

Identification
The dik-dik is a cloven-hoofed, miniature antelope.

The upper coat area is a yellowish grey to reddish brown colour. The underside, flanks and legs are lighter.

The head is large, in comparison to the size of its body. There is a small, upright tuft of hair on the top of its head that conceals two small, pointed, ringed horns. The horns slope backwards and are only present in the male. The ears are large.

White hair surrounds the large dark eyes, and is found beneath the chin. On the inner corner of each eye there is black spot under which lies a specialised preorbital gland that secretes a dark sticky substance. The dik-dik is able to scent mark its territory by inserting either a twig or grass stem into this gland.

The pointed, elongated snout is mobile and has nostrils that point downwards. A combination of blood flowing through the snout that is air cooled, and panting, helps to lower the dik-dik's bodily temperature and minimise water loss.

The dik-dik has delicate, spindle-like legs with small rubbery hooves that help to maintain its grip and balance when running over uneven, rocky ground.

The dik-dik has a short tail.

The dik-dik has excellent eyesight, hearing and sense of smell.

Female dik-diks are slightly larger than the males.

Head & Body Length: 55-72cm
Shoulder Height: 30-45cm
Tail Length: 4-9cm
Weight: 2.7-6.5kg
Horns: 4-11cm

Life Span
Three to four years in the wild.

Habitat
Dik-diks are found in a variety of locations ranging from savannahs and open plains to dense forests. They need low-growing, dense ground cover to feed on, and to hide in from predators. Always alert and on the lookout for predators, if the grasses and shrubs grow too tall for them to see over, they will move on.

Behaviour
Dik-diks are shy, graceful, elusive animals that spend a lot of time hiding in the bush. They are territorial and both sexes scent mark the territory with secretions from glands on their feet and head, urine and faeces. Their dung heaps (middens) can be up to 30cm in diameter and are used regularly. Only the male defends the family territory. Well-used, worn trails through the bush form part of their territory.

Dik-diks are vigilant, agile animals that react to the alarm call of other animals. They usually zig zag from side to side if startled and on the run. If in danger they can reach speeds of 42km/h but more often than not they will go into hiding. When the danger has passed by, they rub noses and begin scent-marking their territory.

Dik-diks are primarily nocturnal, but are considered to be diurnal as well. They feed early morning and late afternoon and rest at midday.

Diet
Dik-diks are adaptable herbivores, and are grazers and browsers, grazing on succulent grasses and browsing on roots, tubers, herbs, shrubs, shoots, leaves, buds, fruit and berries. The dik-dik is not water-dependent and is able to extract sufficient moisture from the plants it feeds on to meet its needs.

Communication
Dik-diks use a variety of vocalisations to communicate with each other. Visual signals, bodily postures, movement and scent marking are also used.

Reproduction
Dik-diks are monogamous and give birth to two litters a year, in the months of November/December and April/May. Although the female (ewe) does not seek to mate outside the life-long, bonded pair, the male (ram) will guard and protect her from other males when she is in oestrus.

The gestation period is up to 174 days. The female gives birth to a single fawn, which is suckled within 15 minutes of being born. The fawn is hidden in dense undergrowth for two to six weeks. The hiding place may change every few days. The female returns several times a day to feed the fawn. The male regularly licks and grooms the fawn. The young are weaned after three to four months and are fully grown by seven months old. Remaining with their mother until the next young is born, they are then forcibly driven away by either parent to find a mate and establish their own territory.

Females reach sexual maturity between six to eight months old. Males reach sexual maturity between eight to twelve months old.

Mortality for the young is 50%.

Predators/Threats
Dik-diks are natural prey for baboons, leopards, lions, cheetahs, hyenas, jackals, African wild dogs, crocodiles, monitor lizards, eagles and pythons. The young are preyed upon by baboons, eagles and genet cats. They are hunted and trapped by humans for their hide. The small bones of the legs and feet are used to make traditional jewellery. They are classified as a *species of least concern* (2016).

Trivia
♦The dik-dik is able to survive long periods without water, consequently their faeces are very dry and hard, and the urine is concentrated.

♦Salt is important to a dik-dik's diet and wellbeing.

♦The dik-dik makes a whistling noise when disturbed, which alerts the other animals to the presence of predators or hunters.

♦The dik-dik gets its name from the noise it makes when alarmed.

Greater Kudu
(*Tragelaphus strepsiceros*)
Swahili:*Tandala mkubwa*

Identification

The greater kudu is a graceful woodland antelope and is the world's third largest antelope (behind the eland and bongo).

It has a long, narrow body and long legs. The muscular shoulder and neck muscles continue to grow throughout the male's life. The short smooth coat is a brown bluish grey colour that fades with age. Bald patches also appear with age. Six to ten thin, white vertical stripes are present on the body.

The head is darker in colour. A chevron of white hair is present between the eyes. A single white diagonal cheek spot is present on either side of the face. A short upright mane extends from the top of the head to the shoulders.

The male has a long fringe beard that extends underneath the throat.

The mobile pink ears are large, round, and with a fringe of white hair on the periphery.

The horns begin to grow when the male is six to twelve months old and continue until it is six years old. The long, large spiralled horns have two and a half twists present, and in exceptional circumstance three twists are present.

Females are hornless.

The bushy tail has a black tip, the underneath side is white.

The greater kudu has excellent hearing and eyesight.

The male is larger than the female.

Head & Body Length: 1.85-2.45m
Shoulder Height: 1.0-1.6m
Tail Length: 30-55cm
Weight: 120-317kg
Horns: 1.8m

Life Span

Seven to eight years in the wild. Up to 23 years in captivity.

Habitat

Greater kudus are usually found in on the edge of forests, woodlands, bush lands, thorny scrubland, lowland hills and mountains up to 2,400m.

Behaviour

Greater kudus are reputed to be the most peaceful animal in Africa, and are non territorial. Females live in small non-hierarchical herds of six to ten individuals that include the calves and sub adults. The males either live in a bachelor herd or remain solitary. Dominance amongst the bulls is based on size and fighting ability. The males are rarely aggressive, but on the odd occasion that they do engage in fighting their twisted horns can become interlocked, and this results in death. They engage in social licking, and this occurs in family groups and bachelor herds. The herds congregate together in the dry season and disperse in the wet season.

Greater kudus are diurnal. They feed early morning and late afternoon and rest in the shade at midday. Masters of camouflage, they can stand motionless for prolonged periods and then silently disappear in the blink of an eye into the undergrowth. They are shy, highly alert and very difficult to approach.

They are strong swimmers, are nimble, and can jump 3.5m. When alarmed, they curl their tails up over their back so that the white underside is exposed. This alerts the rest of the herd to the presence of predators. They are not fast runners, they lack stamina and are unable to outrun a persistent predator. They often make the fatal mistake of stopping in their tracks to check on the position of the chasing predator.

Diet
Greater kudus are herbivores and browsers, and feeds on herbs, tubers, roots, vines, leaves, flowers, berries and fruit. They can exist for long periods without drinking water as they are able extract sufficient moisture from their food.

Communication
Greater kudus use low grunts, humming, gasping and clicks to communicate with each other. When they are alarmed they emit a loud sharp bark. Males are more vocal than females

Reproduction
It is only in the mating season that the male (bull) and female (cow) come into contact with each other. During this period the male spends his time sniffing the females' genitals and tasting her urine to see if she is in oestrus. The male only mates once with the female he has selected. After mating the male and female go their separate ways.

The gestation period is up to 240 days. The mother leaves the herd to give birth to a single calf in the long grass. She remains with the calf for a day before returning to the herd. The calf remains alone in the bush for four to five weeks. The mother returns every three to five days to suckle the calf. By the time the calf is three to four months old it is constantly with its mother. The calf is weaned and independent by the time it is six months old.

Females are sexually mature by the time they are 18 months old, and first calve between the ages of two to three years old.

Males are sexually mature by the time they are 22 months old, and begin to mate between the ages of four and five years old.

Predators Threats
Greater kudus are natural prey for African wild dogs, leopards, lions and spotted hyenas. They are susceptible to rinderpest. They are hunted by the locals for their meat and precious horns. The horns can be used as musical instruments, and as symbolic containers in ceremonial rituals as they are believed to be the dwelling place for spirits. They are also a symbol of male potency. Trophy hunters hunt the greater kudu for their prized horns. Habitat loss and climate change is also a threat to the greater kudu's survival.

The greater kudu is classified as a *species of least concern* (2016).

Trivia
♦The greater kudu is the most commonly hunted species of antelope in South Africa, and is often top of the trophy hunters' hit list.

♦The name kudu is derived from the indigenous Khoikoi language of South Africa. The scientific name is derived from Greek and means - he goat, deer, twisting horn.

♦The greater kudu is known as the grey ghost.

♦Images in this section were taken in Etosha National Park, Namibia

Lesser Kudu

(*Tragelaphus imberbis*)
Swahili:*Tandala Ndogo*

Identification

The lesser kudu is a graceful forest antelope.

It has a long thin body, with 11 to 14 irregular white stripes (that are connected to the white spinal stripe) on either side. The female's and juvenile's coat is reddish brown in colour. The juvenile male's coat changes colour to slate grey by the time it is two years old. A crest of long hair runs the length of the spine, as does a single white stripe.

The brown bushy tail has a white underside and a black tip.

The long slender legs are fawn coloured, with black and white patches present.

Two distinct white patches are present on underside of the long neck.

A white stripe runs from each eye to the centre of the face. The area round the lips is white, and four black spots are present on the lower jaw.

The ears are large and rounded.

Horns are only present on the male. The horns begin to grow when the male is six to nine months old, and stop growing by three years. The spiral horns are dark brown with a whitish tip, and have two to two and half twists present.

The lesser kudu has excellent hearing, very good eyesight and sense of smell.

Males are larger than females.

Head & Body Length:		1.1-1.4m
Shoulder Height:		90cm-1.1m
Tail:		25-40cm
Weight:	Male	60-90kg
	Female	50-70kg
Horns:		50-70cm

Life Span

Ten to 15 years in the wild. Between 15 to 20 years in captivity.

Habitat

Lesser kudus are usually found in heavily forested, woodland areas that provide plenty of shade. They do not like large open areas with long grass as they feel insecure in this environment.

Behaviour

Lesser kudus are shy, wary and elusive. They are primarily nocturnal, active at night and early morning, and sheltering in shaded thickets at midday when it is hot.

They are non territorial. Females are gregarious and live in small groups of three to four individuals. Males either live in a leaderless bachelor herd that is non hierarchical, or live in isolation. The desire to live a solitary life increases with age. It is extremely rare for male kudus to engage in a fight. If confronted, males either interlock their spiral horns and do a lot of pushing and shoving until one of them submits, or they make themselves as tall as possible in an intimidating manner until one of them gives way.

When alarmed lesser kudus stand motionless, blending in with the surrounding vegetation, as they are perfectly camouflaged. Their thin bodies allow them to walk through dense vegetation with ease. Should the need arise they can walk backwards through dense vegetation with their head extended and their horns resting on their back.

When threatened they bark hoarsely, jump up to two metres in the air, and with an upraised tail take flight. They rarely use their horns on a predator. They can run at speeds of 70km/h, and can jump a distance of 9m and 2.5m high.

Diet

Lesser kudus are herbivores and a pure browsers. They feed on succulent plants, tubers, herbs, shrubs, bushes and trees, eating their roots, shoots, twigs, branches, leaves, flowers, fruit and berries. They can exist for long periods without drinking water as they are able to extract sufficient moisture from its food.

Reproduction

Lesser kudus breed all year round. During the rutting season the male spends time testing the urine of any female that he encounters to see if she is in oestrus. The female responds by urinating. If the female is in oestrus, the male will rub her rump, chest, head and neck and will attempt to grasp her with his lips. He then mounts the female and mates, after which he moves on in search of another female.

The gestation period is up to 222 days. The female (cow) leaves the herd to give birth to a single calf in isolation. The calf remains alone in the bush for four to five weeks with the female returning once a day to feed it. The female checks the calf each time by sniffing its rump or neck, she licks and cleans the perianal region and may eat its excrement. After five weeks the calf will accompany its mother and join the herd. Growing rapidly, it is independent by the time it is six months old. Males remain with their mother until they are 18 months old. Fifty per cent of the calves die within the first six months of their lives. The main cause of juvenile mortality is predation, and white muscle disease, which is due to a lack of vitamin E and selenium. White muscle disease causes muscle weakness and problems with mobility. Another 25% will die before the age of three.

Lesser kudus are sexually mature by the time they are 18 months old. Males mate when they are four to five years old.

Predators/Threats

Lesser kudus are natural prey for African wild dogs, leopards, lions and spotted hyenas. Cheetahs, small cats, eagles and pythons prey on the young.

They are hunted for their meat, hide and horns. The horns are used to make musical instruments and honey containers, and are a symbol of male potency. Loss of habitat due to human settlements, overgrazing and charcoal burning, as well as the effects of climate change, are a threat to their survival. Lesser kudus are one of the most sought after targets for trophy hunters.

The lesser kudu is classified as a *near threatened species* (2016).

Trivia

♦Edward Blyth, an English zoologist was the first person to describe the lesser kudu in 1869.

♦It was believed until the 1960s, that the lesser kudu's natural habitat included Saudi Arabia. Scientists discovered that lesser kudus were transported there for hunting purposes.

♦The horns of the lesser kudu are believed to be the dwelling places of powerful spirits.

Differences between Greater and Lesser Kudu

♦The greater kudu is bigger than the lesser kudu.

♦The greater kudu has a fringe like beard that runs underneath the throat. It is absent in the lesser kudu.

♦The greater kudu has six to ten vertical white stripes on the sides of its body. The lesser kudu has 11-14 vertical white stripes on the sides of its body.

♦The lesser kudu has two white patches underneath its neck.

♦The greater kudu has a white chevron between its eyes. The lesser kudu has two white stripes that run from the eyes to the centre of the face.

♦The greater kudu, because of its weight, cannot jump. The lesser kudu can jump 2.5m high.

Lesser Kudu. Meru National Park, Kenya.

Greater Kudu. Chobe National Park, Botswana.

Beisa Oryx/East African Oryx
(Oryx beisa)
Swahili:*Choroa*

There are 4 sub species of oryx. Three are native to Africa and one is native to the Arabian peninsula. The Arabian oryx is found on Sir Bani Yas Island, United Arab Emirates, Qatar, Bahrain, Israel, Jordan and Sauda Arabia. It is classified as a species that is vulnerable. The scimitar oryx inhabited Northern Africa and is believed to be extinct in the wild, although several thousand are held in captivity around the world. The gemsbok oryx inhabits Southern Africa and is classified as a species of least concern. The East African/beisa oryx is found in East Africa and is classified as a species that is endangered.

Identification
The beisa oryx is a large, beautiful, majestic antelope that has a muscular body and thick neck with a short mane. A thin black stripe runs from the base of the mane to the tip of the tail.

The coat is a light grey brown colour that reflects the heat of the sun. Striking black and white markings are present on its body, face and legs. A narrow black stripe is present on its lower flank. The underside is white. Black bands are present above the knee of the front legs. The tail has long black tassels.

The black facial markings are distinctive. A black strip extends laterally from the base of the horn, through the eye and lower cheek to above the muzzle. A black triangle is present above the muzzle, with the apex between the eyes. The base of another black triangle lies between the horns and the apex meets the apex of the former triangle. The nose has a dense network of capillaries which cool the blood that travels to the brain. This prevents the brain from overheating.

The ears are long and narrow.

The ringed, parallel v-shaped horns are long and narrow and are made of keratin. Both sexes have horns. Female horns are more slender.

The oryx has an excellent sense of smell.

Body Length:	1.6-1.9m
Shoulder Height:	1.1-1.2m
Tail:	70-80cm
Weight:	150-100kg

Life Span
Twenty years in the wild. Drought reduces their life expectancy. Twenty-two years in captivity.

Habitat
Beisa oryx are true desert antelopes that thrive in hostile, arid environments. They are found in dry plains, semi arid deserts, arid grasslands, dry thorny bushes, woodlands and savannahs.

Behaviour

Beisa oryx are sociable and live in unstable, hierarchical mixed herds of five to 40 individuals. They are alert and wary. The dominance hierarchy is based on age and size. The males (bulls) use ritualistic behaviours to establish their dominance. This involves prancing, walking, galloping and use of their horns. Once their dominance is secured, the fighting ceases. Although not strongly territorial, the dominant male will mark its territory with dung. When the herd is on the move a female beisa oryx (cow) will be at the front leading the way, in single file, with the alpha male at the rear. When threatened by predators, it is the beisa oryx's natural instinct to run away, but if it is cornered it will defend itself by lowering its head so that the horns point forwards. It is a formidable opponent and is more than capable of killing a lion. They can run at speeds of up to 60km/h.

Older males live alone.

Diet

Beisa oryx are herbivores that graze on coarse grasses and browse on leaves, buds, fruit and thorny shrubs, they will also dig for tubers and roots to eat. They have adapted to living in harsh, arid habitats, and will dig a shallow hole in the ground to rest and cool down if the temperatures start to rise. If water is in short supply they are able to absorb the moisture in a variety of ways, from the food they are eating, and by licking the early morning dew off their coats, the surrounding vegetation and rocks. They are able to store water by raising their body temperature to prevent them from perspiring. Beisa oryx have the unique ability to detect rainfall from a distance and will walk in the direction of fresh plant growth.

Beisa oryx eat early morning, late afternoon and early evening, as that is the time when the moisture content of the plants is at its highest.

Reproduction

Beisa oryx are polygamous and breed all year round. The gestation period is 240 days. The female leaves the herd to give birth to a single calf that remains hidden away from the main herd for the first two to three weeks of its life. During this period the female returns several times a day to suckle the calf. The newly born calf weighs 10kg, is brown coloured and is able to run about. The calf joins the herd when it is two to six weeks old, during which time the characteristic black markings start to appear. It is weaned by the time it is three to five months old.

Males leave the maternal herd when they are two years old to join bachelor herds.

Females are sexually mature between 18- 24 months old

Males are sexually mature at five years old.

Predators/Threats

Beisa oryx are natural prey for the African wild dog, hyenas, leopards and lions. They are hunted by humans for their meat and hide. Their horns are used to make charms. Loss of habitat and the effects of climate change are a threat to their survival. The beisa oryx is classified as an *endangered species* (2018).

Trivia

♦The oryx is the national animal and symbol of Qatar.

♦The female beisa oryx is able to mate as soon as the calf is born, and is able to produce a calf every nine months.

♦The beisa oryx has two nicknames which are directly linked to its horns, it may be known as the spear antelope because of the shape of the horns or the sabre antelope because the horns can inflict serious injury or kill.

♦The dominant male is known as tail end Charlie.

♦The image in this section was taken in Ol Pejeta Conservancy, Kenya.

Thomson's Gazelle

(Eudorcas thomsoni/Gazella thomsoni)

Swahili: *Swala tomi*

Identification

The Thomson's gazelle is a medium-sized antelope. It is the smallest gazelle, and the second fastest land animal after the cheetah.

The Thomson's gazelle's upper coat is a light tan-fawn colour. The chest and underside are white. A broad, black, horizontal stripe runs along the side of the body from the shoulders as far as the flank. The legs are long and slender, with a long ankle and foot bones.

The white patch on the rump, which is bordered by an extremely fine black stripe, extends to just beneath the short black tail.

The head is small in comparison to the size of its body. The ears are large and the eyes, also large, are encircled by white hair. A broad, black band extends from below each eye, across the cheeks as far as the upper corner of the mouth. There is a distinct dark patch above the nose, which lightens as it extends upwards towards the forehead. The muzzle is narrow and the chin and under throat are an off-white colour.

The male has long, pointed, ringed horns that curve backwards, but with tips that gently curve forwards. Horns are usually absent on the female, but if they are present they are short and narrow.

Thomson's gazelles have excellent eyesight, hearing and a keen sense of smell.

Males are slightly bigger than females.

Length:		81cm-1.2m
Shoulder Height:		56-68cm
Tail Length:		15-20cm
Weight:	Male	17-30kg
	Female	12-24kg
Horns:	Male	25-43cm
	Female	8-15cm

Life Span

Between 10 and 15 years in the wild.

Habitat

Thomson's gazelles like open spaces and are usually found in savannahs, grasslands, open plains and woodlands. They always live near water.

Behaviour

Thomson's gazelles are sociable animals living in all-female herds with their young, all-male herds, or mixed herds of up to 200 individuals. Membership of the herds is fluid and can change by the hour.

Travelling alongside wildebeest and zebras while searching for food and water, they are involved in the annual cyclical migration from the Serengeti to the Maasai Mara. Their numbers may be as high as 500,000.

Thomson's gazelles are territorial animals. Males, who usually remain territorial throughout their adult life, scent-mark their boundaries with urine and dung heaps (middens), and by depositing secretions on blades of grass from a small pre-orbital scent gland situated beneath each eye.

The male will regularly engage in combat fights to establish dominance and defend its territory, especially during the breeding season. Young males are tolerated in a herd as long as they ignore the females. The dominant male will attempt to retain any females who randomly stray into his territory.

Thomson's gazelles are prey to all of the major predators. They are extremely graceful and agile and are able to leap 3m high and jump distances of 9m. They have the ability to run at speeds of 65-80km/h and outrun the predators, as well as constantly dodging, twisting, turning and changing direction quickly, makes them extremely difficult prey to catch. While on the run they leap high in the air with all four legs leaving the ground; this alerts other gazelles to the presence of predators.

Thomson's gazelles are diurnal and nocturnal. They are active early morning and late afternoon.

Diet
Thomson's gazelles are migratory herbivores and are primarily grazers feeding on succulent, short green grasses, but when these are absent they will browse on shoots, shrubs, seeds and leaves. They are water-dependent and need to drink every one to two days, particularly in the dry season, however if the need arises they are able to extract sufficient moisture from the plants they feed on.

Communication
Thomson's gazelles are unusually quiet and use bodily postures (holding their head high, pointing in the direction of predators), visual displays (contracting the underlying skin of the horizontal black body band to increase its size and make it more visible), stamping feet, scent marking and the occasional snort to communicate with each other.

Reproduction
Thomson's gazelles are polygamous and may give birth to two litters each year. The peak season for giving birth is after the rainy season.

The gestation period is between 150-185 days. The female leaves the herd to find a secluded spot to give birth to a single fawn. Occasionally two fawns are born. The fawn is hidden in long grass for up to three weeks, it is particularly vulnerable at this point in time to predation, and must remain perfectly still to avoid being detected. The female returns several times a day to feed the fawn. As soon as it is able to run, it will join the herd. The fawn is weaned by the time it is four months old. To prevent in-breeding, males leave the maternal herd to join a bachelor herd.

Mortality for the young is as high as 50%.

Predators/Threats
Thomson's gazelles are natural prey for lions, cheetahs, leopards, African wild dogs, jackals and crocodiles. The young are preyed upon by baboons, birds of prey, jackals, pythons and serval cats. They are hunted by humans for their meat and hide. Loss of habitat and the effects of climate change are a threat to their survival. The Thomson's gazelle is classified as a *species of least concern* (2018).

Trivia
♦The Thomson's gazelle is nicknamed "Tommie".

♦The Thomson's gazelle is similar in appearance to the Grant's gazelle, but is easily distinguished by the horizontal black band on its side.

♦The Thomson's gazelle is named after the Scotsman Joseph Thomson, who explored Africa in the 1890s.

♦The Thomson's gazelle's tail is in continuous motion, swinging to and fro and from side to side.

Topi
(Damaliscus lunatus)
Swahili: *Nyemera/Paa*

Identification
The topi is a hardy, medium-sized antelope that has a distinctive appearance and colouration.

The topi looks awkward and ungainly with its short neck, humped shoulders, sloping back and long slender legs. The black head is long and narrow, with a narrow muzzle that has tan-coloured lips. The ears are narrow and slender.

The glossy coat is a red-purple-brown colour with blue-purple patches straddling the flanks, shoulders and upper legs. The lower half of the legs are a gingery tan colour. The rump and tail are paler. A tuft of hair is present on the tail.

Both sexes have thick, ringed, lyre-shaped horns.

Female topis are a lighter colour.

The topi has good eyesight and hearing.

Body Length:	1.5-2.0m
Shoulder Height:	1-1.3m
Tail Length:	40-60cm
Weight:	75-160kg
Horns:	72cm

Habitat
Topis are usually found in lowlands, savannahs, flood plains, woodlands and semi-deserts.

Behaviour
Topis are sociable and territorial, and often found in close proximity to other herds of antelopes.

Females live in small herds of between 15-20 individuals, with their offspring and a single, dominant male. Males either live in loosely formed bachelor herds of between 8-20 individuals, or they can be solitary. The herds merge temporarily when migrating to form mega herds. Whenever the herds stop moving, the males begin to establish small territories and round up the females.

Males become territorial between the ages of four to five years old and mark their territory with urine, dung heaps (middens) and secretions from their pre-orbital glands. They spend a considerable amount of time on their own, overseeing and guarding their territory, usually on the summit of a termite mound.

Topis are able to run at speeds of up to 70km/h if required.

The topi is diurnal.

Diet
Topis are highly selective herbivores that graze on grass and very rarely on leaves. They have a preference for succulent green grass. If they eat dry, coarse grasses they need long rest periods to chew their cud in order to aid digestion. Topis are able to survive for long periods without water providing they have access to succulent green grass, otherwise they will need to drink daily.

Communication

Topis use a variety of vocalisations, visual signals, bodily postures, movement and scent marking to communicate with each other.

Reproduction

Mating is dependent on favourable weather conditions and availability of food. During the breeding season the male establishes small territories and rounds up as many females as possible to mate with. The dominant male is easily recognised as he struts around with an upright posture and head held high.

The gestation period is between 225-240 days. If environmental and climatic conditions are not favourable the female is able to delay the birth of the calf. The female gives birth to a single calf, which is hidden in vegetation for between 3-12 days before joining a kindergarten; the females take it in turn to watch over the calves while the others go in search of food. The calf, which has a sandy brown coat, is able to walk within 15 minutes of being born. Horns appear when they are three months old, and at the same time their coat begins to take on the adult colouration. Weaning is complete by the time the calf is four months old.

Females reach sexual maturity between 18-24 months old.

Males reach sexual maturity between 36-48 months old.

Predators/Threats

Topis are natural prey for cheetahs, lions, leopards and African wild dogs. They are highly selective herbivores that feed almost entirely on grass - this means that when there is a lack of available grass, or competition for grass from other herbivores, they will be at risk of starvation. Topis are hunted by humans, despite being difficult to catch. Loss of habitat and the effects of climate change are a threat to the topi's survival. The topi is classified as a *species of least concern* (2016).

Trivia

♦The topi is also known as the *sassaby*.

♦If the topi is lucky and does not fall foul of predators, it will die when its teeth fall out.

♦Male topis usually live a solitary life, and even if part of a herd they will be on their own overseeing, patrolling and guarding the territory - this makes them more likely to be taken by predators.

♦Images in this section were taken in the Maasai Mara National Reserve, Kenya.

Waterbuck
Common or Ringed Waterbuck *(Kobus ellipsiprymnus ellipsiprymnus)*
Defassa Waterbuck *(Kobus ellipsiprymnus defassa)*
Swahili: *Kuro*

Identification
The waterbuck is a large, robust, muscular antelope.

The coat is long, coarse and shaggy. Sweat glands in the skin secrete an oily, brown, tar-like substance that waterproofs the coat. It has a distinct, lingering odour - described as musk-like.

There are two species of waterbucks in Tanzania:

The common waterbuck, which is greyish brown in colour. It has a distinct, circular white ring on its rump that encircles the tail, with a darker patch in the centre.

The defassa waterbuck, which is reddish brown in colour. It has a solid, white circular patch on either side of its rump.

Males are darker than females. The colour of the body darkens with age.

The short, strong legs are darker in colour than the body, and there are white rings above the hooves.

The waterbuck has a long body with a straight back. The ears are large, prominent and rounded. The eyes are placed on either side of the head, and horizontal, elongated pupils allow for all-round, peripheral vision. White hair is present above the eyes, inside the ears and on the muzzle. There is a rough mane around the neck, and a creamy-white patch under the throat.

The male waterbuck has long, pointed, spiral, ringed horns that sweep up and back. The female does not have horns.

Waterbucks have excellent eyesight and a keen sense of smell and hearing.

Head & Body length:		1.7-2.3m
Shoulder Height:		1m-1.4m
Weight:	Male	200-300kg
	Female	150-200kg
Tail Length:		22-45cm
Horns:		55-100cm

Life Span
Between 14-18 years in the wild.

Habitat
Waterbucks are usually found in savannahs, grasslands, forests and woodlands. They are always found near water.

Behaviour
Waterbucks are quiet, sedentary, territorial animals. They are not migratory, and usually remain within the same home range year round, living in herds of between 5-30 individuals. Membership of the herd is fluid and changes day to day.

Young males (bulls) form bachelor herds of between five to ten individuals from the age of two years old. This is a hierarchical closely knit group based on seniority, size and strength. Remaining in the herd until they have matured, which is between the ages of six to seven years old, they then become territorial.

The females (cows) and calves live in a loosely formed nursery group of between 5-25 individuals. A dominant male may or may not be present. Females may also be seen alone or in pairs. Mature, dominant males are territorial, and will try to keep any females that stray into their domain, although they are rarely successful.

The dominant male aggressively defends his territory until the age of ten. The territory is not scent marked, as their bodily odour is sufficient to advertise their presence.

Waterbucks are nocturnal and diurnal. They feed early morning and late afternoon.

Diet
Waterbucks are herbivores, they are primarily grazers but will also browse, grazing on a variety of medium and short coarse grasses, and browsing on herbs and leaves from shrubs and trees. Waterbucks are water-dependent and need to drink daily.

Communication
Waterbucks use a variety of vocalisations, visual signals, bodily postures and movement to communicate with each other.

Reproduction
Waterbucks are polygamous and breed all year round. The peak season for giving birth is in the rainy season. The dominant male may have a harem of cows and may be challenged by other males for mating rights.

The gestation period is up to 280 days. Several days before the birth, the female finds a secluded spot away from the herd, and gives birth to a single calf. Within 30 minutes of being born the calf is able to stand up and walk. The calf is hidden in dense thickets and long grass for two to four weeks, with the female returning several times a day to feed it. Each time she leaves the calf, she grooms it thoroughly to remove any lingering odours that may attract predators. The young are weaned after six to seven months. Horns first appear on the male when they are eight to nine months old. The young males wander off to join all male groups but the females remain with the maternal group.

Females reach sexual maturity between 12-14 months old. Males reach sexual maturity between 14-18 months old.

Predators/Threats
Waterbucks are natural prey for lions, leopards, cheetahs, hyenas, jackals, wild dogs and crocodiles. Loss of habitat and the effects of climate change is a threat to their survival. They have been known to be hunted for their meat. The common waterbuck is classified as a *species of least concern* (2016). The Defassa waterbuck is classified as a *species that is near threatened* (2016).

Trivia
♦The meat of the waterbuck is tough, and has an unpleasant odour and taste; it is believed that this deters many potential predators.

♦The waterbuck is the most water-dependent of all the antelopes.

♦Waterbucks are strong swimmers and take refuge in water if threatened by predators.

♦The waterbuck's long shaggy hair attracts ticks, and they are prone to foot-and-mouth disease, anthrax and rinderpest.

Wildebeest
(*Connochaetes taurinus*)
Swahili: *Nyumbu Ya Montu*

Identification
The wildebeest is a large antelope and is synonymous with the annual migration of animals between the Serengeti in Tanzania and the Maasai Mara in Kenya.

The wildebeest has a long, black, narrow head with large nostrils, and a wide muzzle equipped with incisors suited to eating short grass quickly. It has a shaggy mane of long, black, thick hair and a beard that goes underneath the throat. The ears are long and narrow.

The coat is short and glossy and is a grey-brown colour. Males are darker in colour than females. Vertical bands of long black hair are present on the neck and forequarters.

The cow-like horns are long, curved and sharp. The horns of the male are larger than the female's, and are joined by a shield (*boss*) that covers the forehead.

The wildebeest looks cumbersome and ungainly, with muscular, heavily built forequarters and disproportionately slender hindquarters. The legs are long and spindle-like with hooves. The wildebeest is agile and able to run at 65km/h.

The tail is long, black and hairy.

Wildebeest have good eyesight, sense of hearing and smell.

Length:		2.4-3.4m
Shoulder Height:	Male	1.25-1.45m
	Female	1.15-1.42m
Tail:		45-56cm
Weight:	Male	165-300kg
	Female	140-230kg
Horns	Male	55-80cm
	Female	45-63cm

Life Span
Twenty years in the wild.

Habitat
Wildebeest are usually found in grasslands, plains and open woodland. They are always found near water.

Behaviour
Wildebeest are sociable and territorial, living in herds that are constantly on the move searching for fresh food and water. The wildebeest that live in the Serengeti are migratory and are renowned for their annual, cyclical migration from the Serengeti to the Maasai Mara. Trekking over 19km a day alongside the zebras and antelopes, 250,000 wildebeest will perish - the very young, lame, sick and old.

Wildebeest live in mixed herds (within a mega herd) comprised of:

♦Bachelor herds made up of young males and bulls without territories that live on the fringes of the herd. Males (bulls) leave the bachelor herd when they are four to five years old and become territorial.

♦Small herds of females (cows), calves and yearlings of 10-100 individuals. Males leave between the ages of one and two years old to join a bachelor herd.

♦Territorial bulls, who may be solitary.

As food becomes scarce the herds lose their individual identities and merge.

Territorial males mark the boundaries of their territory with dung heaps and secretions from their preorbital gland and hooves. When competing for territories either on their own or in small groups, territorial males display aggressive behaviours, grunting and bellowing, pawing the earth, standing erect and thrusting and tossing their horns about.

Wildebeest are primarily diurnal but can be considered nocturnal as well. They are active early morning and late afternoon.

Diet

Wildebeest are nomadic herbivores, feeding on short grass. They are water-dependent and need to drink every day.

Communication

Wildebeest are noisy animals and will use a variety of vocalisations to communicate with each other. Visual signals, scent marking, tactile behaviours (sniffing and touching noses, neck and genitals) are also used. When threatened or when they are required to assert their dominance, males will utilise agonistic behaviours, (tilting their heads, horn sweeping, leaping, bucking and spinning).

Reproduction

Wildebeest are polygamous. Mating begins at the end of the rainy season (March-April) with males competing for territories and females. The females will mate with several males during this period.

The gestation period is between 240-250 days with 80-90% of calves been born in a 2-3 week period in February and March. Although the young are easy prey for the predators, their high numbers (500,000 in the Serengeti) ensure that more of them will survive.

The female gives birth to a single calf, usually within the herd rather than in isolation, and almost always before midday. Within minutes of being born the calf is able to stand up and walk about, and is able to keep up with the herd within two days. They are able to eat grass after ten days and are suckled between six to twelve months.

The female spends one to two days imprinting herself on the calf so that she is able to recognise its scent. The calves are initially a light brown colour, but by the time they are nine weeks old they begin to take on the adult colouration. Their tiny horns are initially upright, but begin to grow sideways after they are eight months old. Calves remain close to their mothers, and if they lose contact, they are actively rejected by all of the other females and their days are numbered. Males are driven away from the herd when the next calf is born, but females remain with the maternal herd.

Females are sexually mature between two and a half and three years old. Males are sexually mature between three and four years old.

Predators/Threats
Wildebeest are natural prey for lions, hyenas, cheetahs, leopards, African wild dogs and crocodiles. Loss of habitat and the effects of climate change, (intense droughts in particular), are a threat to their survival. The wildebeest is classified as a *species of least concern* (2016).

Trivia
♦Wildebeest are sometimes referred to as *gnus*.
♦The majority of new born wildebeest are female.
♦Wildebeest are the commonest animal to live on the African plains.
♦Wildebeest live in the highest concentration of all known mammals.
♦On an evening, wildebeest sleep in rows on the ground for safety and security.
♦Wildebeest can live in enormous "mega" herds of up to 1 million animals.

Migration

The annual wildebeest migration across the plains of the Serengeti in Tanzania to the Maasai Mara in Kenya and back is the greatest wildlife spectacle on earth. This is a never-ending, epic journey with the animals driven on in the relentless search for fresh food and water. It is a fight for survival. Trekking over 19km a day, 250,000 wildebeest will perish on this annual pilgrimage - the very young, lame, sick and old. Hot in the pursuit of the migration are the predators - carnivores and scavengers alike.

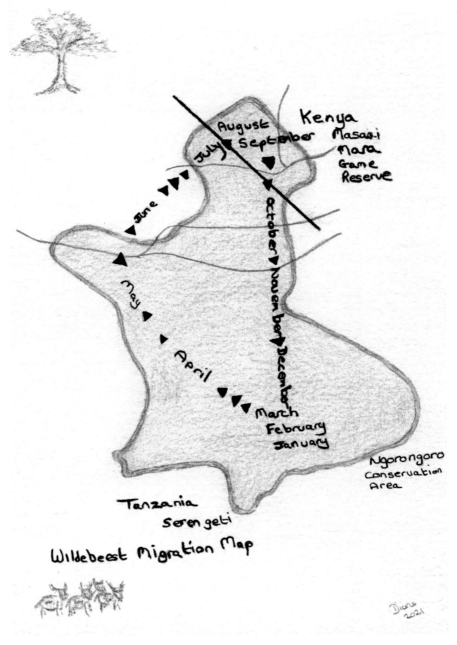

January-February

The months of January and February find over 1.5 million wildebeest and 300,000 zebras and antelopes congregated on the Salei and Ndutu plains, which are located in the southern part of the Serengeti, adjacent to the Ngorongoro Conservation Area.

Zebras give birth to their young in January. The wildebeest give birth to 500,000 calves within the space of two to three weeks in February.

March

March sees the arrival of the long rains from the north. The southern plains are stripped bare of grass and the migration needs to move on in search of food and water.

April-May

The migration travels northwards towards the central area of the Serengeti, with a large number of animals present in the Seronera, an area popular with safari operators. They continue through the long grass plains and woodlands towards the Western Corridor, alongside the Mbalageti River and towards the Grumeti Controlled Area, where the long rains have now set in.

Towards the end of May the rains die away and the rutting season begins.

June

The migration is now firmly established in the Western Corridor and crosses the Grumeti River towards the Ikorongo Controlled Area. Some animals travel in a different direction towards the Lobo area.

It is now the dry season.

July

The migration arrives at the Ikorongo Controlled area and proceeds to cross the notorious Mara River towards the Maasai Mara (Kenya). Many hundreds will die as they cross the river, searching for a safe and suitable crossing point, either breaking their legs on the sides of the steep, slippery banks or being trampled to death in the ensuing, panic-stricken stampede. Waiting eagerly, either in the water or the banks of the Mara River, are the Nile crocodiles who make quick work of any fallen prey.

The crossing of the Mara River is spectacular because of the high volume of water that is present, whereas the Grumeti River is made up of a series of intermittent pools and channels. The migratory herd now enters the Maasai Mara, in their continued search for food and water.

August-September

The migratory herds reside in the Maasai Mara from July through to October where there is a plentiful supply of water.

October-November

The migration slowly starts to leave the Maasai Mara, crossing the Mara River once again and heading towards the southern plains where the new rains are starting.

December

The migration continues moving back along the Loliondo boundary, towards the regenerated grasses of the southern plains They will remain in the southern plains throughout the months of January, February and March before the annual, cyclical migration begins once more.

Primates

Black-and-White Colobus Monkey
(Colobus guereza)
Swahili: *Mbega mweupe*

Identification
The fur of the black and white colobus monkey is very distinct: glossy black with a long white mantle on the sides of the body, and a white beard that surrounds the face.

The skin on the face is hairless and grey in colour.

The tail is long and has a bushy white tuft at the tip.

Calluses on the rump allow it to sit for extended periods on tree branches.

Unlike other primates, the black and white colobus monkey does not have a thumb, only four fingers which provide a strong grip allowing it to move quickly and gracefully from tree to tree

Black and white colobus monkeys are able to make amazing and spectacular leaps of up to 15m. through the tree tops. Their trailing black and white hair and long tail act as a parachute.

Head & Body Length: 45-72cm
Tail Length: 52cm-1m
Weight: 5-14kg

Life Span
Twenty years in the wild.

Habitat
Black and white colobus monkeys are usually found in forests, woodlands or wooded grasslands, both in lowlands and coastal mountains (up to 3,300m), and along water courses in arid, savannah regions. They are relatively rare in Tanzania, so consequently all images in this section were taken at various locations in Kenya.

Behaviour
Black and white colobus monkeys live in limited, well-defined territories. They are arboreal, and are rarely seen on the ground, spending the majority of their time high up in the tree tops where they are extremely well camouflaged.

The troops are small and social, consisting of up to 15 animals made up of the dominant male, several females and their offspring. The females remain in the group for life. Young males leave the group before they reach sexual maturity, their departure may be voluntary or may be initiated by the lead male. These young males may lead solitary lives or band together with other males. Where territories overlap with other troops of black and white colobus monkeys, they are vigorously defended by the males and this may involve physical contact. At night time they take it in turns to guard the troop and their territory from predators.

Black and white colobus monkeys are diurnal.

Diet
Black and white colobus monkeys are herbivores, and exist on a diet that consists mainly of leaves, blossom, leaf buds, flowers, fruit, stems, bark, twigs and aquatic plants.

Their large, complex, two-chambered stomachs support bacterial micro floral colonies and this allows them to digest large quantities of difficult, mature, toxic foliage. The leaves, although plentiful, are a source of low energy and nutrition and result in the black and white colobus monkey being relatively inactive. Their dependence on foliage restricts them to forest habitations, however they will eat agricultural crops in inhospitable environments.

Communication

Males are very noisy and vocal, particularly at dawn, and this is used as a means of communication to segregate the groups. Their calls are very distinctive, and have been described as: roars, snorts, purrs, honks and screams.

Visual signals and body postures are also used as a means of communication. Tactile communication includes social grooming, playing and fighting.

Reproduction

There is no distinct breeding season. Black and white colobus monkeys are polygamous, and females initiate the mating process by attracting the male through lip smacking. The gestation period is six months and the female gives birth to only one offspring, which is born with its eyes open. For the first month the young have a pink face and their body is covered with white fur which soon begins to change colour, with the final black and white colour of adulthood being achieved by the age of six months.

The female suckles the young for one year, although the infant clings to both the mother's and father's abdomen. Both parents participate in rearing the young infant and may also involve other female members in the group. These substitute mothers, known as "allo" mothers, will suckle the young infant and also carry it around on their abdomen.

Females reach sexual maturity at between four to six years old. Males reach sexual maturity between four to eight years old.

Predators/Threats

Black and white colobus monkeys are natural prey for hawk eagles, leopards and the occasional chimpanzee. They are hunted illegally for their beautiful fur and for their meat. Their skin is used to make dance costumes, hats and capes. The main threat to survival is loss of habitat as forests are cut down for logging, human habitation and agricultural purposes. Climate change is also a threat to their survival. The black and white colobus are classified as a *species of least concern* (2016).

Trivia

♦*Colobus* is a Greek word that means "mutilated" or "docked", and refers to the absence of a thumb.

♦Colobus monkeys are sacred icons to the gods of the Hindu and Buddhist religions.

♦The colobus monkey is also affectionately known as the *"Messenger of God"*, as it basks in the tree tops in the early morning and late afternoon sun.

Olive Baboon
(Papiocynocephalus anubis)
Swahili: *Nyani*

Identification
The olive baboon is the most widespread of the baboon family and gets its name from its dark green-grey colour.

It has a large muscular body covered in thick, grey-green-brown fur. The female is duller than the male. The back slopes downwards and the males have a long tapering mane of hair around the neck. Calluses, which are thickened patches of skin, are present on the hairless rump. The tail is non-prehensile.

The face is dog-like with close-set eyes, a prominent eyebrow ridge and rounded ears. The hair on the face is fine and is dark grey to black in colour. The muzzle is hairless, long and pointed. The jaws are strong and powerful with long, pointed canine teeth up to 5cm long. Large cheek pouches enable the baboon to eat while on the move, as well as getting their fill when competing for scarce food.

The olive baboon has long, powerful arms and legs and is able to move about on four limbs. Five fingers are present on the hands of the arms, and five toes are present on the hind legs, all of which are used for grasping.

Males are larger than females.

Head and Body Length:	60-86cm
Tail:	41-58cm
Weight:	22-37kg

Life Span
Up to 30 years in the wild.

Habitat
Olive baboons are adaptable and are usually found in savannahs, grasslands, rocky areas, open woodlands, forests and semi-arid areas - all of which will be close to water.

Behaviour
Olive baboons are sociable and live in a highly organised, complex, hierarchical group of between 30-80 individuals, called a troop. These troops can be as large as 200 in number. The troop is made up of adult females and their offspring, and adult males. There are several dominant males within the troop and each member has a ranked position.

The dominant male (alpha male) uses his physical prowess to protect, defend, dominate and maintain order within the troop, ultimately deciding on the movement of the troop, what they will eat and where they will sleep. A linear, hierarchical social order exists amongst the females, and is in order of birth and kin. This ensures that the dominant females' offspring assume the same privileges of social ranking.

86

Olive baboons are terrestrial, spending the majority of their time foraging for food early morning and late afternoon and resting at midday. When they are not foraging for food they sit in small groups grooming each other, looking for and removing parasites, dead skin and dirt. Grooming reinforces social bonds, with subordinates grooming dominant members. Males groom females in particular when they are seeking sexual access.

When threatened, olive baboons may run away, but they are also capable of being quite ferocious - they will either bark or bare their large canine teeth, and have even been known to attack humans. Mobbing predators if the young are threatened, male baboons are a formidable force to be reckoned with and more than capable of inflicting serious injuries.

Olive baboons are diurnal and retreat to the safety of the trees, cliffs and rocky outcrops at night.

Diet

Olive baboons are omnivores. They are opportunistic foragers and feed primarily on aquatic plants, grasses, lichens, roots, tubers, bulbs, bark, bark sap, leaves, blossom, berries and seeds. They supplement their diet with insects, small mammals (rodents, vervet monkeys), birds, fish, shell fish, lizards and snakes. They need to drink water every day or two.

Communication

Being extremely noisy they use up to 30 vocalisations to communicate with each other, such as clicking, barking, grunting, roaring, screeching and screaming. Facial expressions or visual displays are used to communicate their mood and intention, these may be staring, smiling, baring teeth, raising eyebrows, narrowing eyes, yawning, head shaking and lip smacking. Bodily postures and tactile/sociable greetings (grooming, embracing each other, nose to nose greetings), are also used as a form of communication.

Reproduction

Olive baboons are promiscuous, breeding throughout the year with a multitude of partners. The female comes into heat once a month during which time the rump changes colour from grey to a bright pink. There is a lot of competition and aggression between the males to gain attention and access to the female at this time. The female initiates the mating process by presenting her pink swollen rump to the males. She gives birth to a single infant once a year, after a gestation period of 180 days. The infant is born with pink skin which darkens with age and is covered in black fur. By the time the infant is six months old it will have taken on adult colouration and will be an olive green colour. The infant remains in close contact with its mother by clinging to her stomach for the first four weeks of its life, after which it will ride jockey style on her back, as well as that of other members of the troop. This continues until the infant is one year old. Both male and female care for the young, but the majority of the care is provided by the mother and other female members of the troop. Males will assist by gathering food and grooming.

By the time the infant is four to six months old it will be spending most of its time playing with the other juveniles. The young are weaned by the time they are one year old, and are independent by the time they are 18 months old.

Females are sexually mature between the ages of four to six years old and remain with the maternal group for life.

Males are sexually mature between the ages of five to seven years old. Before they reach sexual maturity they leave the maternal group to join a new troop, gaining acceptance into the new troop by befriending a female over many months.

Predators/Threats

Olive baboons are natural prey for African wild dogs, cheetahs, chimpanzees, crocodiles, hyenas, lions and leopards. They are hunted by humans if they are considered to be a pest by raiding crops and being present in large numbers. Loss of habitat is a threat to their survival. The olive baboon is a *species of least concern* (2020)

Trivia

♦The olive baboon is also known as the *savannah baboon* or *Anubis baboon.*
♦Baboons have the same dental pattern and number of teeth as a human.
♦Baboons will wade into swamps for water lily tubers.
♦Baboons are fond of raiding agricultural crops.

Vervet Monkey
(*Chlorocebus pygerthrus*)
Swahili: *Tumbili/Ngedere*

Identification
The vervet or green monkey is a medium-sized primate.

The body is long and slender. The coarse dorsal fur is either a greyish olive-green or brown colour. The underside and the inside of the arms and legs are covered with white fur. The skin on the abdomen is blue.

Vervet monkeys have a small, hairless black face encircled by elongated whiskery white hair. The canines are long and sharp and there are cheek pouches for storing food.

The arms and legs are approximately the same length and this allows the vervet monkey to walk on all four limbs. The hands and feet are black and hairless.

The tail is long with a black tip that curves downwards when the tail is held upright.

The male has a bright blue scrotum and red penis.

Male vervet monkeys are larger than the females.

Height:	Males	45-85cm
	Females	40-60cm
Tail:		50 cm-1.1m
Weight:	Males	3.5-7.5kg
	Females	2.5-5.5kg

Habitat
Vervet monkeys are adaptable and widely distributed, and are found in savannahs, grasslands and woodlands up to altitudes of 3,000m, usually in close proximity to streams, rivers and lakes. They rarely stray more than 460m away from the safety of wooded areas.

Behaviour
Vervet monkeys are highly sociable and live together in a close-knit group called a troop. There can be between 6-80 individuals in a troop, although the average size is 25. The troop is made up of one or more males, females and their offspring, and has a highly developed hierarchical social order that dominates all aspects of the monkeys' lives. The dominant male (alpha) and female (matriarch) maintain their authority by using aggressive behaviours, and they are given priority when foraging for food, eating and when engaged in grooming.

The alpha male protects the troop and has access to all high ranking females. He has a second in command, the beta male, whose duty is to scout for food and warn the troop of the

89

presence of intruders or predators. Other adult males are allowed to remain in the troop as long as they do not engage with the females.

The linear hierarchical social order that exists among the females is in order of birth and kin and ensures that the dominant females' offspring assume the same privileges of social ranking. Other adults are submissive to the juveniles that belong to a family of a higher social status. Physical affection is especially important among family members. Grooming in particular reinforces social bonds, with the monkeys spending many hours every day grooming each other, and looking for and removing parasites, dirt and dead skin.

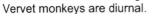

Vervet monkeys are semi-arboreal and semi-terrestrial, spending the majority of their time during the day foraging for food on the ground. They usually walk about on all fours but will stand upright on their hind legs to get a better view. On an evening they retreat to the safety of the trees to sleep.

When food is scarce both sexes become territorial and scent-mark their territory with secretions from their facial glands, by rubbing their chins and cheeks on trees and rocks. When there is an abundance of food they relax and concentrate on foraging.

Vervet monkeys are diurnal.

Diet

Vervet monkeys are omnivores and feed primarily on grasses, herbs, bulbs, roots, shoots, bark, leaves, buds, flowers, and fruit, supplementing their diet with small birds, eggs, insects and rodents. Close to human habitation they become a nuisance as they regularly raid vegetable plots, lodges and camp sites. Vervet monkeys need to drink water daily.

Communication

Vervet monkeys are very vocal and use a wide range of vocalisations to communicate with each other and their offspring, from barking, woofing, squealing, purring and chirping to grunting (19 sounds in total). Facial expressions (staring, head bobbing, rapid glancing), tactile communication (nose to nose touching), bodily postures (penile display) and tail signals are also used as an indication of their mood or the presence of predators.

Reproduction

Vervet monkeys breed throughout the year. Only the alpha male is allowed to mate with the females and he defends this right fiercely.

The gestation period is between 160-165 days. The majority of births take place at night, and during the rainy season when there is an abundance of food. The female gives birth to a single infant and is very protective towards her offspring. After licking the infant clean the female will bite off the umbilical cord and proceed to eat the afterbirth. The infant is born with its eyes open, a pink face and covered in black fur. The infant remains in close contact with its mother by clinging to her stomach for the first three weeks of its life, after which it will venture out to play with other youngsters. Fifty per cent of the infants do not make it to adulthood, they die from poor nutrition or predation.

Males do not participate in rearing the young, this is left to the mother, other siblings and females.

The young are weaned by the time they are six months old and are independent by the time they are one year old.

Females are sexually mature when they are four years old and begin to reproduce when they are five years old. Females remain with the maternal group.

Males are sexually mature when they are five years old, at which point they leave the maternal troop to go in search of another troop with no female relations. This is a difficult time as male outsiders are never welcome and meet with considerable aggression. Male vervet monkeys may change troops several times throughout their lives, always during the mating season.

Predators/Threats

Vervet monkeys are natural prey for lions, leopards, cheetahs, caracals, serval cats, baboons, eagles, crocodiles and pythons. They are hunted for their meat and are used in traditional medicine. They may be poisoned, trapped or shot when close to human habitation as they are seen as a pest regularly stealing food and raiding crops. Game farms may use vervet monkeys as target practice. Loss of habitat and the effects of climate change are a threat to their survival. The vervet monkey is classified as a *species of least concern* (2016)

Trivia

♦Vervet monkeys are used in scientific research. Their tissue is used in the production of the smallpox and polio vaccine. They are especially useful in research into high blood pressure, cancer, organ transplants, immunology, pharmacology and psychology.

♦A bereaved mother will often keep the body of her infant with her for several days after its death.

♦Pythons usually wait at the bottom of a tree to ambush a vervet monkey as it climbs head first down a tree.

♦Vervet monkeys are able to swim.

♦Vervet monkeys are intelligent and possess cognitive skills, being able to demonstrate and express emotion through mime.

♦Vervet monkeys are particularly vulnerable to parasitic skin diseases.

Common Birds

African Fish Eagle
(*Haliaeetus vocifer*)
Swahili: *Furukombe*

Identification
The African fish eagle is a large raptor found throughout sub Saharan Africa.

The head, breast and tail are white. Its body is brown and its large powerful wings are chestnut brown to black. It is a handsome, majestic bird.

The eyes are dark brown to pale brown in colour. The African fish eagle has five times more light sensitive cells present in its eyes than a human. It has excellent colour vision and can spot camouflaged prey easily.

The yellow coloured, hooked shaped beak has a black tip and is made from keratin. The strong powerful beak is rarely used to kill prey, it is primarily used to pull the scales off the fish or to shred prey.

The legs are strong and muscular, with large feet that are covered in thick, scaly skin that is yellow in colour. Three toes point forwards, and a fourth toe points backwards. The sharp, curved talons are 5cm in length. Sharp barbs called spiricules are present on the soles of its feet, this allows the eagle to get a firm grasp on slippery prey in the water and fast moving ground prey.

The African fish eagle has good hearing.

Females are larger than males.

Length:		63-77cm
Wingspan:	Females	2.4m
	Males	2m
Weight:	Females	3.2-3.6kg
	Males	2.0-2.5kg

Life span
Between 12 to 14 years in the wild.

Habitat
African fish eagles lives near fresh water rivers, lakes, lagoons and reservoirs where there is a plentiful supply of food. They are absent from arid regions where there is little or no large areas of open water.

Behaviour
African fish eagles wake before sunrise and start their day with a resonating, raucous, shrill call. They are sedentary birds and spend the majority of the day perched on a horizontal branch near the water's edge searching for prey near the surface of the water. They are highly skilled, opportunistic hunters. Swooping down at 32km/h with extended feet and talons, they deftly lift unsuspecting slippery prey out of the water. They will scavenge and steal prey from other birds.

African fish eagles are territorial all year round (especially the female), and will not tolerate intruders encroaching on their territory. They are often seen in pairs inside and outside the breeding season and are very loyal birds.

African fish eagles are diurnal.

Diet
Ninety per cent of the African fish eagle's diet comprises of live fish, catfish and lung fish in particular. They also feed on lizards, frogs, turtles, terrapins, baby crocodiles, snakes and water birds (ibis, herons, lesser flamingoes, spoonbills, and storks). They are not averse to eating carrion or domestic fowl.

Communication
African fish eagles are very vocal. They are constantly communicating to each other in order to establish and maintain their territory and to create and strengthen their bond.

Reproduction
African fish eagles are monogamous, breeding for life and only reproducing once a year. The breeding season starts during the dry season when the water levels are low. The breeding pair are always in sight of each other and can be heard singing a duet, and displaying courtship behaviours that involve aerial diving, swooping and claw grappling in mid air. When the female is ready to mate she lies with her body parallel to the ground, with her head lowered and her tail elevated. The male either jumps on or flies onto her back to complete the mating process.

The nest is usually located near water in a large tree. It is built from sticks and is lined with grass, reeds, papyrus and leaves. The nest is reused every year and gets bigger and bigger with time. It can be up to 2m wide and 1.2m deep.

Both birds participate in incubating and rearing the chicks. The female lays one to three white eggs. One egg is laid every two to three days. The eggs are incubated for 44 days. The chicks have white down and pink legs. Once all of the chicks are hatched, the strongest eaglet kills the weaker eaglets to eliminate competition for food and ensure its own survival. The eaglet fledges when it is 65 and 75 days old and is independent of its parents eight weeks later.

Juvenile African fish eagles' plumage and eyes are paler than the adults. They achieve full adult plumage when they are five years old.

Only five per cent of African fish eagles reach adulthood.

Predators/Threats
Over fishing, pollution from factories and townships and the indiscriminate poisoning of bait intended for other species of wildlife is a threat to the African fish eagle's survival. Loss of habitat and the effects of climate change resulting in the lowering of water levels are also a threat to its survival.

The African fish eagle is classified as a *species of least concern* (2016).

Trivia
♦The African fish eagle is the national bird of four African countries - Zimbabwe, Namibia, Zambia and South Sudan.

♦The African fish eagle is strong and can lift prey up to ten times its own body weight, but it can only fly short distances before it has to land in a safe place to eat its catch.

♦The call of the African fish eagle is known as the "Call of Africa". Once heard, it can never be mistaken for the call of another bird. It is distinctive and very evocative. Magical.

Flamingo

Greater Flamingo
(*Phoenicopterus roseus*)
Lesser Flamingo
(*Phoenicopterus minor*)
Swahili: *Heroe*

Identification

There are six species of flamingo in the world, two of which are found in the African continent. They are the greater flamingo and the lesser flamingo.

The flamingo is a wading bird with long, pink, spindle-like legs and small webbed feet.

The large body is covered in pink feathers. The colour originates from the bacteria spirulina, which is found in the blue green algae of the salt water lakes, diatoms, small crustaceans and alpha and beta carotene.

The neck is long and flexible with a small head. The eyes are small and are a yellow-orange colour. The bare skin between the eyes and the beak is pink. The large, hook-shaped beak is pink with a black tip.

The flamingo has large wings and a short tail. A gland near the base of the tail produces an oil-like substance that the flamingo spreads over its feathers when preening.

Males are larger than females.

There are two species of flamingo present in Tanzania:

Lesser Flamingo

The lesser flamingo is the commonest, smallest and brightest of all the flamingos. The lesser flamingo plumage is an evenly coloured deep pink. The bill is dark red with a black tip. The legs are red and a hind toe called a hallux is present.

Height: 90cm-1m
Wing Span: 99cm
Weight: 1.5-2kg

Greater Flamingo

The greater flamingo is the largest and most widespread of all the flamingos. The greater flamingo is taller than the lesser flamingo and is a pale whitish-pink colour with red patches. The primary and secondary feathers are black. The bill is pale pink with a black tip. The legs are pink.

Height: 1-1.5m
Wing Span: 1.3-1.6m
Weight: 2-4kg

Habitat

Flamingos live in areas of shallow salt water such as lakes, dams, lagoons, swamps, mangroves, estuaries, salt pans and tidal flats. They are able to live at high altitude and tolerate extreme ranges in temperature.

The lesser flamingo is found in Africa and India.

The greater flamingo is found Europe, Asia, Africa, North and South America.

Behaviour

Flamingos are nomadic birds that live in large, closely packed flocks all year round, comprising tens of thousands of individuals.

Flamingos usually fly at night to avoid predators. Reaching speeds of 50-60km/h they are capable of covering long distances of up to 600km. Flying with their head, neck and legs outstretched they either fly in a V formation or in a single line. To become airborne the flamingo has to run forwards while flapping its wings, and when landing it will run several steps before it stops. When resting they always face into the wind to prevent the rain and wind penetrating their feathers, they rest by either sitting down with their legs tucked underneath them or by standing on one leg. It is not unusual to see a flock of flamingos floating on the surface of the water.

Diet

Flamingos are filter feeders that flourish in salt lakes. Webbed feet, which prevent the flamingo from sinking, disturb the underlying mud when searching for food. The beak of the flamingo turns sharply downwards two thirds along its length, this means that when feeding the head has to be lowered into the water in an upside down position allowing it to ladle up water and food particles. The pump like action and roughened surface of the tongue, and tiny hair-like projections (*lamellae*) on the inside of the beak aid the filtration process.

Greater flamingos are omnivores and feed on aquatic plants, worms, insect larvae, small molluscs, crustaceans and blue-green algae.

Lesser flamingos are herbivores and feed on aquatic plants and blue-green algae on the water surface.

Flamingos drink fresh water.

Communication

Flamingos are noisy and communicate with each other by making grunting, growling, honking sounds.

Reproduction

Flamingos are monogamous and only breed in the presence of large numbers. Mating is initiated by a spectacular courtship ritual that involves a lot of marching to and fro, standing tall and erect, stretching their necks in an upward direction, flapping their wings and repeated head turning, before they eventually pair off. A volcanic-shaped nest of mud, stones and feathers is built by both birds on the salt lake deposits. The nest can be as high as 30cm and takes six weeks to complete.

The female lays a single chalky coloured egg that is guarded and incubated by both parents for a period of up to 31 days. The chicks are a grey-white colour, and have a straight red bill, their eyes are initially grey but turn a yellow-

orange colour by the time they are one year old. The short, stocky legs are a pink-red colour. Both parents are able to recognise their chick's call and feed it on crop milk until it is two months old. Crop milk has a high fat and protein content, it is dark red in colour and is produced by glands in the upper digestive tract. When the chick is seven days old it will fledge and join a crèche watched over by other adults/babysitters while its parents go in search of food. The chicks are able to walk about on the salt flats, however if thickened salt-like deposits form around the chicks' ankles it makes it difficult or impossible for them to walk about and condemns them, with time, to a certain death.

By the time the chick is two to three months old its beak is sufficiently developed to allow it to filter food. As soon as the chicks are big enough they are taken by the adults on to the lake to be taught how to swim. They are able to fly by the time they are four months old, and by the time they are three years old they have taken on the adult pink colouration.

Flamingos reach sexual maturity between the ages of three and five years old. They begin to breed when they are six years old.

Predators/Threats

Flamingos are defenceless, and when threatened they will fly away. They have few natural predators due primarily to the remote, hostile, inhospitable environments in which they live. Their main predators are other birds such as marabou storks and African fish eagles, wildcats, and the occasional python. The eggs and chicks are preyed upon by the marabou stork and vultures. The marabou stork is particularly cruel and will kill the chicks without actually feeding on them. The main threat to the flamingo's survival is loss of habitat and polluted water. The greater flamingo is classified as a *species of least concern* (2018). The lesser flamingo is classified as a *species that is near threatened* (2018).

Trivia

♦A combination of strong, intense sunlight, high temperatures, flamingo droppings, alkaline water and plankton encourage the growth and formation of the algae responsible for the unique pink colouration of the flamingo.

♦The colour of the flamingo is a good indicator of its health. A pale flamingo is under nourished and unhealthy, whereas a vibrantly coloured flamingo is well nourished and in good health.

♦The flamingo is nicknamed the flame bird.

♦The legs of the adult flamingo are longer than the body.

♦The brain of the flamingo is smaller than its eye

♦Flamingos are able to drink water that is close to boiling point.

♦Salt is excreted from salt glands situated in the nostrils.

Grey Crowned Crane
(*Balearica regulorum gibbericeps*)
Swahili:*Ndege korongo*

Identification
The grey crowned crane is an elegant, graceful bird that is found in East Africa and is extremely striking in appearance.

Its elongated neck and body are covered in a slate grey plumage. The feathers on the neck are lighter.

The wings are white, and streaked yellow with black and chestnut colouring present. The primary and secondary feathers are dark grey.

A crown of stiff yellow feathers with black tips sits on top of the head, from whence it gets its name. The head is black. A white cheek patch is present on the side of the face, and vibrant red facial skin is present above this patch. A red inflatable gular sac is present below the chin. The eyes are light blue. The bill is short and grey.

The black-grey legs are long and thin with large feet. A prehensile hind toe enables the crowned crane to grasp branches on trees.

Males are slightly larger than females.

Height:	91cm-1.2m
Length:	1-1.1m
Wing Span:	2m
Weight:	3.5kg

Life Span
Twenty two years in the wild.

Habitat
Grey crowned cranes are usually found in savannahs, open grasslands, grassy wetlands and marshes near streams, rivers, ponds, lakes and swamps.

Diet
Grey crowned cranes are omnivores and feed on plants, grains, seeds, insects, earthworms, small mammals, fish, frogs, snakes and eggs.

Behaviour
Grey crowned cranes are sedentary, non-migratory birds and spend all day searching for food and preening others, this preening strengthens bonds between the birds. When searching for food they will stamp their feet heavily on the ground to disturb the insects, and then flush them out. They usually lives in small flocks of three to five individuals, although larger flocks of 30 to 150 individuals are not uncommon. During the day they rest in trees, and return to roost at night, this keeps them safe from predators. They are terrestrial and arboreal.

Communication
Grey crowned cranes communicate by honking. Body postures and displays are also used to communicate their mood.

Reproduction
Grey crowned cranes are monogamous and mate for life. Breeding at any time of the year they engage in a ritualistic 'Nuptial Mating Dance" that involves lots of head bobbing, deep bowing, wing fluttering, dancing, leaping and jumping. The gular sac

may be inflated in the process. Either sex can initiate the mating dance and it is an integral part of the courtship. Both parents are involved in constructing a large platform-like nest made from grass, in tall wet vegetation, and both share responsibility for incubating the eggs and caring for the young. The female lays between two to five muddy white coloured eggs that are incubated for up to 31 days. The chicks all hatch at the same time, and are able to run as soon as they are born. Within 12 hours the chicks can swim and float, they start eating food within 24 hours and are able to follow their parents foraging for food at two days. They communicate to their parents with a shrill peeping noise. The chicks fledge when they are between 50-90 days old, and once fledged they join a juvenile flock. Young grey crowned cranes reach their full adult colouration when they are 20-24 months old.

Grey crowned cranes are sexually mature when they are three years old.

Predators/Threats
Loss and degradation of habitat and the effects of climate change are a threat to the grey crowned crane's survival. They may be caught in live traps for food, their eggs collected illegally or they may be poisoned if they come into conflict with humans.

The grey crowned crane is classified as an *endangered species* (2012).

Trivia
♦The grey crowned crane is also known as African crowned crane, East African crane, East African crowned crane, golden crested crane, golden crowned crane and South African crane.

♦The grey crowned crane is the national bird of Uganda.

♦The grey crowned crane is the only crane that can roost in a tree.

♦The grey crowned crane can fly short distances.

♦The red gular sac can be inflated to store fish and food.

♦Primitive species of grey crowned cranes have been discovered in fossils that date back to the Ecocene epoch period 56.5-34.5 million years ago.

Kori Bustard
(Ardeotis kora)
Swahili:*Tandacuala*

Identification
The kori bustard is Africa's heaviest and largest flying bird.

The kori bustard's plumage allows it to blend in with the environment providing perfect camouflage. The body, back and tail are light brown and the underparts are dark brown to buff coloured. Multiple layers of black and white spots are present near the front of the wings. Broad greyish brownish bands are present on the tail and the flight feathers.

The kori bustard has a black crested head with moveable feathers. A white stripe is present above the brownish yellow eyes and the yellowish beak is straight and pointed. Loose fluffy white feathers with fine black lines are present around the chin throat and neck. The neck is long.

The pale brown-grey coloured legs are long and strong with transverse scales. Three short, forward pointing toes are present that have evolved to accommodate a terrestrial life style that involves a lot of running. The absence of a hind toe means that the kori bustard is unable to grasp and perch on a tree branch.

Males are more brightly coloured than females.

The male is twice as heavy as the female.

The kori bustard has excellent eyesight.

Height:	60cm-1.2m
Length:	80cm-1.5m
Wingspan:	60-70cm
Weight:	5.5-19kg

Life Span
Unknown in the wild. Between 26-28 years in captivity.

Habitat
Kori bustards are usually found near water in semi deserts, open grasslands and lightly wooded savannahs at altitudes between 700-2000m. They like to live in areas where the grass is short so that they can survey the surrounding vicinity easily.

Behaviour
Kori bustards are sedentary, shy, ground dwelling birds that are reluctant to fly. They only fly if they are threatened, and they need a large area to take off. They fly with measured, deliberate strokes, with the neck extended and legs folded. They land with outspread wings that fold in as their feet touch the ground. Kori bustards spend the majority of their time foraging for food, walking along slowly picking up insects and small mammals with their bills. The preening gland (uropygial gland) which produces preen oil that is essential for water proofing and maintaining good feather condition in birds, is absent in the kori bustard. They produce powder down and engage in sunbathing and dust bathing. They need to live in habitats where there is plenty of sun to dry out damp, wet feathers.

Kori bustards are not migratory and only leave an area if there is a shortage or absence of food and water.

They are usually seen alone or in small flocks.

Kori bustards are diurnal.

Diet
Kori bustards are opportunistic omnivores and feed on insects, small mammals, lizards, snakes, carrion, seeds and berries. Unlike other birds that scoop water up with their bills, they use a sucking motion.

Communication
Kori bustards are usually quiet birds. They will make a barking noise if alarmed or threatened, a low pitched booming noise when engaged in their courtship ritual and snorts or growls if the young are threatened. The chicks make soft cooing noises to communicate with their mother.

Reproduction
Kori bustards are polygamous and only produce one clutch of eggs a year. Mating lasts between 23-30 days.

Courtship begins early morning or late afternoon with the male inflating its neck up to four times its natural size, dropping its wings and deflecting its tail feathers upwards and forwards. Dancing and bowing before the female, making a high pitched booming noise, and snapping its beak, the male works hard to attract her attention. Mating lasts for a few seconds. On completion the male immediately begins searching for another available female. The male attempts to breed with as many females as possible.

The male takes no part in incubating the eggs or rearing the chicks. The female makes a shallow nest in the ground in which she lays one to two pale olive, brown speckled coloured eggs. The eggs are incubated up to 24 days. The newly hatched chicks are well camouflaged, they have a mottled, tawny brown coloured body and a black mottled head. Initially the female feeds the chicks on soft food that is easily digested. Within weeks they are able to forage for their own food and are fully fledged when they are five weeks old. They are confident fliers by the time they are three to four months old and usually remain with their mother until they are one to two years old. Up to 82% of kori bustard chicks die in the first year of their life.

Kori bustards reach sexual maturity when they are two years old.

Predators/Threats
Kori bustards are natural prey for caracals, eagles, jackals, leopards, lions and serval cat. Humans pose the greatest threat to their existence. Loss of habitat due to urbanization, farmers acquiring land for livestock, poisoning, pollution and hunting are a continuous threat. The kori bustard has a slow reproduction rate, and during dry years this is reduced even further. Climate change is a threat to their survival.

The kori bustard is classified as a *near threatened species* (Oct. 2016).

Trivia
♦Bustard means "birds that walk".

♦Fishermen use the feathers of the kori bustard for fly fishing.

♦The kori bustard is nick named the "Christmas Turkey" in Namibia and the "Kalahari Kentucky" in South Africa.

♦The kori bustard is hunted for its meat.

Marabou Stork

(*Leptoptilos crumeniferus*)
Swahili: *Batamaji*

Identification

The marabou stork is an extremely large wading bird and is one of the world's largest land birds that is able to fly.

Both sexes have a black plumage. White plumage is present behind the head, on the chest and belly and as tail feathers.

The head is bald with a sparse covering of downy feathers that extend as far as the nape of the neck. The skin on the head and neck is a pink-purple-red colour and is covered with irregular red-black spots. A large, pendulous reddish-pink throat wattle hangs down from its neck and is used in courtship rituals. The eyes are a greyish-brown colour. The beak is large, pointed and conical.

The bones of the legs and toes are hollow and the skin is naturally black, although it usually appears to be white because the marabou stork regularly defecates down its legs, (this is believed to help regulate its body temperature as well as having strong antiseptic properties).

Males are taller and larger than females.

Height: 1.5m
Wing Span: 2.6m
Weight: 9kg

Habitat

Marabou storks are usually found in savannahs, grasslands and marshland, near rivers, fishponds and lakes. They can also live close to human habitation in the vicinity of rubbish dumps and slaughterhouses.

Behaviour

Marabou storks are lazy, slow-moving birds that spend a lot of time standing still. They can have a solitary existence but usually live and breed in colonies alongside ibises, egrets, pelicans and storks, and their numbers can range from 20 to 1000s. They are aggressive eaters, often found alongside vultures and hyenas feasting on carrion. In the presence of a grass fire they will wait at the edge of the blaze hoping to capture fleeing prey.

When in flight they keep their legs extended but retract their necks, and they have the ability to soar at high altitude above the African plains.

Diet

Marabou storks are scavengers feeding on carrion, scraps from refuse heaps and slaughterhouses, small birds and mammals, reptiles, eggs, nestlings, amphibians, fish and insects. Indigestible food is regurgitated.

They are able to access food more easily during the dry season as animals congregate in high concentrations around dwindling water supplies.

Communication

Marabou storks are usually quiet, only making croaking noises or engaging in bill rattling during the mating season. When threatened they will emit a noise called beak clacking.

Reproduction

Marabou storks mate for life, and breed during the dry season. Their nests are made from twigs and are situated on treetops or ledges. The nest is never left unattended as other marabou storks will steal the twigs for their own nests. The nest is shallow and the centre is lined with smaller sticks and greenery. The female lays between two to five chalky-white eggs that are incubated for up to 31 days.

Both parents share the responsibility of incubating the eggs, feeding the young regurgitated food and teaching them how to fly and hunt.

The chick's down is short and white and is replaced after eight days with a second coat that is the same colour. They achieve the full adult black plumage between the ages of three to four years old.

The chicks make a lot of noise, croaking, whistling, whining and clattering. They are able to fly when they are two months old and are fully fledged by the time they are three to four months old, after which they break any maternal bonds that they have with their parents.

Marabou storks reach sexual maturity when they are four years old.

Predators/Threats

The marabou stork is classified as a *species of least concern* (2016).

Trivia

♦The marabou stork is nick-named the undertaker bird due to its shape - it has cloak-like wings and skinny legs.

♦The marabou stork is the only species of stork to feed on carrion, they will also eat faeces.

♦Scavengers such as marabou storks usually have bald heads. When they are actively engaged in devouring a carcass their head will be covered in blood, other bodily fluids and matter that would be difficult to clean and be a source of infection if they were covered in feathers.

♦The feathers and down of the marabou stork are used to trim clothing and hats.

♦Marabou storks are sometimes considered to be a pest, but they do a marvellous job cleaning up carcasses that may be a source of disease.

♦Marabou storks can become tame when living close to human habitation.

♦The images in this section were all taken in Kenya.

Ostrich
(Struthio camelus)
Swahili: *Mbuni*

Identification
The ostrich is the largest and heaviest land bird in the world. It is also the fastest animal on two legs.

The male's plumage is black with the tips of the wings and tail feathers coloured white. The female's plumage is a dusty brown-grey colour. Between 50-60 tail feathers are present. The plumage is soft and has strong insulating properties. Ostriches are able to tolerate extreme variations in temperature.

The ostrich is a flightless bird. Strong stiffened wing and tail feathers required for flight are absent. Its wings are extremely short but very strong. Two claws are present on the tips of the wing fingers and are used in self defence.

The ostrich's head, long narrow neck and legs are bald, with a sparse covering of down. The skin on the female's neck and legs is tinged a pink-grey colour, whereas the male's is a grey-blue colour. The eyes are large and coloured brown, and are protected from the elements by long eyelashes. The broad, flattened pink beak has a rounded tip.

The legs are long and powerful with two toes on each foot. A sharp claw is present on the inner toe and assists in self defence and running. The ostrich can run at speeds of up to 70km/h and is able to maintain a constant speed of 50km/h when required.

The ostrich has excellent eyesight and hearing.

Height: Male   1.8-2.7m
           Female 1.7-2m
Wing Span: 2m
Weight: 100-155kg

Life Span
Up to 50 years in the wild.

Habitat
Ostriches are usually found in dry grasslands, savannahs, semi-deserts and desert areas.

Behaviour
Ostriches are nomadic, travelling alongside other grazers in the constant search of food, although males are territorial. They either live alone or in pairs, but during the mating season they may live in herds of between 5-50 individuals, led by a top hen.

In the presence of predators, ostriches will either lie flat on the ground with their necks outstretched, appearing as a mound of earth on the ground, or they will run away. They are capable of outrunning any of the predators such as leopards, hyenas and lions. When threatened, the ostrich can deliver a single powerful blow with its legs that is capable of disembowelling and killing any predator.

Ostriches are diurnal and are most active early morning and late afternoon.

Diet
Ostriches are omnivorous, feeding primarily on grasses, shrubs, shoots, fruit, seeds, leaves, and nuts, supplementing their diet with invertebrates, (locusts, grasshoppers), and vertebrates, (small birds, lizards, frogs). Small stones and sand are swallowed to aid digestion. Ostriches requires very little water and are able to extract sufficient moisture from the plants they feed on to meet their needs.

Communication

Ostriches use a variety of vocalisations to communicate with each other from whistling, hissing, growling, grunting and snorting to a low booming sound that it emits during the mating season. Bodily postures are used to intimidate rivals and warn off any predators.

Reproduction

Ostriches are polygamous and iteroparous. Mating commences between the months of March to April and ceases by September. The males (roosters) fight to win over a harem of between two to six females (hens). The dominant male (alpha male) initiates the mating process with an elaborate courtship ritual. He makes a lot of hissing noises, beats his wings repeatedly and pokes the ground with his beak to attract a female, before proceeding to mate. The male mates with all of the females but will only form a pair bond with the dominant female.

Ostriches are oviparous and lay their eggs in a communal nest over a three week period. The nest is constructed by the male, who scratches and scrapes the ground to create a hollow that is up to three metres in diameter and 30-60cm deep. The dominant female, who is able to recognise her own eggs, lays her eggs first in the centre of the nest and these are surrounded by eggs laid by the other females. Eggs on the periphery that are surplus to requirements are discarded. The eggs are a creamy-yellow colour and the surface of the shell is pitted. There will be between 15-60 eggs in the nest, and they are incubated for up to 45 days by the dominant female during the day and by the male during the night.

When the chicks are ready to hatch, they call to their parents from inside the egg. Within minutes of being hatched the chicks are able to run around. Both parents play an active role in providing the chicks with food, water, shelter and shade, as well as protecting and defending them from predators. Growth is rapid and the chicks are independent by the time they are one year old.

Ostriches reach sexual maturity between two to four years old.

Predators/Threats

Ostriches are hunted by humans for their feathers, meat and skin, and when they are perceived by locals to be in competition with domestic livestock for grass. The feathers are used as feather dusters and are also used in the clothing industry. The meat, which tastes like beef, is low in cholesterol. The skin is used for leather goods. The fat and bone marrow are used in traditional medicines to treat conditions such as arthritis and rheumatism. The eggs are used to make jewellery and receptacles for carrying water. The young are preyed upon by hyenas, jackals and vultures. The ostrich is classified as a *species of least concern* (2018).

Trivia

♦An ostrich is only able to kick forwards.

♦The ostrich's eyes are up to 5cm in diameter and are the largest of all known birds.

♦The ostrich is fond of water and likes to bathe in it.

♦The ostrich lays the largest eggs in the world, they are 18-23cm long, 11-15cm wide and weigh 1.3kg.

♦It takes a large pan and two hours to cook an ostrich egg to perfection.

♦Ostriches are bred commercially in some parts of the world for their meat, feathers and skin.

♦Ostriches are able to secrete urine separately from their faeces - an unusual trait for a bird.

Secretary Bird

(Sagittarius serpentarius)
Swahili:*Katibu ndege*

Identification

The secretary bird is a large raptor distantly related to buzzards, harriers, kites and vultures.

It has a small eagle like head, and the small eyes are yellow to dark brown in colour, with long black eyelashes that are modified feathers without the barbs. The featherless face is a brilliant orangey red colour. The small hook shaped beak is grey. Twenty black crested feathers sit behind the head. Black feathers are present at the base of the neck.

The plumage is light grey and the flight feathers are black. The wedge shaped tail is black. Two elongated tail feathers are present and touch the ground.

The long, powerful legs have black feathers present half way down. The lower leg is covered in a layer of thick, pink scales. The short blunt toes have short curved talons at the end. The secretary bird is unable to grasp objects.

Height:	90cm-1.5m
Length:	1.12-1.52m
Wing Span:	1.9-2.2m
Weight:	2.3-5kg

Life Span

Ten to 15 years in the wild.

Habitat

Secretary birds are grassland specialists and are usually found on open grasslands, shrub land and savannahs throughout sub Saharan Africa from sea level to 3,000m.

Behaviour

Secretary birds are solitary. Successful, opportunistic hunters, they spend the majority of the day on foot searching for food. They are efficient runners and it is believed that they have evolved to accommodate their unique strutting and stomping style of hunting. Hunting either alone or as a loose pair they stomp through the tall grass flushing prey out. They are often observed on the periphery of a bush fire capturing escaping prey. When attacking prey they spreads their wings out wide and raise their feathered crests at the back of their heads. The beak is used to strike the prey, and the feet to stun the prey unconscious. The force they use to kill prey is five times their own body weight. This is one, very powerful bird. Secretary birds then swallow their prey. When digestion is complete they regurgitate pellets consisting of fur, feathers, bones and invertebrates' exoskeletons.

Secretary birds are primarily terrestrial. They rest in the shade at midday away from the heat of the sun, and roost in a tree at night. They can fly, but need a long take off run prior to taking to the air. They fly with their legs extended.

They are non migratory.

They are diurnal.

Diet

Secretary birds are carnivorous and feed on insects, small mammals, mice, hares, mongooses, crabs, lizards, snakes, tortoises, small birds and birds' eggs.

Communication
Secretary birds are quiet raptors. They croak when courting, defending their nests, chicks and territory. They emit a single croak when alarmed.

Reproduction
Secretary birds are monogamous and mate for life. Breeding all year round, they engage in a ritualistic courtship display that involves flying high in the sky, soaring in a circular manner, swooping and claw grappling in mid air. They also chase each other on the ground, and mating is completed either on the ground or in a tree.

Both parents are involved in constructing a large platform like nest made from sticks and twigs in a thorny tree. The nest is 1.0-1.5m wide and 30-50cm deep, and is lined with grass, leaves, animal fur and dung.

Both parents share responsibility for incubating the eggs, (the female does the majority of incubating), and caring for the young. The female lays two to three elongated, rough textured chalky blue to white eggs. The eggs are laid at two to three day intervals, and are incubated for up to 45 days. The eggs hatch in the sequence in which they were laid. During the first few weeks of the chick's life one of the parents is always present near the nest, safeguarding them from predators. Both birds feed the chicks in the nest for the first few weeks of their lives on liquefied regurgitated food that is stored in the crop. At 40 days old the chicks can eat small mammals and reptiles that are dropped into the nest by the parents. Sibling rivalry is absent.

The chick's down is initially a dusty white colour which changes to duck grey by the time it is two weeks old. The crest and long eyelashes appear when the chick is three weeks old. The chick is fully feathered at seven weeks old.

The chick's development is very slow. It is able to stand at six weeks old, at nine weeks it begins to exercise its wings by flapping them up and down, momentarily lifting it up from the floor of the nest, and it is fully fledged at 12 weeks. The chick courageously throws itself out of the nest and glides down to the ground below. It will remain near the nesting tree for another 62-105 days while its parents teach it how to hunt and forage for food, essential skills to ensure its survival. Once the chick is independent of its parents, it flies off to make a life of its own.

Predators/Threats
Adult secretary birds have no natural predators. The eggs and young chicks are preyed upon by crows, hornbills, kites, large owls and ravens. Loss of habitat and climate change (severe weather in particular) is a threat to the secretary bird's survival.

The secretary bird is classified as a *vulnerable species* (October 2016).

Trivia
♦The secretary bird appears on the coat of arms of Sudan and South Africa.

♦The secretary bird is also known as the devil's horse.

♦The secretary bird is famous for its snake hunting abilities. Its taxonomic name means archer of snakes.

♦The secretary bird got its name from the resemblance of an 18th century clerk, with a quill wedged behind the customary wig.

Vulture
Swahili: *Tai*

Identification
Vultures are found in every continent in the world apart from Antarctica and Australia.

Vultures are medium to large-sized birds and are unique in that they scavenge for food and do not hunt and kill like other birds of prey. They fall into one of two group classifications:

New World Vultures:
There are seven species of New World vulture and they belong to the family Cathartdae. They are closely related to ibises and storks and are found in North, Central and South America.

Old World Vultures:
There are 15 species of Old World vulture and they belong to the family Accipitridae. They are closely related to buzzards, eagles, hawks and kites and are found in Africa, Asia and Europe.

Old World vultures are characterised by their bald head, short neck, long, broad, powerful wings and rounded tail. The beak is strong, sharp and hooked, and assists in stripping the flesh from a carcass. They have excellent eyesight that has evolved with time, and the centre of the eye has a magnifying area that allows the vulture to accurately locate food. The ear is protected by a fine layer of skin that prevents blood and other bodily matter collecting in it when its head is inside a dead animal during feeding. The feet are strong with sharp talons. A back claw called a hallux is present, and this acts like a thumb enabling the vulture to manipulate objects.

Both male and female are a similar size and colour (black-brown), and are hard to distinguish from each other.

Length: 1m
Wingspan: 1.5-3.7m

Habitat
The vulture's dependence on its eyesight for locating food has restricted the habitat in which it is able to survive. They are usually found in open countryside such as savannahs, semi-arid and desert areas.

Diet
Vultures are opportunistic, carnivorous scavengers that feed on carrion. Soaring high in the sky on warm thermals they spend many hours a day scanning the surrounding countryside, searching for food. Once food is located they land en masse. Food can be stored in a pouch in the throat called a crop, and is digested at a later time or regurgitated for the chicks. Strong, corrosive digestive juices enable the vulture to feed on carcasses that are in the advance stages of decay and contaminated with deadly bacteria and parasites that other animals are unable to tolerate (hog cholera, anthrax, TB and botulinum toxin). Vultures have a very strong, robust immune system. Never knowing when they will eat again, they gorge themselves in a frenzied, chaotic feeding session.

After feeding, a lot of grooming and preening takes place before they retreat to a nearby tree to recover and digest their food.

Communication
Vultures are sociable yet shy, and are usually quiet, apart from when they are feeding.

Reproduction
Vultures are monogamous. The male initially attracts the attention of the female with a display of his flying skills before they pair off. The nest is made of leaves, twigs and sticks, high up in the hollow of a tree or on a cliff, and may be used for several years. Up to two eggs can be laid and both parents share the responsibility of incubating, feeding the young regurgitated food and teaching them how to hunt and fly. The incubation period is up to 50 days. When food is scarce, if two chicks are present the larger chick will kill the smaller one. The chicks are able to fly by the time they are three to six months old, until then they are relatively docile.

Predators/Threats
Vultures are perceived as being aggressive, ugly, ungainly and cumbersome creatures, associated with scavenging on carrion. Their breeding grounds and nests are destroyed, and they are killed for body parts to be used in witchcraft and traditional medicine. Locals using poisoned bait to kill livestock predators (lions, cheetahs and feral dogs) indiscriminately kill large numbers of vultures. Poachers actively poison carcasses to entice and kill the vultures. Circling vultures alerts the authorities attention to the presence and location of poachers.

The vulture plays an invaluable role in ridding the environment of dead, decaying and diseased animals. Their demise will see a rise in diseases that can be easily transmitted by flies, dogs (rabies in particular) and rats that can infect humans and animals. Lack of food, loss of habitat and the effects of climate change are also a threat to their survival. Fifty per cent of old world vultures are classified as a *vulnerable, endangered or critically endangered species.*

Trivia
♦There are eight species of Old World vultures in Africa.

♦Scavengers such as vultures usually have bald heads. When they are actively engaged in devouring a carcass their head will be covered in blood, other bodily fluids and matter that would be difficult to clean and be a source of infection if they were covered in feathers.

♦It is extremely rare for a vulture to kill a live animal. If food is scarce, they may attack a newborn, or a sick, wounded animal.

♦Contrary to popular opinion vultures are not aggressive birds.

♦The consumption of poisoned bait by large numbers of vultures results in the vulture population declining faster than any other species.

♦Projectile corrosive vomit can be used as a deterrent when threatened.

♦Vultures urinate down their legs as the uric acid present in their urine kills bacteria and acts as a coolant.

♦A group of vultures on the ground is called a wake, committee or venue. When circling in the air a group of vultures is called a kettle.

♦Vultures are able to reduce a small mammal down to its skeleton in less than 30 minutes.

Reptiles

Agama
(Agama agama)
Swahili: *Mjusi kafiri*

Identification
Agamas are agile, small to medium-sized, non-poisonous lizards native to Africa, Asia and Europe.

It has a large triangular-shaped head, with large eyes that have rounded pupils, and ears surrounded by clusters of spines. It has sharp, incisor-like teeth, with two fangs present in the upper jaw and a sticky tongue suited to catching prey. The body is covered in small scales, and long toes are present on all four limbs.

The tail is long, and the skin colour varies from a green-grey-brown colour to bright blue, pink or red, and they are consequently nicknamed "rainbow lizards". Some may have a stripe present down the centre of the back. The underside is a whitish colour. Males are always more brightly coloured than females.

Depending on species the length of the agama ranges from 12-38cm.

Habitat
Agamas are terrestrial and arboreal and are usually found in rocky outcrops, hillsides and semi-desert areas. They live and hide in rocks or the thatched roofs of mud huts, emerging to feed on prey.

Behaviour
Agamas are docile by nature and live in small groups of 10 to 20 individuals. Several females are present in the group alongside sub males who are led by a highly territorial dominant male (cock). Agamas do a lot of head nodding and head bobbing.

Frequent bouts of fighting occur when the dominant male is challenged by a subordinate or if a male wanders into its territory. The dominant male may change colour, do a lot of bobbing about, lash out with its tail and open its jaws wide to intimidate and confuse any rival. Agamas will run on their hind legs when threatened. Agamas are diurnal.

Diet
Agamas are primarily insectivores and feed mainly on ants, grasshoppers, beetles and termites, but will also eat grass, berries, seeds and the eggs of small lizards.

Reproduction
Agamas are polygamous and mate between March and May. During the mating season the male may change colour and will do a lot of head bobbing to attract and impress a female. Agamas are oviparous. Between June and November the female lays between 7-18 eggs in a warm, damp, sandy, shallow hollow about 5cm deep, and have an incubation period of eight to ten weeks. Females are sexually mature between 14-18 months old. Males are sexually mature at two years old.

Predators/Threats
Agamas are natural prey for snakes.

Chameleon
(*Chamaeleonidae*)
Swahili: *Kinyonga*

Identification
Chameleons are small to medium-sized arboreal lizards. There are between 80-150 different species and they are native to India, Sri Lanka, Spain, Madagascar and other areas of Africa.

The head is triangular with a pointed crest. Depending on species, horns and spines may be present. The eyes are tiny and situated on a large, conical protrusion. A small, yellow ring surrounds a black eye. The eyes are able to rotate, and move independently of each other, but will face forwards when focused on prey. External ears are absent.

The chameleon has a long, sticky, elastic, prehensile tongue that curls up inside its mouth. The tongue can actually be the full length of its body, it is fast moving and is used to catch prey. Teeth are present on the lower jaw.

The body is flattened laterally. It has a long prehensile tail that wraps itself around the tree branches to help maintain balance.

The legs are long and slender. Five toes are present on all four limbs and are fused together in bundles of two or three, this affords the chameleon a pincer-like grip with which to hold onto the branches of trees as it slowly rocks forwards. Sharp claws are present on each toe.

The dry, rough skin has varying shades of green-grey-brown. The colour of the skin changes involuntarily, and is stimulated by temperature, light and emotion. Hot temperatures, bright lights and anger darkens the colour of the skin. Cold temperatures, darkness and excitement or fear lightens the colour of the skin. The chameleon has excellent eyesight.

Body Length: 2.5-68cm depending on species.

Habitat
Chameleons mostly live in trees and bushes, and are found in tropical and mountainous rain forests, woodlands, savannahs, semi-deserts and deserts. Some species live on the ground.

Diet
Chameleons are insectivores and feed on locusts, flies, mosquitoes, crickets, beetles and grass hoppers. Larger species may eat small birds.

Reproduction
Chameleons may be oviparous or ovoviviparous. The gestation period, incubation period and number of eggs laid varies from species to species.

Predators/Threats
Snakes (boomslangs and vine snakes in particular) are the main natural predators of the chameleon, followed closely by birds. Garden and agricultural pesticides either poison the chameleon or they starve to death because of the lack of food. Grass fires quickly destroy their habitat.

Monitor Lizard
(*Varanidae*)
Swahili: *Kenge*

Identification
Monitor lizards are large reptiles found in the tropical and sub-tropical regions of Africa, Asia and Australia. They are usually found in deserts, forests or grasslands.

They have a long flexible neck, a small head and large, powerful jaws that enable large prey to be swallowed. The flickering forked tongue is used to sniff the air and collect airborne particles to pass onto sensory tissue in the Jacobson's organ which is in the roof of the mouth. This tells the monitor lizard all it needs to know about prospective prey, the presence of predators and the environment. The body is large and heavy with four short, strong legs equipped with long powerful claws. The tail is long and powerful. Despite its cumbersome appearance it is surprisingly agile and is able to climb, swim and burrow with ease. Depending on species the body length ranges from 20cm to 3m, and an individual may weigh up to 165kg. Some monitor lizards, such as the Komodo, are venomous.

Habitat
The majority of monitor lizards are terrestrial, some are arboreal and others semi-aquatic or aquatic.

Behaviour
By nature monitor lizards are aggressive, ill-tempered and hostile. They will avoid confrontation where possible and seek flight, but where there is no alternative they will use bodily postures, hiss a lot, enlarge their throat and expand their ribs while lashing out wildly with the tail to ward off any predators. Monitor lizards are diurnal.

Diet
Monitor lizards are carnivorous and feed on birds, small mammals, crayfish, eggs, frogs, turtles, snakes, crocodile hatchlings and invertebrates. Close to human habitation they will feed on domestic livestock (cats, dogs, pigs, goats, chickens) as well as carrion.

Reproduction
Monitor lizards are oviparous and lay a clutch of between 2-60 eggs, either in a burrow in the ground or in the hollow of a tree. The eggs incubate for a period of 56-70 days. The young use an egg tooth to break the shell.

Predators/Threats
Loss of habitat and the effects of climate change are a threat to the monitor lizard's survival. They may be hunted for their hides to make fashion accessories.

Trivia
♦The monitor lizard is unable to grow its tail back if it loses it.
♦The bacteria in the mouth of the monitor lizard is highly toxic and can be fatal to the victim if bitten.
♦The image in this section was taken in Lake Baringo, Kenya.

Nile Crocodile
(*Crocodylus niloticus*)
Swahili: *Mamba*

Identification
The Nile crocodile is a large, amphibious, lizard-like reptile. It has a long, streamlined body and tail, with four short legs equipped with sharp claws. There are five toes on the forelegs that are suited to digging in the sand, and four webbed toes on the hind legs that assist with swimming.

The head is large with a broad, elongated, tapering snout. The eyes, ears and nostrils are placed high on the crocodile's flattened head, allowing it to see, hear, and smell above the surface of the water when it is submerged. The tiny eyes are green and the pupils are vertical. A third eyelid protects the eyes under water.

The jaws are strong and powerful, and the long, conical teeth, which can number up to 66, are designed to endure the stresses and strains of firmly holding on to struggling prey. The teeth interlock and are clearly visible when the crocodile's mouth is closed. The fourth tooth in particular, protrudes from the lower jaw and fits into a notch on the upper jaw. The teeth continue to grow throughout life.

The hide is thick, rough and scaly. Rows of ossified, overlapping raised horny scales (*scutes*) run the length of the back and tail. The scutes offer camouflage, protection and help control body temperature. A fine mesh of blood vessels runs up and down through the scutes to the surface, absorbing energy from the sun, which increases the crocodile's body temperature.

Juveniles are dark brown/olive green in colour with dark crossbands on the body and tail. The adults are darker with crossbands that fade as they age. The underbelly has smooth scales that are a yellow-grey colour.

Nile crocodiles have excellent eyesight, hearing and sense of smell.

Males are 30% larger than the female.

Nose to Tail Length: Male 3.5-5m
Female 4m
Weight: Male 500-550kg
Female 300-350kg
NB: Large males can be up to 1,000kg

Life Span
Forty-five years in the wild.

Habitat
Nile crocodiles are found in waterholes, ponds, lakes, rivers, estuaries, freshwater marshes and swamps. They usually remain in the same territory throughout their natural lives, only moving when drought conditions cause the water to dry up.

Behaviour
Nile crocodiles are sociable animals and usually live in a small group called a bask.

Both the male (bull) and female (cow) are territorial, especially during the mating season. They do not like intruders and defend their territories aggressively.

Nile crocodiles are cold-blooded creatures. They are inactive when cool, and active when warm. They spend a considerable amount of time during the day on the banks of the river, sliding up onto the banks on their bellies to bask in the sun, usually with their mouths wide open, venting off heat. They return to the water when they need to cool down, or when they are startled. Nile crocodiles can lift their bellies up off the ground and high walk. They can run at speeds of 17km/h over short distances, but tire quickly. Small crocodiles can bound like a rabbit.

Nile crocodiles are the ultimate predator, highly skilled, effective and opportunistic, either hunting on their own or as part of a team. Moving with ease through the water they can swim at 32km/h. They lie in wait, submerged beneath the water, waiting for the unsuspecting prey to approach the water's edge, before launching a speedy, surprise attack.

Locking their powerful jaws on to the prey they drag it underwater. They then spin the body round to disorientate and drown the prey. This is known as the crocodile death

roll. Nile crocodiles are unable to chew, so by spinning the body in the water they are able to tear off chunks of flesh, which they swallow whole. The Nile crocodile has two aortas. The additional aorta saturates the blood in carbon dioxide - a vital ingredient for the production of stomach acid, which is necessary for the digestion of the massive prey they hunt.

Nile crocodiles are nocturnal, but can be observed basking in the sun during the day.

Diet

Nile crocodile are carnivorous, capable of eating half of their body weight. The majority (70%) of their diet is made up from large fish. They will eat any animals, including humans, that come their way - warthogs, antelopes, zebras, Cape buffalo, wildebeest, hippos, porcupines, large cats, reptiles and carrion. If the crocodile's body temperature falls below 24°C it loses its appetite and ability to digest food.

Nile crocodiles swallow small stones to aid digestion and can survive long periods without eating.

Juveniles feed on insects, frogs and small reptiles.

Reproduction

Nile crocodiles are polygamous, mating in the dry season with the young hatching in the wet season.

Mating takes place in water and is a noisy affair; the male (bull) attracts the female's attention by bellowing, expelling water out of both nostrils and slapping the surface of the water with its snout.

The female lays between 25-100 eggs in November and December, in a nest that is 50cm deep, and several metres away from the water's edge. The eggs are left to incubate for 80-90 days. During this time, the male and female closely guard the nest, as they are frequently raided by hyenas, water mongoose, baboons, monkeys, monitor lizards and humans. When the hatchlings are ready to hatch, they call to their parents from inside the egg. A horn or egg tooth that is present on the tip of the snout helps to break the egg shell. Both parents assist the hatchling by gently cracking the egg shell open with their mouths. The female carries the hatchlings in her jaws to the water's edge.

If threatened, the female will protect the young by placing them inside her mouth or on her back. The young crocodiles live in a family group until they are two years old. Monitor lizards, turtles, catfish, baboons, honey badgers, white tailed mongoose, marabou storks, herons, and ibises are the main threat to the survival of the young crocodile.

Females reach sexual maturity when they are 2.5m long and are usually ten years old. Males are sexually mature when they are 3-3.1m long and are also usually ten years old.

Communication
Nile crocodiles are the most vocal of all the reptiles. They use a variety of vocalisations to communicate when distressed, when mating, when patrolling its territory and when threatened. Visual signals, bodily postures, touch and scents are also used to communicate with each other.

Predators/Threats
Nile crocodiles do not have any natural predators. They are hunted for their valuable hide and meat. They are in competition with local fishermen for food, and regularly get tangled up in their fishing nets from which they cannot escape, and death follows quickly from drowning.

Loss of habitat and the effects of climate change are a threat to the Nile crocodile's survival.

The Nile crocodile is classified as a *species of least concern* (2017).

Trivia
♦It is believed that crocodiles evolved from dinosaurs, and have inhabited the earth for over 240 million years.

♦Crocodiles do not shed their skin like other reptiles; instead they grow with it.

♦The crocodile is Africa's largest predator and is top of the food chain.

♦The crocodile has the most powerful bite in the animal kingdom.

♦The crocodile is able to close its nostrils underwater.

♦The temperature in the nest determines the sex of the crocodile. Temperatures below 31.7°C or above 34.5°C produce females. Males are born in the narrow temperature range between 31.7°C and 34.5°C. Usually the eggs at the top of the nest are female and those lower down are male.

♦Crocodiles can remain underwater for 30 minutes when threatened. The diaphragm, which is attached to the ribs and the pubic bone (part of the hip bone), pulls the liver backwards and allows the pleural cavity to expand to increase the volume of air entering the lungs. The ability to increase or decrease its centre of buoyancy allows the crocodile to adjust its position in the water without making a ripple or splash.

♦Crocodiles do not have sweat glands. Keeping their mouths open while sleeping or basking on river banks helps to reduce their temperature.

♦Locals perceive crocodiles as being very dangerous, hostile creatures.

♦Crocodiles are immune to anthrax.

Snakes
Swahili: *Nyoka*

Snakes are found in every continent in the world apart from Antarctica, inhabiting a variety of environments that range from equatorial rain forests, tropical jungles and temperate forests to savannahs, grasslands deserts, swamps, seas and oceans.

Snakes are legless reptiles with long, narrow bodies. Depending on species, body length ranges from 13cm to 11m and weight from 1g to 226kg. The musculoskeletal system of snakes is made up of a skull and 130-500 vertebrae, with attached ribs. Flexible, elastic ligaments allow movement between the small bones of the skull, as well as allowing the upper and lower jaws to open as wide as 150°, enabling the snake to swallow large prey.

Their eyesight is poor, but they are sensitive to movement. A protective transparent cap (*brille*), covers the lidless eyes and restricts movement.

External ears are absent. A small bone in the ear (*columella*), detects vibration and the body is also sensitive to vibration.

Some snakes have specialised heat sensing organs present in the upper and lower jaws to detect warm-blooded prey. This is especially useful during the hours of darkness.

The snake's flickering, forked tongue is used to sniff the air and to collect airborne particles to pass on to sensory tissue in the Jacobson's organ. The Jacobson's organ is found in all vertebrates, it is located in the roof of the mouth and is well developed in reptiles, especially snakes. It tells the snake all it needs to know about its prospective prey or the presence of predators, as well as informing the male of the reproductive status of nearby females.

Despite its shiny, slimy appearance the skin of a snake is actually very dry. Numerous small, thin scales are present on the back and sides and help to protect it from abrasions and dehydration. The scales (*scutes*) on the underside are fewer in number and thicker, and they protect and support the tissues that are in direct contact with ground. Snakes frequently shed their skin as they outgrow it, and those that grow rapidly shed their skins more frequently. Before a snake sheds its skin it will go into hiding, this is due to the skin over the eyes becoming opaque and blurring its vision, so it is particularly vulnerable to predators at this time.

The young shed their skin at least 50-60 times during their first year of life. The snake's scales, colour and unique patterns provide excellent camouflage from predators and prey alike.

Powerful muscles on the underside grip the ground surface to help propel the snake forwards. Snakes cannot move backwards.

Snakes are cold-blooded vertebrates and are most active at temperatures between 25-32°C. The high temperature in the tropics causes them to grow more rapidly than in cooler parts of the world. It is worth bearing in mind that the higher the temperature, the greater the risk of a chance meeting, and it is common to find snakes on roads and paths, especially at night, where the temperature is higher than in the surrounding bush.

Snakes are carnivorous. Depending on species they eat worms, small and large invertebrates, small mammals, birds, eggs, fish, reptiles and amphibians. They either kill their prey by constriction or by a venomous bite. When constricting prey, the snake coils itself round the victim and each time the victim breathes out the snake tightens its grip until the victim dies of asphyxiation or cardiac arrest.

Non-poisonous snakes, which are usually the constrictors, have two rows of teeth in the upper jaw and one row of teeth in the lower jaw. The teeth break easily but are quickly replaced. The teeth, which are short, sharp, and curved backwards towards the throat, prevent live prey from escaping. Snakes do not chew their food, they swallow their prey whole, regardless of whether it is dead or alive. Digestion of prey is assisted by powerful digestive enzymes. If disturbed or threatened shortly after eating, a snake will regurgitate its food so that it can escape.

Venomous snakes have one row of teeth in the upper jaw and have a pair of grooved-out fangs that the venom flows down, or hollowed-out fangs that the venom flows through. Hollowed-out fangs can either be fixed or folded. Folded fangs are located at the front of the mouth, they fold back into the mouth when closed, but open up when the mouth is open. Fangs inject venom into the prey from glands located at the back of the upper jaw or on top of the head. Fangs fall out several times a year and are then replaced. During the digestive process, the snake is relatively inactive. Plant matter, hair and claws are indigestible and are excreted. Snakes have a low metabolic rate so they do not need to continually eat large amounts of food.

Snakes live alone and only meet up to mate. This may be quite a tortuous process for the male, sometimes lasting many days before he succeeds. Depending on species the female either:

♦Lays soft-shelled eggs that hatch after a period of incubation (oviparous).

♦Gives birth to young that have developed in an egg inside the mother's body, which break free within minutes of being born (ovoviviparous).

♦Gives birth to live young (viviparous) that are independent from the moment they are born and are as deadly as their parents.

Snakes reach sexual maturity between nine months and up to three years old.

Snakes only bite when cornered, threatened, startled or provoked and such attacks are used as a means of defence or self preservation. Venomous snakes have the ability to decide whether or not to inject venom into the aggressor. They do not want to waste precious venom on unsuitable prey as it takes four days to three weeks to replenish. On such occasions they deliver a dry bite.

Snake venom is a deadly, toxic cocktail consisting of proteins, toxins and enzymes and it acts in one of four ways to subdue, immobilise and eventually kill its prey. It is either: haemotoxic, cytotoxic, neurotoxic or cardiotoxic. In some species it can be a combination.

Effects of Snake Venom on Humans
Haemotoxic Venom (Heart and Cardiovascular System)

The effects of haemotoxic venom are immediately evident. There is severe pain, marked swelling and discolouration of the soft tissues at the site of the bite. Haemotoxic venom affects the ability of the blood to clot, resulting in loss of blood from the body's external orifices, and eventual death from severe internal haemorrhaging and major organ failure.

A haemotoxic bite is the most painful of all snake bites.

Cytotoxic Venom (Localised effect)

Cytotoxic toxic venom initially results in localised tissue damage. The body responds to the presence of venom in the soft tissues by sending plasma to the site of the bite in an attempt to dilute it. There is marked swelling and a reduction or loss of circulation to the body part, which may precipitate gangrene. If this bite is not treated promptly it can result in amputation and eventual death.

A cytotoxic bite is extremely painful.

Neurotoxic Venom (Central Nervous System)

Neurotoxic venom is extremely fast acting and affects the central nervous system. The transmission of nerve impulses to muscles involved in swallowing, respiration, speech and sight are affected, and this results in paralysis. If untreated, death is inevitable and will occur between 20 minutes and 4 hours after the bite. The victim dies of cardiac or respiratory arrest.

A neurotoxic bite is not particularly painful. Symptoms are not always obvious and may appear some time later.

Cardiotoxic Venom

Cardiotoxic venom directly affects the heart and to leads to circulatory failure and shock.

Trivia

♦Snakes are unable to chew food because of the curvature of their teeth.

♦The hedgehog, mongoose, secretary bird and honey badger are immune to an ordinary, average dose of snake venom.

♦It is impossible to distinguish male and female snakes from each other as their markings and coloration are identical. They all look the same!

♦A snake that has hatched from an egg is known as a hatchling. A newly born snake is known as a neonate or snakelet.

♦Snakes continue to grow until they die.

♦Children are usually bitten by snakes when playing in the bush.

♦Adult humans are often bitten by snakes when they are working in the fields or when they have entered their homes during the night. In the rainy season (April to June), when the weather is cooler, puff adders and cobras are forced out of their burrows and will enter houses in search of warmth and food. Traditional dwellings such as mud huts provide easy access.

♦The majority of snake bites are to the lower leg, so when walking in the bush it is advisable to wear long trousers and leather boots that go above the ankle, this makes it more difficult for a snake bite to actually penetrate the skin. Snakes rely on detecting movement, so if they are encountered in the bush it is best to stand still and wait for them to move on. The boomslang and twig snake are able to see and recognise stationary objects as prey.

♦Snake venom has been used medicinally for thousands of years by the ancient Egyptians, and as an aphrodisiac by the Chinese. Modern medicine is currently researching the possible benefits of snake venom in the treatment of cancer and high blood pressure.

♦The major threat to the snake's survival is loss of habitat. They are hunted by humans for their skin and meat.

African Rock Python
(*Python sebae*)
Swahili: *Chatu*

Identification
The African rock python is the largest snake in Africa and the third largest snake in the world. It is potentially a very dangerous snake to encounter - its strength, and the speed at which it can strike should never be under estimated.

The background colour of the skin is light brown/tan to grey brown, on which there are numerous irregular, light brown to olive green transverse blotches outlined in black. The underside is a creamy white colour. There are two dark bands on the tip of the tail.

The African rock python has a triangular head. A tan, V-shaped band extends from the snout to just above each eye.

The absence of a breast bone, combined with flexible ligaments that allow the upper and lower jaw to open wide, enables it to swallow large prey. The African rock python is non venomous and does not possess fangs. Its teeth are short, sharp and curved backwards towards the throat, preventing prey, if still alive, from escaping.

Length:	Males	7-8m
	Females	4-6m
Weight:		45-90kg

Habitat
African rock pythons are found in savannahs, woodlands, forests and grasslands at altitudes of up to 2,300m. They live alone in rocky outcrops, deserted termite mounds and underground animal burrows. Dependent on water, they are found in close proximity to lakes, rivers, streams and swamps. They are terrestrial but can climb trees if required.

Juveniles live in drier areas, but as they mature they move towards water.

Behaviour
African rock pythons are solitary, bad-tempered, vicious and unpredictable. Easily provoked, when threatened or harassed they are capable of delivering a swift, painful bite before constricting their victim.

They are opportunistic predators which hunt alone at twilight. Heat-sensing organs present in the upper and lower jaws, and sensory tissue in the Jacobson's organ enable them to detect warm-blooded prey, and compensate for their poor eyesight. Stalking their victim patiently, they strike with astonishing speed. Wrapping their coils round the victim, they tighten their grip with each exhalation, until the victim dies of asphyxiation or cardiac arrest. They swallow their prey head first and whole. Strong acids in the stomach digest the prey. While digesting their food they are vulnerable to predators, such as hyenas and wild dogs. After eating a large animal they do not need to eat for a long period of time - in some instances this may be as long as a year.

African rock pythons are dependent on water in which to cool down and are fast swimmers. They are able to remain submerged for long periods when hunting prey in water.

They are nocturnal, occasionally basking in the mid day sun. They estivate (hibernate) during the dry season when temperatures are high, taking refuge in deserted, underground animal burrows. They eat well before they estivate, usually selecting medium-sized mammals such as antelopes.

Juveniles are active at dawn and dusk.

Diet
African rock pythons are carnivorous and feed on small to medium sized mammals (hyrax, hares, antelopes, monkeys, goats, gazelles), fish, lizards, birds, livestock and, very rarely, humans.

Juveniles feed on small mammals such as rats.

Reproduction
African rock pythons are only seen together during the mating season between November and March, during which time they do not eat. They are oviparous (lay eggs). Three months after mating the female lays between 20-100 eggs in a tree hollow, deserted termite mound or underground animal burrow. Coiling herself around the eggs, keeping them warm and safe from predators (monitor lizards, mongoose), she only leaves them for a short period of time to drink water. Throughout this period the female continues to fast until the eggs hatch. The incubation period is between 60-80 days.

The young (hatchlings) are independent at birth, have identical markings to the adults, but are more striking and vibrantly coloured. The female remains with the young for another two weeks, or until they have shed their first skin.

Females reach sexual maturity between three and five years old and mate when they are 2.7m long.

Males reach sexual maturity between three and five years old and mate when they are 2.1m long.

Predators/Threats
Adults do not have any natural predators. They are hunted for their skin, meat and fat. Small African rock pythons are hunted by monitor lizards, crocodiles, birds of prey, badgers, mongooses, cats and pigs.

Trivia
♦African rock pythons continue to grow all of their lives. The more they eat, the faster they grow and the bigger they get.

♦Although terrestrial, they can be found resting in acacia trees in swampy areas such as in Tarangire National Park.

♦They are good at pest control, as they keep the number of rodents down.

♦They have been known to constrict and consume humans, although this is extremely rare.

Black Mamba

(Dendroaspis polylepis)
Swahili: *Koboko mweusi*

Identification

The black mamba is the largest and deadliest venomous snake in the African continent. It is the fastest moving land snake, capable of speeds of 20km/h.

The black mamba is a large, streamlined snake. Its skin is dark, and is either grey, olive green or brown coloured. The underside is lighter, and is either creamy, or a pale olive green colour. The colour of the skin darkens with age.

The black mamba's face is paler than the body and the eyes are either green, brown or black. The inside of the mouth is black. It has two long, hollow, fixed, venomous fangs.

Length: 2.4-3m

Habitat

Black mambas are usually found in savannahs, grasslands, open woodlands and semi-arid deserts below 1,500m. They live in rocky outcrops, tree hollows, deserted termite mounds and underground animal burrows. Black mambas are terrestrial but can climb trees if necessary.

Behaviour

Dangerous, easily angered and aggressive when threatened, black mambas are highly unpredictable under these circumstances. Normally they will avoid confrontation and will quietly slither away. However when cornered they will hiss repeatedly as a warning, expand a narrow cobra-like hood near their neck, flick their tongue and raise their body by up to one third from the ground. Movement causes the mamba to strike, which is why potential human victims are usually advised to keep perfectly still. Black mambas strike and deliver their deadly poison with incredible precision, and are capable of up to 12 multiple strikes. The venom is neuro- and cardio-toxic.

Bold, aggressive hunters, black mambas identify, and then patiently and silently stalks their prey. When the opportunity arises, they will strike their prey once or twice, and then allow it to wander off to die. Death is usually swift, after which the prey is swallowed whole.

Black mambas live in a permanent lair. Creatures of habit, if left undisturbed they will occupy the same lair for many years. They also have regular, daily basking spots.

Black mambas are diurnal.

Diet
Black mambas are carnivorous and feed on small mammals (voles, rats, mice, hyraxes, squirrels and bush babies), reptiles and the occasional bird.

Reproduction
Black mambas mate once a year in the spring and lay their eggs in the summer.

Males locate the female by following her scent trail, and after inspecting her entire body with his flickering tongue, their bodies intertwine and they begin the long, drawn out mating process. They part company shortly afterwards and return to their lairs.

Black mambas are oviparous. The female waits up to 60 days before laying 10-25 eggs in a warm, damp burrow after which she abandons them. The young use an egg tooth to break the shell open between two to three months after incubation. They are independent from the moment they are born and are as deadly as their parents. Growth is rapid.

Black mambas reach sexual maturity when they are 0.9-1.2m long.

Predators/Threats
Adult black mambas have few predators. Their deadly venom makes them a formidable proposition for any potential predator. They may be killed by the secretary bird or birds of prey, and out of fear, by humans. The main threat to their survival is loss of habitat. The eggs and the young are subject to predation by birds of prey, mongooses, crocodiles, monitor lizards, foxes and jackals.

Trivia
♦The black mamba is the second largest venomous snake in the world after the King Cobra.

♦Local people call the black mamba the "seven step snake", as that is as far as you will be able to walk after you have been bitten before feeling the effects of the deadly venom.

♦A bite from the black mamba is known as the kiss of death. Before the development of anti-venom, a bite from a black mamba was 100% fatal, with the victim dying within 20 minutes to 4 hours later. Other snakes' venom can take several days to take effect and kill the victim.

♦The venom of the black mamba is yellow in colour.

♦The faeces of the black mamba smells of curry powder.

♦Black mambas are often considered to be good pest controllers as they help to keep the number of rodents down.

Boomslang
(Dispholidus typus)
Swahili: *Kijoka mti/Kimkufu*

Identification
The boomslang is a highly venomous, agile and fast-moving snake, and is long and slender. Females are usually a brown-olive colour. Males are more brightly coloured than females and are usually black, brown or green. Juveniles are darker with a distinct, lighter underside.

Its most distinguishing features are the disproportionately large eyes with rounded pupils, pointed snout and relatively small, egg-shaped head.

It has large, grooved fangs located at the back of the mouth, and is able to open its jaws to 170° allowing it to bite large objects such as a human leg or arm. The boomslang has good eyesight.

Length: 1-1.5m

Habitat
Boomslangs are usually found in savannahs, grasslands and woodlands. They are arboreal and live in trees, bushes and shrubs, occasionally hunting prey at ground level.

Behaviour
Boomslangs are good-natured, placid and timid. They are well camouflaged and rarely seen. If startled, threatened or provoked they will inflate their neck to double its size and will strike instantly. Boomslangs are diurnal.

Diet
Boomslangs are carnivorous and feed on small mammals, chameleons, lizards, frogs, birds and birds' eggs.

Reproduction
Boomslangs are oviparous. The female lays between 8-25 eggs in the late spring to mid-summer, either in a tree hollow or on a mound of leaves. The incubation period is between 70-100 days. The hatchlings are initially a greyish colour with blue specks, taking on adult colouration several years later.

Predators/Threats
Loss of habitat.

Trivia
♦The wide variations in the skin colour make it very difficult to identify the boomslang. This would be critical if you were bitten by a snake out in the bush. The boomslang's venomous bite is difficult to treat as it requires a specific anti-venom to be effective.
  ♦Boomslangs mate in the trees.
  ♦Boomslangs have the widest variation of skin colour of all the African snakes.

♦Boomslangs hibernate for short periods in cool weather.

♦The venom of the boomslang is highly potent, slow acting and haemotoxic.

♦A bite from a boomslang is extremely rare, but must be taken seriously. Medical treatment should commence immediately, even though the individual feels well. Symptoms may take 24-48 hours to manifest, by which time it will be too late.

♦The venom of the boomslang is more toxic than the venom of the black mamba, but because it is delivered in a reduced quantity it takes longer to take effect on its victim.

Puff Adder
(Bitis arietans)
Swahili: *Kifutu*

Identification
Common and widely distributed, this dangerous and highly venomous snake is responsible for 60% of all fatalities in the African continent.

The puff adder is a large viper with a thickened body and shortened tail. The background colour of the puff adder's skin is yellow-orange to brown-grey. Black chevrons with pale outer edges run the full length of the back. The underside is a pale yellow-white colour, on which blotches may be present.

The puff adder has a large, broad, flat, triangular-shaped head with a blunt rounded snout and two large nostrils that point in an upwards direction. A dark V-shaped band extends from the snout to above each eye, and its pupils are vertical.

The teeth of the puff adder are extremely sharp, and two long, hollow, erectile fangs are situated at the front of the mouth.

Males are larger than females and have longer tails.

Length:	1m
Fang Length:	2cm
Weight:	4-6kg

Habitat
Puff adders are usually found in savannahs, grasslands and open woodlands, they have a particular liking for rocky outcrops. They are terrestrial, but can climb trees and swim if required.

Behaviour
Bad-tempered, lazy, slow-moving and well camouflaged, puff adders make no attempt to move out of the way when they can sense the vibrations from your footsteps as you travel towards them. Basking in the sun they are usually found on or close to footpaths and roads, and will not hesitate to strike if startled, provoked or accidently trodden on. When threatened they may attempt to retreat backwards towards cover, but usually they inflate their body with air, do a lot of hissing and puffing as a warning, and then strike. If required they can strike a second time. The long fangs enable puff adders to deliver their lethal, cytotoxic venom deep into the soft tissues. The bite is extremely painful and produces extensive swelling and discolouration of the soft tissues within 10-30 minutes.

Puff adders use "wait and see" tactics to ambush their unsuspecting prey, which are usually rodents. After striking, they let go of their victim, and allow it to wander off to die before moving in to swallow it whole.

Puff adders are diurnal and nocturnal.

Diet
Puff adders are carnivorous and feed on small mammals (rats, mice and voles), amphibians, lizards, small snakes and birds.

Reproduction
Puff adders are viviparous. The gestation period is between 210-270 days with the female giving birth to 20-60 snakelets in the late summer. The young are as deadly as their parents, capable of delivering a venomous bite.

Predators/Threats
Puff adders have few predators. They may be killed by birds of prey, other snakes, badgers, warthogs and out of fear by humans. Loss of habitat, especially in coastal areas is a threat to their survival.

Trivia
♦The puff adder may act dead, but will strike back when it gets the opportunity. Its nervous system remains active for some time after death, during which time it is still able to bite.

♦The fangs of the puff adder are able to penetrate soft leather.

♦Puff adders are frequently found on roads and footpaths as these areas are warmer than the surrounding bush. Animals are also attracted to the footpaths, as they like to bask, walk, run and wallow about in open spaces.

♦Leaving traces of their fur, feathers and scent, these animals attract puff adders to the vicinity, with potentially deadly consequences.

♦Before the puff adder sheds its skin, there is a reduction in skin colour; after it has shed its skin, its original colour and vibrancy returns.

Other wildlife that you may come across

African Wild Dog
(*Lycaonpictus*)
Swahili:*Simbambangu*

Identification
The African wild dog is a medium sized canine and is a species of wild dog.

The brightly coloured, mottled coat is short and sparse. The colours of the coat are brown, black, orange, yellow and white. The African wild dog loses its fur as it ages.

The head is broad, with a short black muzzle. Brown patches are present on the cheeks and forehead. The ears are large and rounded.

The body is lean and the legs are long and slender. Unlike other canids the African wild dog only has four toes present on each foot.

This adaptation increases the length of its stride and the speed at which it can run when pursuing prey. Rapid muscle recovery makes the African wild dog an endurance hunter.

The tail is long with a large plume of white fur on the tip.

Males are larger than the females.

The African wild dog has excellent sight and hearing, and a keen sense of smell.

Head & Body Length: 70cm-1.2m
Shoulder Height 60-75cm
Tail Length: 31-41cm
Weight: 16-23kg

Life Span
Eleven years in the wild.

Habitat
African wild dogs are usually found in savannahs, deserts, grasslands, forests, woods, bushes and swamp like flood plains. They are extremely rare in Tanzania, but can be found in Ruaha National Park and Selous Game Reserve. Images in this section were taken in Chobe National Park, Botswana.

Behaviour
African wild dogs are highly sociable and live in a tightly knit pack of up to 40 individuals. They rarely fight with each other. Males outnumber the females in every pack. They are nomadic and only settle in an area when they are denning and rearing pups. There is a strict hierarchy that has a dominant alpha mating pair in charge.

African wild dogs are highly intelligent, formidable endurance predators. They are Africa's most successful predator with an 80% success rate. This is due to the fact that they are a highly organised, efficient team when it comes to hunting. They identify the intended prey and work towards separating it from the main herd. They spread out and cut off any escape routes. Running at speeds of 66 km/h they chase the prey to the point of exhaustion. Along the way they will bite the legs, belly and rump at every opportunity to slow the prey down until it finally succumbs. The teeth of African wild dogs are adapted to enable them to swiftly tear meat from the bone, and their powerful bite crushes and breaks bones. They eat the meat and organs but leave the skeleton and skin behind for the scavengers. They rarely fight over food - the old, sick and young are always fed before the rest of the pack.

African wild dogs are diurnal.

Diet

African wild dogs are carnivorous and hunt and feed on medium sized mammals (gazelles, greater kudu, impalas, warthogs, wildebeest and zebras), rodents, lizards, birds and insects. They have a large stomach and long intestines which allows them to absorb sufficient moisture from food so that they can survive long periods without water. They are well adapted to living in the desert and semi arid environments.

Communication

African wild dogs are very vocal, and chatter nonstop to each other using a variety of vocalisations to communicate. A short bark is used as an alarm, howling is used to rally the dogs together and a deep throated growl is used when they are angry. Sneezing is used to vote on hunting decisions. They also communicate by touching and licking each other and wagging their tails. Elaborate greeting ceremonies involve lots of leaping about, grunting and tail wagging. Subordinates expose their bellies and throats to the dominant male.

Reproduction

There is no particular breeding season, but the majority of births take place between April and June. Only the dominant alpha pair in the pack breed, and they are monogamous. If the beta pair manage to breed and produce pups, the pups will be killed shortly after birth by the alpha pair.

The gestation period is up to 72 days. The female gives birth to between six and sixteen pups in a den, (usually a disused aardvark den). She remains with them for the first few weeks of their life. Other members of the pack are not allowed near the pups until they are three to four weeks old, which is when they leave the den. They are weaned by the time they are five weeks old and are fed on regurgitated meat by all members of the pack. The pups are the centre of attention in the pack and take priority. When the pups are eight to ten weeks old they are able to follow the adults when they are hunting, and it is at this point that the den is abandoned. The pups are the first to eat at a kill. Older members of the pack wait patiently for them to finish before they can start to eat. This arrangement ceases when the pups are 12 months old.

African wild dogs become sexually mature between 12 to 18 months old, and when the female reaches sexual maturity she will leave the pack and go in search of a male.

Predators/Threats

African wild dogs are one of the world's most endangered animals. There were only 6,600 alive in the wild in 2016. They are natural prey for lions and hyenas and are considered to be vermin by humans who shoot them, poison them, or use snares to trap and kill them. The main cause of their demise however is their intense social behaviour, which facilitates the rapid transmission of infectious diseases through the entire pack, (rabies, canine distemper and parvovirus). Loss of habitat and the effects of climate change are an increasing threat to the African wild dog's survival.

The African wild dog is classified as an *endangered species*, (2019).

Trivia

♦The African wild dog is also known as the African painted dog, African hunting dog, cape hunting dog and painted wolf.

♦The African wild dog has a great mistrust of humans and cannot successfully be tamed.

Banded Mongoose
(*Mungos mungo*))
Swahili:*Nguchiro milia*

Indentification

Despite its weasel like appearance the banded mongoose is closely related to the civet cat.

It has a small triangular shaped head, with small flat broad ears. The snout is darker.

The shaggy fur is a greyish brown colour. A series of dark banded stripes traverse the upper body from the mid back to the base of the tail. The underside is lighter.

The long tapered tail has a black-dark brown tip.

The banded mongoose has short muscular limbs with dark feet. Five long curved claws are present on the front feet and are used for digging. The four claws on the hind feet are shorter and not as curved as the front claws.

The banded mongoose has excellent eyesight, hearing and sense of smell.

Head & Body Length: 30-45cm
Tail Length: 15-30cm
Weight: 1.5-2.25kg

Lifespan
Ten years in the wild. Seventeen years in captivity.

Habitat
Banded mongooses are found in a variety of locations ranging from savannahs, grasslands, thorny bush lands and rocky outcrops to open forests.

Behaviour
Banded mongooses are highly sociable and live in a mixed sexed pack (colonies, mobs) of up to 40 individuals. Aggression within the pack is low and usually occurs when females are in oestrus. Females live in hierarchies based on age. If the pack gets too large, older members of the pack may force some of the females out. The rejected female may form a new pack with subordinate males.

Encounters with neighbouring packs can be highly charged and aggressive as each perceives each other as competitors for food, resources and females. Ensuing fights may result in injuries and fatalities on both sides.

Banded mongooses live, travel and fight together, they are nomads. They never stay in one particular den for more than a few days or weeks. They frequently return to their favourite sites. They like to live in natural rocky crevices, thickets, gullies, old abandoned burrows or warrens and termite mounds. They like dens that have multiple entrances and passages. There is usually a central sleeping chamber with several adjacent smaller chambers. They can if required dig their own burrow. If they are unable to find shelter they will form a tight knit group and sleep with their heads touching and pointing outwards.

Banded mongooses are terrestrial, and foraging for food is a group activity. This takes place early morning and late afternoon, with a prolonged rest at midday when it is particularly hot. They may travel up to eight km. a day searching for food. Foraging with their nose to the ground, they are possessive of any food they find. They are individual foragers and do not share food. Occasionally there are disputes over food.

Banded mongooses are diurnal.

Communication

Banded mongooses are noisy, they chatter incessantly to each other, grunting or squeaking every few seconds. They use their anal and cheek glands to scent mark their territory as well as greeting each other when they have been separated or feel threatened.

Diet

Banded mongooses are omnivores and have a varied diet feeding on ants, beetles, caterpillars, centipedes, earwigs, grasshoppers, millipedes, slugs, snails, earthworms, termites, eggs, frogs, lizards, scorpions, snakes, birds, small rodents and fallen fruit. Placing hard food objects between their hind legs and throwing the object either vertically or backwards enables them to break open objects such eggs. They like to live in close proximity to water.

Reproduction

Banded mongooses are polygamous. The dominant male mates, and aggressively defends receptive females. Spending two to three days guarding each female they will challenge any male that approaches the female. Females are polyandrous and will attempt to escape from the dominant male, and mate with subordinate males within the pack as well as males from rival groups. All females are able to breed and usually give birth simultaneously within a few days of each other.

The male initiates the courtship by chasing the female with his tail held high. He then circles around her and covers her with secretions from his anal glands. The female lies on her back and wrestles with the male.

The gestation period is between 60-70 days. The female gives birth to two to six pups. Older females give birth to larger litters. Newborn pups are blind and open their eyes after 10 days. The pup remains within the confines of the den for the first four weeks of its life, and is looked after by a non breeding male or a breeding female whilst the rest of the pack goes foraging. At five weeks old the pup will start accompanying the adults on foraging trips. Each pup is looked after by a single adult, who helps the pup to find food and protects it from danger. The pups are independent at three months old.

Females reaches sexual maturity between nine to ten months old.

Predators/Threats

Banded mongooses are not an endangered species as they adapt easily to their environment. They are natural prey for African wild dog, black backed jackals, hyenas, leopards, marabou storks, snakes and birds of prey. Agricultural developments have a positive effect on banded mongooses as the farmed crops provide additional food. The banded mongoose is classified as a *species of least concern* (2015).

Trivia

♦When a predator approaches a pack of banded mongooses they will bunch together and move as a group, creating the illusion of a single large animal. The individuals in front may even stand on their hind legs and lunge forwards in the direction of the predator.

♦The mongoose was introduced in Hawaii and the Caribbean in the 19th century in an attempt to control rodents and snakes. Instead, it caused the extinction of many bird species.

♦Mongooses are famous for their ability to challenge and kill snakes.

♦Mongooses can become tame pets if they are hand reared.

Bat-Eared Fox
(*Otocyon megalotis*)
Swahili: *Bweha masigio*

Identification
The bat-eared fox is a small African fox, that has a jackal-like appearance.

The body is small and slender with a long, grey-brown bushy coat and a paler underside. The tail is long and bushy with a black upper surface and tip.

It has a small face with a broad forehead, enormous conspicuous ears and a short, pointed muzzle. The teeth, of which there are up to 50, are small and are suited to eating and grinding down insects. The face is black below the eye with white patches around the eyes and muzzle. The backs of the ears are black with lighter fur on the inside. Blood circulating thorough the capillaries in the ears is cooled, preventing the bat-eared fox from overheating.

The short, black, slender legs are equipped with powerful, non-retractable claws for digging. There are five toes on the forefoot and four toes on the hind foot.

The bat-eared fox has excellent hearing.

Head & Body Length:	46-60cm
Shoulder Height:	30-40cm
Tail:	30-35cm
Ears:	13-14cm
Weight:	3-5kg

Habitat
Bat-eared foxes are usually found in savannahs, grassland, lightly wooded areas and semi-deserts.

Behaviour
Bat-eared foxes are very shy and sociable and live in a small family group of up to six individuals. The family consists of the mated pair and their offspring, and they live together in a den, which is usually an abandoned burrow. If the need arises they are capable of digging and making a den of their own underground. The den usually has several entrances and numerous, underground interconnecting tunnels. They occasionally scent mark their territory with urine.

Bat-eared foxes are agile and capable of running fast in a zigzag manner when pursued by predators, before swiftly disappearing underground to the safety of their den.

Bat-eared foxes are primarily nocturnal. Emerging from their dens at dusk they will initially play together and groom each other before going to forage for food. Walking alone, slowly and quietly, with their ears cocked forwards and their noses to the ground, they listen intently for the underground movement of insects, stopping only to dig up prey when it is located. They may be active early morning and late afternoon, and will rest at midday.

Diet
Bat-eared foxes are omnivores, feeding primarily on termites, beetles, scorpions, centipedes, grasshoppers, ants, crickets and locusts, supplementing their diet with

small birds and mammals, lizards, snakes, eggs and fruit. They are able to extract sufficient moisture from the food they eat.

Communication
A sociable animal, the bat-eared fox uses a variety of vocalisations (whistling), facial expressions (particularly the ears), and bodily and tail postures to communicate with other foxes.

Reproduction
Bat-eared foxes are monogamous and breed once a year. It is not unusual for a male (reynard) to live with two females (vixen) in a shared communal den. Both parents share the responsibility of caring, protecting, grooming and playing with the cubs.

The gestation period is between 60-70 days. The female gives birth to a litter of two to six cubs, usually at the start of the rainy season when there is an abundance of insects to feed on. Newborn cubs are a light grey colour and are born blind, with their eyes opening after nine days.

The female only has four nipples to suckle the cubs on. She actively kills some of the young to increase the remaining cubs' chances of survival.

The cubs emerge from the den when they are two to three weeks old and are looked after by the male while the female is out foraging for food - this is because she needs to maximise the amount of milk she produces as the cubs are not fed on regurgitated food. Weaning begins when they are one month old and is complete by the time they are 15 weeks old. The cubs reach adult size by the time they are six months old and may remain with their parents until they are one year old.

Sexual maturity is reached when they are nine months old.

Predators/Threats
Bat-eared foxes are natural prey for African wild dogs, hyenas, cheetahs, lions, leopards, jackals, pythons and birds of prey. They are not a threat to livestock, but this does not stop them from being hunted for their meat and hide or being mistaken for a jackal. The bat eared fox is classified as a *species of least concern* (2014).

Trivia
♦The bat-eared fox derives its name from its large ears that closely resemble those of a bat.

♦Bat-eared foxes eat approximately 1.15 million termites a year.

♦The bat-eared fox has more teeth than any other canine.

♦Bat-eared foxes are found in close proximity to plains game such as zebras and antelopes as they feed on the insects that land and feed on their excrement.

♦Bat-eared foxes usually seek out a new den each year before they mate.

♦Bat-eared foxes closely resemble jackals and are sometimes mistaken and killed by locals as a result.

♦The images in this section were taken in Amboseli National Park, Kenya, and the Namib Desert, Namibia.

Black-Backed Jackal
(Canis mesomelas)
Swahili: *Bweha nyekundu*

Identification

The black-backed jackal has a long, thin, pointed, fox-like face. Its eyes are large and the ears are large, pointed and upright.

It has a slender body, slender legs and large feet.

Its fur is a gingery, reddish-brown colour. A prominent, well-defined silvery grey saddle of fur runs the length of its back from the back of the neck to the base of the tail. The chest is white and the throat and underside are a gingery white colour. Scent glands are present on the face and around the anus and genitals.

The long bushy tail is black.

The black-backed jackal has excellent sight, hearing and a keen sense of smell.

Males are larger and more vibrantly coloured than the females.

Body Length	70-90cm
Shoulder Height:	38-50cm
Weight:	5-10kg
Tail Length:	25-35cm

Life Span
Between 8 and 13 years in the wild.

Habitat
Black-backed jackals are adaptable, independent of water and are able to survive in dry, arid countryside. They are usually found in savannahs, grasslands and woodlands.

Behaviour
Black-backed jackals are semi-solitary, either living on their own, as a bonded pair, or as a member of a small family group. Family groups consist of the mother and father, older offspring and the latest litter of cubs. Wary, cunning and adaptable they will either hunt alone, as a mated pair or in a loosely formed pack of five to eight individuals to bring down larger prey (Thomson's gazelles). They can scavenge in order to survive. They are able to run at speeds of up to 55km/h, and maintain a steady running speed of 12-15km/h for longer periods when foraging for food.

They are very territorial, especially a bonded pair who will defend and scent mark the boundaries of their territory with urine and secretions from their scent glands.

Black-backed jackals are diurnal as well as nocturnal.

Diet
Black-backed jackals are omnivores and feed on small to medium-sized mammals (rats, mice, mongooses, spring hares), fish, reptiles, birds and insects, as well as fruit, berries and grasses. They are also a scavengers feeding on carrion and on refuse when close to human habitation.

Communication
Black-backed jackals are noisy and will use a variety of vocalisations to communicate with each other - screaming, yelling, growling, whining, woofing, howling and yelping. A loud-pitched howl indicates that prey has been located. When separated from each other they will call out to one another.

Reproduction
Black-backed jackals are monogamous, remaining together for life as a bonded pair, reproducing annually during the dry season (July-October). Both parents are actively involved in rearing the young. The gestation period is between 60-65 days, with the female (vixen) giving birth underground to two to six cubs. Newborn cubs are blind and helpless. Their eyes, which are initially blue but gradually darken with time, open by the time they are 10 days old. The cubs are hidden in dense thickets or underground burrows for the first few weeks of their life. To avoid the cubs being discovered by predators the females change dens every two weeks, and during this time the male has sole responsibility for defending the territory and hunting. The young are fed regurgitated food until they are two months old and are weaned by the time they are 10-13 weeks old.

By the time the cubs are three months old the den is redundant and they accompany their parents on hunting trips, being able to hunt successfully on their own by the time they are six months old. Between the ages of eight to ten months old they may leave their parents and establish their own territories. Some of the offspring will remain with their parents until they are 18-24 months old before leaving, and others that have left the family group may return to act as helpers, assisting their parents in rearing the latest litter. This affords the cubs some degree of protection from predators and allows the parents to go foraging for food.

Black-backed jackals are sexually mature at eleven months old.

Predators/Threats
Black backed jackals are natural prey for eagles, hyenas, lions and leopards, and may be killed by humans for their fur and meat and if they are a threat to live stock. The majority of the young are killed in the first 14 weeks of life. Loss of habitat and the effects of climate change are a threat to their survival. The black backed jackal is classified as *species of least concern* (2014).

Trivia
♦The black-backed jackal is also known as the silver-backed jackal or saddle-backed jackal.

♦They have been known to cache food and return 24 hours later to feed on it.

♦They are wary of humans and are not aggressive towards large predators.

♦Black-backed jackals are considered to be vermin by locals as they carry and spread rabies, the canine distemper virus and canine parvovirus.

Caracal

(*Caracal caracal*)
Swahili: *Simba mbangu*

Identification

The caracal is robust, medium-sized wild cat. The short, dense fur coat is a tawny, sandy brown to a brickish, wine red colour. The fur on the underside is whiter. Its uniformly plain coat provides perfect camouflage when it is threatened in an open exposed habitat. It will lie down flat and patiently wait until the threat has moved on.

The caracal has a small face with dramatic facial markings. A black spot lies directly above the large, yellow brown eyes that are surrounded by a rim of white fur. The pupils are circular. A narrow black stripe runs directly from the eyes to the nose. Dark spots are present on either side of the muzzle. The canine teeth are long and sharp. The fur on the chin and throat is white.

The ears are elongated, tapered tufted. The backs and bases of the ears are black, and white fur lines the inside. The ears are mobile and highly flexible.

The legs are long and slender. The hind legs are longer and stronger than the front legs and this enables it to leap up to three metres in the air. The forelegs have five digits and the hind legs have four digits, with each having long, sharp retractable claws. Stiff hairs located between the individual foot pads enable the caracal to walk on soft sand without sinking. The bushy, bobbed tail is relatively short and is used as a rudder in mid air.

The caracal has excellent hearing, very good eyesight and a moderate sense of smell. Females are lighter and smaller than males.

Head & Body Length:	Males	75cm-1.05m
	Females	61cm-1.02m
Shoulder Height:		40-50cm
Tail Length:		18-34cm
Weight:	Males	11-18kg
	Females	8-15kg

Life Span

Twelve years in the wild. Between 16 to 17 years in captivity.

Habitat

Caracals are adaptable and inhabit a variety of habitats ranging from semi deserts, arid scrublands, savannahs, marshy lowlands and evergreen forests to mountain forests. They do not need to drink large quantities of water and are tolerant of dry, arid environments. They can live up to altitudes of 3,000m

Behaviour

Caracals are elusive, solitary and secretive. It is extremely rare to spot a caracal in the wild. Being highly territorial they will remain in one area for their entire lives and will aggressively defend it. Their territory is marked by spraying urine and depositing faeces on rocks and vegetation. Special scent glands that are situated between the toes mark the territory when they sharpen their claws on trees.

Caracals are highly skilled, opportunistic, acrobatic predators that hunt alone at night, and are capable of taking prey down two to three times their own size. Their agility allows them to chase animals that change directions whilst running, otherwise they will stalk their prey to within five metres before pouncing on it. The prey is killed with a bite to the throat or back of the neck. They are capable of running at 80km/h. The kill is consumed immediately with the entrails been discarded. They are unable to digest fur. Larger prey may be cached away up a tree or buried in sand to return to at a later date.

Caracals are primarily nocturnal, spending most of the day sleeping, hidden away in bushy thickets, abandoned burrows or trees. They may be seen at dusk or dawn.

Diet
Caracals are carnivorous, and hunt and kill small mammals (gerbils, spring hares, hyraxes, mice, mongooses, monkeys) rodents, small antelope and their offspring (dik-diks, impala, kudu) birds, reptiles (lizards, snakes) and insects. Consuming the body fluids of their prey allows them to survive long periods without drinking water. Should the opportunity arise they will kill domestic livestock, bringing them into conflict with humans.

Communication
Caracals are silent/quiet animals and interactions are limited to the mating period. They use a variety of vocalisations to communicate their mood - purring, meowing, snarling, growling, hissing and bird like chirrups. Ear movements are also used to communicate.

Reproduction
There is no distinct breeding season. The majority of births take place between October and March. Oestrus lasts up to six days. The female mates with several males but has a strong preference for the biggest strongest male. The successful male may remain with the female during this period to prevent other males from mating with her. Once impregnated the female chases the male away.

The gestation period is up to 81 days. The female gives birth to up to six kittens in dense vegetation or an abandoned burrow, and raises them on her own. The kittens are born with their eyes and ears closed. The eyes begin to open at day one, and are fully open by day ten. It takes up to four weeks for the ears to completely unfurl and for the claws to become retractable. The kittens are darker and greyer than adults, and have reddish spots on their abdomen that fade with time.

The kittens begin to explore their surroundings between three to four weeks old. Shortly afterwards they begin to vocalise, making chirping bird like sounds, and will begin to play and interact with their siblings. Weaning is completed by the time they are 10 weeks old. They will make their first kill at three months old. Permanent teeth appear between four to five months old. Juveniles are independent by ten months old and will leave their mother to find and establish their own territory. Caracals reach sexual maturity between 12 to 16 months old.

Predators/Threats
Caracals are natural prey for lions, hyenas, and leopards, and are hunted by humans for their meat and hide, and when they attack livestock. Loss of habitat due to desertification, deforestation and agriculture, plus the effects of climate change, are also a threat to their survival. The caracal is classified as a *species of least concern* (2014).

Trivia
♦Caracal is a Turkish word "Kara Kulak" and means black ears.

♦The Caracal's tufted ears resemble those of a lynx, and it is often referred to as Persian Lynx or African Lynx. It is not a lynx, and the closest genetically related cats are the Serval and the African golden cat.

♦Caracals are called gazelle cats by North African Nomads.

♦The Ancient Egyptians tamed and used the caracal to hunt.

Genet Cat
Large Spotted Genet Cat (*Genetta tigrina*)
Small Spotted Genet Cat (*Genetta genetta*)
Swahili: *Kanu*

Identification
The two species of genet cat most commonly seen in Tanzania are the large spotted genet cat and the small spotted genet cat, and they are very similar to each other.

Large Spotted Genet Cat
The background colour of the large spotted genet cat's fur is yellow-grey. The spots are larger than the small spotted genet cat and are either black or a rusty brown colour. A prominent stripe runs the length of the back and the tail is ringed with a black tip.

Small Spotted Genet Cat
The background colour of the small spotted genet cat's fur is tan to grey. The spots, which are present in rows, are darker than those of the large genet cat. The tail is ringed with a white tip.

Genet cats have a small, fox-like head with large, forward facing, rounded eyes and large, pointed upright ears. Long whiskers are present on the black, pointed snout. The short, soft fur is varying shades of brown. A combination of spots and a ringed tail provides perfect camouflage.

The body is long with short legs. Five digits are present on each foot and are equipped with sharp retractable claws. The tail is extremely long and may be up to one and half times the length of its body. This acts as an effective counter balance enabling the genet cat to balance on narrow tree branches and jump from one tree to another.

Genet cats have excellent night vision.

Males are larger than females

Life Span
Eight years in the wild.

Habitat
Genet cats are usually found in riverine woodlands, forests, grasslands and semi-arid deserts. They are also seen in game lodges and can become habituated when in close contact with humans.

Behaviour
Silent, agile, highly skilled hunters, genet cats are at home hunting prey on the ground as well as in the trees. Their territory is scent marked with urine, claw marks on tree trunks and with a greasy musk-like substance released by the perianal glands. Females are more territorial than males. When threatened they arch their back and may emit a foul smelling musk-like substance that acts as a deterrent. Their faeces are deposited in clearly marked open latrines.

Genet cats are nocturnal and are particularly active at dusk. They are terrestrial and arboreal.

Diet
Being omnivores, they feed on small mammals, birds, bats, reptiles, eggs, frogs, insects, scorpions and fruit. When living close to human habitation, given the opportunity they wilfully kill poultry feeding only on the breast and head.

Communication
A variety of vocalisations are used to communicate their mood, from purring and meowing to spitting.

Reproduction
Genet cats either live in pairs, or if they are solitary they only meet up to mate. The gestation period is 75-90 days. The female can give birth to two litters a year of two to four kittens in a burrow, usually between August and March, and raises them on her own. The kittens open their eyes and ears after ten days and begin to eat solid food at six weeks. They remain with their mother until they are seven to eight months old and are sexually mature at two years old.

Predators/Threats
Genet cats are natural prey for caracals, serval cats, leopards, owls and pythons. The young are also prey to jackals, civet cats and snakes. They are hunted by locals if they are considered to be a pest.

Trivia
♦Genet cats are able to perform a handstand when releasing a musk-like substance from the specialised perianal glands to scent mark their territory.

♦The musky secretions from the genet cat are used in the pharmaceutical and perfume industries.

♦Ancient Egyptians originally used genet cats to catch rodents, until the introduction of the domestic cat, which did not have the problem of the unpleasant musky secretions.

♦Genet cats can be kept as an exotic pet.

♦The large spotted genet cat is also known as the "blotched genet cat", "rusty spotted genet cat" and "cape genet cat".

♦The small spotted genet cat is known as the "common genet cat".

Honey Badger/Ratel
(*Mellivoracapensis*)
Swahili:*Simbambangu/Nyegere*

Indentification
The honey badger has a skunk like appearance and belongs to the same family as the weasel, stoat and otter.

It has a long, muscular body that is broad across the back. The head is short and flat with a short muzzle, and the nose is highly sensitive. Their eyes are small, as are their ears which are located near the back of the head under a fold of thick skin. The honey badger has difficulty hearing long range sounds and is dependent upon picking up ground vibrations.

The jaws are strong and powerful and are equipped with short, sharp canine teeth. The cheek teeth usually show signs of excessive wear and tear. Short backward pointing papillae are present on the tongue, this enables the honey badger to devour and digest all parts of its prey - skin, hairs, feathers and bones.

The short, thick coarse fur is 40-50mm long and is dark brown to black in colour. A distinctive mantle of grey and white hair extends from the top of the head to the base of the tail. The hair on the sides of the face and lower body is black. The flanks, belly and groin have a thin covering of hair. The skin is loose and is up to six mm thick around the neck.

The honey badger has short, strong legs that are adapted for digging. Five toes are present on each foot and are equipped with long powerful claws. The front paws and claws are stronger and longer than the rear claws as they are required for digging. The rear paws sweep the soil away. The claws can grow up to 40mm. The soles of the feet are thickly padded.

The tail is short and bushy and is covered in long hairs.

The honey badger has poor eyesight and an excellent sense of smell.

Females are smaller than males.

Head & Body Length:		55-77cm
Shoulder Height		23-30cm
Tail Length:		20-30cm
Weight:	Males	8-11kg
	Females	5-7.kg

Life Span
Unknown in the wild. May live for 24 years in captivity.

Habitat
Honey badgers are adaptable and opportunistic, living in a wide variety of environments ranging from sea level up to 4,000m. They are usually found in arid deserts, harsh scrublands, savannahs, grasslands, deciduous forests

and tropical rain forests. Honey badgers are found throughout Africa, Arabia, Iran, Turkmenistan and India.

Behaviour
Honey badgers are elusive, yet are fearless, ferocious, tenacious, solitary and non territorial. When threatened they will attack any predator in self defence, regardless of

size. Their thick, loose skin allows them to twist and turn and attack their assailant. The skin is hard to grip and difficult to penetrate. Secretions from their anal glands that are located under the base of the tail produce a foul smelling liquid that is used to warn and repel predators, and mark their territory.

Honey badgers are extremely active, spending their time trotting around, searching for food throughout the day. They can trot at speeds of 25-30km/h for short periods of time, they are good swimmers and are able to climb trees. During the breeding season when they are looking for a female, males may form a small, loose hierarchical group of two to five individuals. The older males out rank the younger males.

Honey badgers are highly skilled diggers and live either in a self dug out hole, an abandoned aardvark or warthog hole, rock crevices or a termite mound. When resting they curl up into a ball. Honey badgers are diurnal.

Diet

Honey badgers are omnivores. They are fierce, aggressive predators that feed on insects, birds, eggs, rodents, meerkats, gerbils, ground squirrels, porcupines, frogs, lizards, snakes, scorpions, tortoises and turtles. They will also eat roots, bulbs and fruit.

Communication

Honey badgers use smell and a variety of vocalisations to communicate with each other. The mother and cub purr to each other. Aggressive males when confronted will scream, snort, growl and emit a death rattle as a warning. A high pitched squeal is used to communicate with older males.

Reproduction

There is no distinct breeding season. They are not monogamous and do not form long lasting bonded pairs. The males (boar) are polygamous and protective towards the female for three days whilst mating takes place. The male emits a loud grunting sound when mating. The gestation period is between 50 to 70 days. The female (sow), in preparation for the birth, digs an underground burrow which she lines with grass. The burrow has a single passage and is between one to three metres long She gives birth alone to a single cub (kit) which is pink, hairless and born blind. After one week the skin changes colour from pink to grey, and at two weeks fine hairs appear. The white stripe appears at three weeks. The cub communicates with its mother by whining.

The female raises the dependent cub on her own. The cub begins to hunt and dig when it is eight months old, and will be independent between 12 and 16 months.

Predators/Threats

Honey badgers are not a threatened species and have few natural predators. The only predators that attack honey badgers are hyenas, lions, leopards and pythons.

Honey badgers are hunted by poachers for their skin and their claws, which are used in traditional medicine. It is strongly believed that the fearlessness and ferocious characteristics of the honey badger will be conferred upon the recipient. They also come into conflict with the small livestock farmers if they raid their beehives.

Loss of habitat is also a threat to the honey badger's survival.

The honey badger is classified as a *near threatened species* (2008).

Trivia

♦Their name honey badger means Honey Eater of the Cape.

♦When raiding a beehive the honey badger uses its anal glands to fumigate the hive. This causes the bees to leave the hive or to become inactive. Their powerful claws then break up the beehive.

♦The image used in this section was taken in Moremi Game Reserve, Botswana.

Hyrax

Rock Hyrax
(*Procavia capensis*)
Bush Hyrax
(*Heterohyrax brucei*)
Swahili: *Pimbi*

Identification

Hyraxes are small rodent-like mammals found throughout most of Africa.

They have a round head, with small rounded ears, large dark eyes and a black truncated nose. Long whiskers are present on their muzzles. They use their molars in preference to their tusk-like incisors to bite food. The incisors are used primarily in defence.

The body is small, rotund and muscular, with short, stubby legs. The feet have smooth, rubbery pads that are moist due to the presence of sweat glands enabling the hyrax to climb difficult rocky surfaces, but are not suitable for digging or burrowing. Four toes are present on the foreleg and three toes on the hind leg. Small hoof-like nails are present on the tip of each toe, apart from the inner toe of the hind foot, which has a claw used for grooming and scratching.

The fur is short and coarse. The bush hyrax is light grey to brown in colour whereas the rock hyrax is light to dark brown. The underside is creamy white. The presence of long tactile hairs over their bodies enables the hyrax to orientate itself in dark, enclosed places. A distinct circular sweat gland on the back is covered by a patch of long hair that may be a black or yellow colour, and becomes erect when the hyrax is excited.

The tail is little more than a stump and is not visible.

The male hyrax is slightly bigger than the female.

Physiology

Hyraxes have difficulty regulating and maintaining their bodily temperature. They rely on basking in the sun and huddling together to generate warmth, and retreating to their shelter to cool down if they overheat.

Life Span

Between 8-10 years in the wild. Females usually live longer than males.

Habitat

Hyraxes are terrestrial and are usually found in savannahs, mountains or forests, and can survive at altitudes as low as 400m below sea level right up to 3,800m above sea level. They are unable to dig, so live in naturally occurring sheltered crevices in kopjes, cliffs and boulders. They are tolerant of arid conditions.

Behaviour

Hyraxes live in colonies of up to 50 individuals. The colonies are made up of several small, stable family groups. The group consists of:

♦A single, dominant, territorial male who may control more than one group.

♦Three to seven females. Females are not territorial.

♦Subordinate males who fall into one of three sub groups.

♦Peripheral males that are tolerated, but live on the periphery of the dominant male's territory, and who in the absence of the dominant male will attempt to take over the group.

♦Early dispersing males who leave the group when they are 16-24 months old.

♦Late dispersing males who leave the group before they are 30 months old.

Hyraxes are shy, but are particularly vicious when threatened. They are found in close proximity to their shelters, either huddling together to keep warm, basking in the sun or feeding. Feeding is a group activity with members facing outwards, looking out for predators. There is also a male or female on sentry duty who will raise the alarm when threatened.

Hyraxes urinate and defecate in the same spot, and their latrines are easily identified by the white deposits of un-dissolved calcium carbonate from the urine that covers the rocks.

Hyraxes are diurnal.

Diet

Hyraxes are herbivores and are able to feed on vegetation of poor nutritional value. They feed on grasses, vegetables, herbs, bark, stems, buds, leaves and fruit. Their kidneys are efficient and enable them to exist on the minimum amount of water.

Communication

Hyraxes use a wide range of vocalisations to communicate with each other from growling, shrieking, squealing, whistling and raucous alarm calls to twittering.

Reproduction

Hyraxes live in a polygamous harem. During the mating season, solitary males will attempt to mate with any available female. Consequently, dominant males are particularly aggressive towards any other males.

The females give birth to between one to four young during the rainy season after a gestation period of 212-245 days

The young are born fully developed, covered in fur and with their eyes open, and are able to run and jump about within one hour of being born. They begin to eat vegetation when they are two days old and are weaned between one and five months old. The young play together in a nursery group.

Hyraxes are sexually mature by the time they are 16-18 months old. Males leave the maternal group between 16-30 months. Females remain with the maternal group.

Predators/Threats

Hyraxes are natural prey for African wild dogs, caracals, serval cats, civet cats, jackals, leopards, lions, mongooses, snakes (pythons in particular) and large birds. They are hunted by humans for their meat and skin. Loss of habitat and the effects of climate change are a threat to the hyrax's survival. The bush hyrax is classified as a species of least concern (2014). The rock hyrax is also classified as a species of least concern (2014).

Trivia

♦Hyraxes are related to elephants, having similar teeth, leg and foot bones.

♦The hyrax's incisors continue to grow throughout life.

♦The bush hyrax is also known as the yellow spotted hyrax.

♦Hyraxes produce vast quantities of dung and urine that is used in traditional medicine to treat epilepsy and convulsions.

♦The burnt hair of the hyrax is mixed with ash and water to make a drink that treats coughs.

Leopard Tortoise
(Geochelone pardalis)
Swahili: *Kobe*

Identification

Leopard tortoises are the second largest species of tortoise in Africa, and the fourth largest in the world.

The background colour of the hard, lumpy, high-domed shell is pale yellow, and is beautifully marked with an array of black squares that have a brown or yellow inner area with a dark spot in the centre. This central spot reduces in size with age. The markings are unique to each individual and provide the leopard tortoise with perfect camouflage. There is a v-shaped opening at the front of the shell, which allows the head and neck to protrude. When threatened, leopard tortoises retract their head and limbs back into the safety of their shells.

The head and limbs are pale yellow.

The leopard tortoise has a hard beak instead of teeth, and this assists in tearing food apart.

The legs are short and are covered by thickened, protective scales. Five claws are present on the paddle-shaped front legs, and four are present on the hind legs. The female's legs are longer than the males and scales are present on the heels of the rear legs to assist with digging.

The tail is short with two to three horny tubercles present and a horny pin.

The tail of the male is longer and thicker than the female's.

Leopard tortoises have very good eyesight, sense of smell and taste. There are no external ear openings; consequently they have poor hearing.

Males are larger than females.

Length: 45-70cm
Weight: 15-20kg

Habitat

Leopard tortoises are widely distributed throughout sub Saharan Africa and are usually found in semi-arid regions, savannahs and grasslands.

Behaviour

Leopard tortoises are solitary and territorial. They are cold blooded and need to bask in the early morning sun to raise their body temperature. In very hot or cold weather they seek shelter in abandoned animal burrows. They are quite nimble and can move surprisingly quickly over large areas when necessary. They can remain under water for up to ten minutes.

Diet
Leopard tortoises are herbivores with a preference for a high fibre diet. They graze on mixed grasses, wild flowers, beans, thistles, pumpkins, toadstools, watermelons and the pads of the prickly cacti.

Reproduction
Mating is a noisy affair with the male making lots of loud husky calls as well as battering and pushing the female about at the same time. The female digs a hole about 25cm deep in which she lays between 5-30 white eggs at 3 weekly intervals over a period of 20 weeks. The incubation period is between 4-18 months. The hatchlings break the egg shell open with their beaks and then have the arduous task of digging their way to the surface.

Leopard tortoises reach sexual maturity between the ages of 12-15 years old

The leopard tortoise is classified a *species of least concern* (2014).

Trivia
♦The upper shell is called the *carapace*.

♦In folklore leopard tortoises are associated with strength and immortality.

♦Surprisingly, leopard tortoises are plagued with ticks, mites and internal parasites.

♦The black spots on the leopard tortoise's shell resemble the markings on a leopard - hence the name.

♦Leopard tortoises are reputed to eat old bones.

Striped Hyena
(Hyaena hyeana)
Swahili:*Fisi miraba*

Identification
The striped hyena is the smallest of the three species of true hyena, (brown, spotted and striped hyenas).

Its most recognisable feature is a sloping back - this is due to the forelegs being longer and more muscular than the hind legs. There are four short claws on each foot that are non-retractable and blunt.

The long, coarse, shaggy, fur coat is light grey to beige in colour. Five to six distinctive vertical black stripes are present on the flank, and horizontal black stripes are on the legs. Coarse guard hairs are present on the flanks, and are 50-75mm long. A mane extends down the centre of the back, from the nape of the neck to the base of the tail.

A large, black throat patch is present under the long muscular neck.

The skull is small. It has a black pointed muzzle and nose, and large black broad pointed ears that are set back on the head. The dark eyes are small.

The long bushy tail is covered in black and white fur.

Males are slightly larger than females.

The striped hyena has excellent eyesight, hearing and sense of smell.

Body Length:	85cm-1.3m
Shoulder Height:	60-80cm
Tail Length:	25-40cm
Weight:	22-55kg

Life Span
Twelve years in the wild. Twenty-three years in captivity.

Habitat
Striped hyenas are usually found in semi deserts, savannahs, grasslands, woodlands, scrub forests, rocky terrain and mountains up to 3,000m. They are well adapted to living in hostile arid, desert conditions.

Behaviour
Striped hyenas are shy, elusive and extremely difficult to spot in the wild. This is due to the fact that they are nocturnal, they forage alone and disappear silently and very quickly into the surrounding vegetation if disturbed.

They are nomadic, and usually live on their own or in a small family unit called a clan. They live in a den for short periods of time, which is usually situated in a cave, rock fissure, eroded water channels or abandoned aardvark burrow. Bones may be present at the entrance. They scent mark their territory with secretions from their anal pouch.

Striped hyenas can run at speeds up to 8km/h. They are nocturnal.

If confronted by a predator, they will turn their anus inside out and spray a foul smelling fluid in its direction. This is a powerful deterrent and usually sends the predator on its way.

Diet

Striped hyenas are omnivores, and are primarily scavengers foraging for food on their own. Being smaller than spotted hyenas, they are physically incapable of taking down large prey. Feeding on the remains of ungulates left by the top predators, (gazelles, hartebeest, impala, topi, wildebeest and zebras), they are able to digest rotting flesh in various stages of decomposition. The high concentration of hydrochloric acid present in their stomach destroys toxic bacteria before it enters the intestines.

Powerful jaws and teeth allow striped hyenas to strip the carcass of skin and hair ligaments, and to crush bones, horns and hooves. This is later regurgitated in the form of pellets. The faeces is white due to the high calcium content. They may cache bones and flesh in shallow depressions in the ground, returning several days later to feed on the decomposing flesh.

Striped hyenas hunt small animals, (porcupine, rabbits, rodents), chasing them and bringing them down by grabbing the flank, groin or leg. They will also eat birds, lizards, insects and fruit, and will frequent human habitation to feed on refuse.

Striped hyenas can drink salt water as well as fresh water, and can survive long periods without water.

Communication

Striped hyenas are not as sociable as spotted hyenas. They are normally silent, but will vocalise by growling, chattering or laughing if excited or threatened. When threatened the mane becomes erect, making it appear to be 30% larger. They greet each other by sniffing each other's noses, pawing each other's throats and licking the mid back region. They may also extrude the anal pouch. Displaying the anal glands is an indication of submissiveness.

Reproduction

Striped hyenas are monogamous, mating any time during the day and breeding throughout the year. The male establishes a den with the female in which to raise the cubs. Both parents are involved in rearing the cubs. The gestation period is up to 91 days, and the female gives birth to two to four cubs. The cubs are born with the markings of the adults - white to grey coloured coats with the highly distinctive black stripes present. The eyes are closed at birth, and open when they are seven to eight days old. The ears are small and the ear canals are closed at birth. They begin to develop teeth at three weeks and start to eat solid food at four weeks, as well as starting to venture outside the den. Weaning is completed by the time they are two months old. The cub remains with its parents whilst it learns how to forage for food. Once the cub is independent it leaves the family unit to go and make a life of its own. The monogamous relationship breaks up, and the parents go their separate ways.

Striped hyenas reach sexual maturity when they are two to three years old.

Predators/Threats

Striped hyenas are natural prey for lions. The main threat to their survival is loss of habitat and the effects of climate change. They are killed by humans if they become a threat to livestock. They may be accidently poisoned, and are many are victims of road traffic accidents. The reduction in number of the top predators seriously affects the survival of the striped hyena, as they are dependent on the animal remains that are left behind. The striped hyena is classified as a *near threatened species* (2014).

Trivia

♦The striped hyena is easily tamed. Ancient Egyptians used them for hunting. Raised in captivity they can form strong bonds with dogs.

♦The striped hyena is the national animal of the Lebanon.

♦The body parts of the striped hyena are believed to have magical powers, and are used as good luck charms.

Warthog
(*Phacochoerus aethiopicus*)
Swahili: *Ngiki/Ngiri/Gwasi*

Identification
The warthog has a large head with a short, thickened neck. It has a muscular, stocky body, long legs with tiny, hoofed feet and is capable of running at speeds of 55km/h.

The large, flat head is out of proportion with its body (one sixth of the total head and body length). The eyes are small and are set high on the head to compensate for its poor eyesight.

The nostrils are located on the end of a long, rounded, rubbery snout and point downwards. This assists the warthog when rooting for food that is underground.

Two pairs of short, sharp tusks protrude from either side of the snout. The upper tusks are long and curve upwards. The tusks are used in self defence and for rooting and digging up food. They have 32-34 long and sharp canine teeth.

Depending on the sex, two or three pairs of facial warts are present. The male has three pairs of warts, one pair beneath the eyes, (these protect the eyes when the warthog engages in fighting), a pair on the snout near the tusks, and a pair on the lower jaw. The female has two pairs of warts (they are absent on the snout). The warts are formed from thickened growths of cartilage that become more prominent with age.

The ears are large and mobile.

The warthog's wrinkled skin is a brownish black colour. There is a sparse covering of hair over the whole body. A long, coarse mane of dark brown hair extends from the top of the head as far as the middle of the back.

There is a tuft of hair on the tip of the long, thin tail.

The warthog has a good sense of smell and an acute sense of hearing.

Body Length:		90cm-1.5m
Shoulder Height:		63-85cm
Tail Length:		25-50cm
Weight:	Male	60-100kg
	Female	45-70kg
Upper Tusk:	Male	3-60cm
	Female	15-25cm
Lower Tusk:		15cm

Life Span
Fifteen years in the wild.

Habitat
Warthogs are usually found in savannahs, grasslands, and woodlands, in or near waterholes. They can be found up to altitudes of 2,000m.

Behaviour
Warthogs usually live in a small, matriarchal group called a sounder, which consists of one to two females (sows), their young (piglets) and yearlings. The sounder can sometimes contain as many as 40 warthogs. Adult males (boars) only associate with the females during the mating season. Male warthogs are not territorial and either live in a bachelor group or have a solitary existence.

Warthogs spend the daylight hours foraging for food, particularly in the early morning and evening. They feed by resting on their forelegs and use their snouts to uproot food. They like to lie close to each other in the shade and to wallow in mud.

They sleep and shelter in abandoned burrows at night time. The young enter the burrow first, followed by the adults who go in backwards. This enables them to defend the burrow from intruders, as well as making a swift exit if predators appear close by. They are extremely fast and agile, and are difficult for a predator to catch.

Warthogs are diurnal.

Diet

Warthogs are essentially grazers, but are also considered to be omnivorous. They feed primarily on roots, grass, herbs, bark, fruit and berries but will also eat insects, scorpions, earthworms, small mammals, birds, reptiles and carrion. Warthogs eat soil, bones and other animal dung to compensate for any trace minerals and elements that may be absent from their diet.

Communication

Warthogs are usually quiet but can use a range of vocalisations to communicate with each other - grunting, growling snorting and squealing. When alarmed or threatened they will retreat to their underground shelter. They also communicate by scent marking.

Reproduction

Mating takes place in May and June. Males are only found in the presence of females when mating. During the mating season they regularly engage in fights with other males to establish mating rights. The facial warts protect them from serious injury.

The gestation period is up to 175 days. The female withdraws from the sounder to give birth to two to four piglets in a grass lined burrow. This occurs during the dry season in October and November. The piglets emerge from the burrow at two weeks old and are completely weaned at three to four months old. When the female gives birth, any remaining piglets from previous litters are driven away, but they may rejoin the group at a later date. Male warthogs leave their mothers at 15 months old, but females may remain with the sounder for life.

Warthogs reach sexual maturity between 18-24 months old.

Predators/Threats

Warthogs are natural prey for lions, cheetahs, leopards, jackal, crocodiles, African wild dogs and hyenas. Eagles and jackals are the main threat to the young. Warthogs are symptomless carriers of African swine fever, and if there is an outbreak, locals will actively hunt and kill them. The same applies if they raid their crops in search of food. Loss of habitat and the effects of climate change are a threat to the warthog's survival.

Warthogs are classified as a *species of least concern* (2016).

Trivia

♦Warthogs are the only swine to defecate together, 4-14 times a day.

♦Warthogs run with their tails up in the air.

♦The warthog's lack of fur and fat means they are vulnerable to the rays of the sun and low temperatures. Shelter is therefore very important and necessary for them.

Translocation

Translocation is the planned or emergency relocation of an individual or group of wild animals from one area to another, and may be for one of the following reasons:

♦In areas that are densely populated, the animals are in direct competition with each other on a daily basis for food and water.

In these cases it is usual to move the animals to areas that are under populated and have abundant supplies of food. Without human intervention the animals could face hunger, starvation and ultimately death.

♦The plains grazers can adversely affect plant life in one of two ways:

-actual damage to the plant itself, such as removal of bark from trees, uprooting of plants or partial damage which prevents a plant from thriving.

-a continued high concentration of animals feeding on the same vegetation can put some plants at risk of extinction.

♦Out on the open plains, there exists a common and mutual interdependency between the plains grazers. The heavy grazers (elephants, hippos, buffaloes) trample and feed on tall coarse grasses, making way for the intermediate grazers (zebras, wildebeest, hartebeest) who feed on shorter grasses. The remaining short grass and shoots are eaten by the smallest and lightest herbivores (dik dik, warthogs, Thompson's gazelle). This delicately balanced relationship can be disrupted by the absence of the heavy or intermediate grazers. The translocation of animals to an area of dense overgrowth can clear the way for the lighter grazers.

♦Animals in national parks and game reserves can come into conflict with the local population, and this has to be managed sensitively. The parks and reserves need to maintain a good relationship, and maintain the good will of the local community. Elephants in particular, in their search for food and water, can break down boundary fences and escape into the surrounding countryside. They destroy the local inhabitants' property, raid their crops and deprive them of their livelihood. They either have to be translocated or have a radio collar fitted. The collar enables rangers to track their movements, so that they can be moved on if they get too close to human habitation.

♦Translocation returns or reintroduces an animal back to its natural environment.

♦The translocation of animals encourages the development of the tourist "safari industry" in developing, underdeveloped and deprived areas. This provides employment for the local population, and vital funds to sustain and maintain the parks and reserves.

♦Animals may be translocated to increase the number of breeding stock and ensure survival of the species.

♦Animals can be translocated if their survival is being threatened by poachers.

The only other alternative to translocation is to cull the animals.

Translocation of animals is a difficult and dangerous job and requires a coordinated, experienced, highly skilled team of experts. The team is made up of pilots, marksmen, vets, winch operators, drivers, groundskeepers and rangers.

A helicopter or light aircraft may be used to identify and locate suitable animals for relocation. The helicopter herds the animal to a suitable area for darting and recovery. The animals may be darted from the air or by a marksman on the ground.

After an individual animal has succumbed to the tranquilliser, it is medically checked, blindfolded, ropes are applied and as it regains consciousness it is manoeuvred into a crate on an awaiting truck.

When a group of animals needs to be translocated, they are rounded up by a helicopter and driven into a boma. A boma is a massive trap with canvas side curtains that act as a funnel. The animals are driven down the funnel and onto the awaiting truck.

On arrival at their destination the animals are "free released" safely back into the wild.

Diseases affecting wildlife

African Swine Fever

African Swine Fever (ASF) is a serious, highly contagious viral disease that spreads rapidly and affects domestic pigs. Although African wild pigs (warthogs, bush pigs, giant forest pigs) are the natural carriers of the swine fever virus, they do not actually go on to develop swine fever. Soft-bodied ticks are also carriers of the virus.

Swine fever is transmitted by direct contact between infected animals whether dead or alive, via bodily secretions, excretions, semen and blood that may be inseminated, ingested or come into contact with mucous membranes or an open wound. The incubation period is between 5-15 days. The onset of the disease is rapid once signs and symptoms appear, with death occurring within 1-7 days. The animal presents with fever, discharges from the eyes and nose, loss of appetite, vomiting, diarrhoea, lethargy and blue/red blotching of the skin of the extremities.

Swine fever is endemic in warthogs and leads to locals killing them in order to protect domestic livestock.

Anthrax

Anthrax is one of the world's oldest and deadliest diseases. An invisible and silent killer, its spores can lie dormant for decades until conditions are right for it to wreak havoc on the animal world.

Anthrax does not necessarily pass from animal to animal, the spores are either inhaled, ingested or enter the body through an open wound or a bite. The spores live in dry soil, and dry weather conditions are perfect, as the animals have to dig and root deeper for food. The spores are disturbed and ingested, and once inside the animal's body they multiply rapidly. Deadly toxins decimate the immune system and cause fatal haemorrhaging resulting in death.

A dead carcass is often a source of infection as it quickly attracts predators, scavengers and blow flies to the scene. Vultures are resistant to anthrax and infected meat passes straight through their acidic digestive system. When feeding on the carcass however, their head, neck and body are covered in the anthrax spores that can be unwittingly passed on to other animals.

Anthrax is often seen as being nature's way of culling wild animals.

Bovine Tuberculosis

Bovine tuberculosis (TB) is one of the most widespread infectious diseases in the world, affecting large numbers of domestic livestock (cattle, pigs, horses, dogs), wildlife (buffalo, wildebeest, topi, kudu) and humans alike.

Tuberculosis is caused by the bacteria *Mycobacterium bovis* and is transmitted between domestic livestock, wildlife and humans, by inhalation (coughing, sneezing), ingestion (eating infected meat or carcasses) and through open wounds.

This is a progressive, debilitating disease that is hard to detect, and primarily affects the respiratory system. Depending on the state of the immune system TB can take years to develop, the disease progresses slowly by initially damaging the lungs, affecting the lymph glands and then spreading to other organs. This is accompanied by weight loss and reduced exercise tolerance, which weakens the animal and results in death.

Out in the wild predators and scavengers can spread the disease to each other by inhaling nasal droplets and oral secretions, eating carcasses and drinking water from the same source.

Foot-and-Mouth Disease

Swahili: *Ugonjwa wa midomo na miguu*

Foot-and-mouth disease (FMD) is a highly contagious, fatal, viral infection that affects cloven-hoofed animals throughout the world.

Foot and mouth disease is caused by the FMD virus *Aphthovirus*, and is capable of spreading rapidly over long distances, affecting domestic livestock and wild animals alike.

The virus is transmitted by animals that have close contact with each other, either directly or indirectly by inhalation, ingestion or through open wounds and mucous membranes. The virus is present in all infected animals' secretions (saliva, expired air) and excretions (urine, faeces) as well as in milk and semen. It may also be present in standing water and in waste food. Humans who have close contact with animals can spread the disease, as the virus may be present on their clothing or body.

Animals are infected within hours of exposure to the virus. The incubation period is between 2-14 days. The animal presents with high fever, excessive salivation and blistering of the lips, tongue and feet.

It is a painful disease, and the animals have difficulty eating and walking. This is accompanied by weight loss, lameness and possible secondary infection from the blisters. The animals recover eventually, but may develop myocarditis in the interim period and die.

Foot-and-mouth disease affects domestic livestock (cattle, sheep, goats, pigs) and wildlife (buffalo, giraffes, zebras, warthogs, camels, wildebeest, kudu).

Wildlife are usually infected by contact with domestic livestock.

Rabies

Swahili: *Kichaa cha mwba*

Rabies, or *hydrophobia*, is one of the most feared viral diseases in the world, affecting all warm-blooded animals (including humans), and is prevalent in the continents of Asia, Africa, America and Europe.

Rabies is contagious and caused by the *Lyssa* virus. It is a disease that can pass freely between animals and humans.

The rabies virus is present in saliva and is transmitted via an animal bite that breaks the skin and

enters the blood stream. It can, on rare occasions, be transmitted by an animal licking an open wound or having contact with the mucous membranes of the eyes, nose, mouth and throat. Once infected the animal can carry the virus for a period of ten days to six months before showing any symptoms of the disease, although sometimes the virus can be carried for several years.

The virus grows undetected by the immune system, in the cells of muscle tissue. It then travels along the nerve pathways towards the brain. The nearer to the brain that the bite takes place, the faster the development of the disease. Once the brain is inflamed (encephalitis) symptoms appear quickly and the disease progresses rapidly, there is no cure or treatment at this point and only one outcome - death. The rabies virus is only present in saliva once the disease has affected the brain. Up to that point a bite from a rabid animal does not carry the risk of infection.

Rabies is difficult to diagnose in wild animals as there are no typical signs and symptoms. There are two forms of rabies in animals:

♦The **furious form** where the animal is initially agitated and aggressive, biting at anything and foaming at the mouth. Shortly before death, the animal becomes paralysed.

♦The other form is **dumb rabies**. The animal is lethargic and depressed. Once again paralysis occurs shortly before death.

Rinderpest
Swahili: *Sotoka*

Rinderpest (RP) is a highly contagious viral disease with a high mortality rate, that affects cloven-hoofed ungulates such as domestic livestock (cattle, sheep, goats, pigs) and some species of wildlife (giraffes). It is particularly common in Africa, the Indian subcontinent and the Middle East.

Rinderpest is caused by the *Morbilliviru* virus. Inhalation of expired air is believed to be the primary source of exposure to the virus, followed closely by contact with nasal secretions, eye discharges and saliva, or urine and faeces of the infected animal. Rinderpest may also be transmitted by ingesting contaminated food and water.

Rinderpest is characterised by its sudden presentation. The incubation period is short, between two to nine days, after which the animal shows symptoms of high fever, inflamed mucous membranes, nasal discharges, gastroenteritis, constipation and later profuse diarrhoea. Death follows swiftly.

The spread of the disease is facilitated by the movement of infected animals in the following ways:

♦The frequent movement of animals by herdsmen in search of new pastures for cattle to graze on.

♦Sales of animals at markets.

♦Illegal movement of livestock across borders.

♦Cattle rustling.

♦Seasonal movement of wildlife in search of food and water, bringing them into contact with domestic livestock.

♦Domestic livestock can wander into national parks and reserves and transmit the disease to wildlife.

♦Cape buffalo, eland, giraffes, kudu, wild pigs and warthogs are highly susceptible to rinderpest.

Antelope and hippopotamuses are less susceptible.

♦Rinderpest does not affect humans.

Habitats

Savannahs

Savannahs or savannas are tropical grasslands found between 5° and 15° north and south of the equator where the average temperature is 28°C and the annual rainfall is between 75-125cm. They are found in Africa, Madagascar, northern South America, India, Australia and Myanmar and Thailand in South East Asia. They are a transitional zone between tropical rain forests and deserts. Savannahs are where the majority of wildlife covered in this book are found, and they are often referred to as the African Plains, with the largest and most well-known being the Serengeti.

Climate
Savannahs are warm to hot all year round (20-35°C) and are characterised by two clearly defined seasons:

♦The dry season (winter), which is a prolonged period of drought.

♦The wet/rainy season (summer), which is a concentrated period of heavy rainfall.
The amount of rain that falls varies from one year to the next.

Soil
The soil of the savannah is called laterite and is porous, acidic and of poor nutritional value. The soil is soaked in the wet season and is baked dry in the dry season, as a result a hardened crust forms which is difficult for plant roots to penetrate. The soil is fragile and is easily broken down and fragmented by the pressure of animals' hooves. Heavy grazing by domestic livestock and cultivation of crops reduces ground cover and depletes the soil of its nutrients.

Termite mounds can be seen on the savannah and are important in soil formation as well as providing food and shelter for animals.

Vegetation
Savannahs are large, rolling, open, semi-arid landscapes, whose plant life has evolved to cope with alternating prolonged periods of drought and seasonal rainfall.

Annual rainfall dictates the type of vegetation that is able to survive in this environment. The plants are all in competition with each other for water.

♦Between 10-20cm of rain per annum only allows grasses to grow.

♦Up to 30cm of rain per annum allows shrubs to grow.

♦Over 30cm of rain per annum allows the occasional tree to grow, such as the acacia tree, which is synonymous with the African savannah.

Above 40cm of rain per annum encourages and supports the growth of trees that are now able to form a canopy, putting the grasses in the shade and restricting their growth.

The open canopy of the savannah encourages the growth of perennial grasses that dominate the landscape. The grasses turn yellow and die back during the dry season but burst back to life at the first sign of rain. Seeds can lie dormant for long periods until conditions are favourable, allowing them to burst into life. The grasses grow vigorously and can be as high as 1.8m.

The trees of the savannah have evolved to survive prolonged periods of drought. Long, deep tap roots enable them to dig deep into the earth to seek out water, and the large trunks are able to store water. Fewer leaves reduces water loss, as do small waxy leaves. Deciduous trees lose their leaves in the dry season to conserve water. Thickened bark, which is either corky or of a smooth resinous consistency, is fire resistant. Some trees like the acacia tree are browser resistant, producing phenols that make the leaves unpalatable and cause the browsing animal to move on. They also produce ethylene, which stimulates surrounding trees to produce phenols.

The bushes have sharp thorns that reduce water loss and deter the browsers.

Fires

The growth of vegetation on the savannah is kept in check by periodic bush fires, which may be natural (electrical storms), or in some cases caused by humankind.

Poachers may set fire to the savannah as a means of exposing and moving the animals. It is not unusual to see a marabou stork standing patiently in front of a wall of fire waiting to capture the escaping wildlife. After a fire all that remains is a fine covering of blackened, powdery ash that makes the soil fertile. The deep, starch roots of the grasses remain unharmed during a fire. When the rains return, the grasses sprout again, and life is restored to the savannah.

Animals

No other environment on earth is able to equal the savannah's ability to support the large numbers and wide variety of mammals that co-exist here. Large herds of browsing and grazing plains game (herbivores), live here under the watchful eye of the ever present predators - the carnivores and scavengers.

Herbivores consume large amounts of food and influence the growth of vegetation on the savannah. The majority of the animals are grazers (wildebeest, zebra, Cape buffalo), some are browsers (giraffes) and some are a combination of both (elephant, impala, duiker, gerenuk). Continued grazing keeps the growth of the grasses in check and promotes the growth of weeds. The individual grazers are highly selective and have a preference for the height and type of grass they will eat. The heavy grazers (elephants, hippopotamuses, roan antelope, sable antelope, buffaloes), have a preference for long, tall, coarse grass, exposing the medium-sized grasses for the intermediate grazers (zebras). The smaller, selective herbivores (gazelles, warthogs) follow in the tracks of the intermediate herbivores, feeding on the remaining short grasses, shoots and roots. This is known as the grazing succession. The animals excrete sodium and nitrogen, which is necessary for plant growth.

The dry season causes the animals to migrate in search of food and water. It is usual at this time to find a high concentration of animals near the waterholes, the grazers and browsers drinking water and the predators waiting to ambush them. As the grasses dry out on the savannah they provide perfect camouflage for some of the predators.

Wooded areas support a reduced number of browsers compared with the grasslands. As a result the browsers are usually solitary or live in small herds. The browsers control the growth and proliferation of woody vegetation, with some trees and shrubs never reaching their full size. Elephants are particularly destructive as they eat leaves and twigs, break branches, strip the bark from the trunk and are ultimately

capable of uprooting a tree. In some areas they may be culled because of the damage they cause to the plant life, whereas in other areas they may be translocated.

The scavengers (hyenas, jackals, vultures) always get a poor press, but actually play a vital role in cleaning up the savannah, ridding it of diseased, sick animals and their remains. Any remaining animal horns or bones provide vital food for the larvae of moths. Dung beetles deal with animal faeces.

Trivia

- Savannahs cover 25% of the land on Earth.
- The savannahs cover 40% of the land in Africa, which equates to about 5 million sq. mi.
- In the savannahs of East Africa the majority of the plains game give birth to their young at the start of the wet season when there is an abundance of food. If the rains fail, this can seriously affect the survival of the newly born calves.
- The word *savannah* comes from a 14th century word that means "land which is without trees but with much grass either short or tall". By the late 19th century its meaning changed to "land with both grass and trees".

Miombo Woodlands

Miombo woodlands are mature, deciduous, tropical woodlands and dry forests found in central, western and southern Tanzania where the average temperature is between 15 and 30°C. The miombo woodlands in central Tanzania are classified as "dry" as they receive less than 100cm of rain per annum, whereas the miombo woodlands in south-west Tanzania are classified as "wet" as they receive more than 100cm of rain per annum. Broad, interspersed grazing depressions are a feature of the miombo woodlands.

The trees have adapted to withstand prolonged periods of drought, variable seasonal rainfall, and well drained soil that is acidic and of poor nutritional value. They lose their leaves in the dry season to conserve moisture, producing new leaves before the wet season starts. Their fruit is used to provide food for livestock, and the wood can be used for crafts, construction or as fuel.

Fires are frequent in miombo woodlands during the dry season. These fires may be natural (electrical storms), or in some cases caused by humankind. Locals seeking fresh pastures for cultivation or grazing will set fire to the woodlands.

Miombo woodlands provide the ideal habitat for a large, diverse number of African animals - African wild dogs, antelopes, black rhinoceroses, Cape buffaloes, caracals, cheetahs, black and white colobus monkeys, duikers, elands, elephants, giraffes, hartebeests, hippopotamuses, hyenas, jackals, kudus, lions, leopards, mongooses, Nile crocodiles, oribis, reedbucks, rhinoceroses, sable antelopes, warthogs, waterbucks and zebras.

Trivia

♦ Miombo woodlands cover one third of the land in Tanzania.

♦ Miombo woodlands are being deforested at an alarming rate, and are not sustainable.

♦ The presence of the tsetse fly, which carries sleeping sickness, deters humans from settling in these areas.

♦Miombo woodlands are only found in Mikumi National Park, Ruaha National Park and Selous Game Reserve.

Semi-Arid Deserts

Semi-arid deserts are inhospitable, rough, rugged environments. The ground is covered with either fine sand or loose, lava-like rocky gravel. Only thorn scrub, hardy grasses, weeds and hardy nomads live here. They have clearly defined seasons:

♦Long, warm, dry summers with drought-like conditions, and temperatures falling to 10°C during the night.

♦A short winter season with erratic, heavy showers where less than 70cm of rain falls per annum.

Semi-arid deserts are found in parts of north-eastern and central Tanzania.

Kopjes

A *kopje* is a rocky outcrop or island that rises abruptly from the African plains. They are made of ancient granite rock and are covered in shrubs, grasses and wild sisal. They offer shade, shelter and sanctuary to wildlife in the wild, hostile and inhospitable environment of the African plains, and are often frequented by cheetahs, dik-diks, rock hyraxes, bush hyraxes, mongooses and snakes.

Termites
Swahili: *Mchwa*

Termites are tiny, soft bodied insects (less than 2mm). They are herbivorous, feeding on dry grass, plant roots, wood, bark, straw and any other plant matter that comes their way. Bacteria produced in the stomach digests the cellulose. The termite's high fat and protein content makes it a valuable source of food for animals such as the aardvark and humans.

The colony, in which up to 5 million termites live, has a highly organised social structure or caste system made up of:

♦A king.

♦A primary queen. This is the first termite to find and establish the colony, she may be over 12cm long and can lay up to 30,000 eggs a day, for 15 years.

♦Secondary queens who take over if the primary queen dies or is killed.

♦Soldiers, who defend and protect the termite mound/nest from intruders, such as ants.

♦Workers, who gather and store food, build and repair the nest and look after the eggs and larvae. They are blind and wingless and die quickly from exposure to the sun if they are outside the nest for any length of time.

♦Reproductives, who have wings and fly round in swarms trying to set up new nests.

Termites produce a chemical called a pheromone, which is used to establish social order and map out trails to and from the nest.

They live and operate underground, building large, elaborate and monumental termite mounds from saliva and particles of soil. The mounds, which are found in the tropics and dry savannahs, are in areas of good drainage and can be up to 6m high and 30m in diameter. Termites can dig to depths of 75m in search of water, bringing everything from below to the surface. This activity aerates the soil and adds nutrients to it. The mound gets higher and higher the more they dig. An active colony is constantly adding to, and repairing, the mound.

The temperature (28°C-30°C) and humidity inside the mound is constant and is maintained by a series of air ducts. Hot air rises and leaves via the air ducts, and outside winds send air currents down into the underground chambers.

The mound is made up of series of chambers with interconnecting tunnels. Faeces and saliva are used to construct the partitioning walls. Inside there are segregated areas for breeding, egg development and gardening.

The mound is usually vacated when the queen dies or is killed, and is either inhabited by a new colony of termites or becomes home to warthogs, squirrels, hyenas, dwarf mongooses, black mambas or porcupines. Termite mounds make useful look out points for leopards and cheetahs.

Trivia

♦Termites are sometimes referred to as white ants, although they are not related to ants.

♦Termites have been known to feed on dung.

♦Termites can devastate crops of maize and millet.

♦Ants may attack the termites and invade their nest.

Vegetation

Acacia Tree
Swahili: *Mgunga*

The acacia tree or umbrella tree is synonymous with the African savannah. A slow-growing, drought-resistant tree, it grows to a height of 20m and thrives in the arid conditions of the savannah, grasslands and sand dunes of Africa. It has a deep, widespread tap root that enables it to survive the dry season, and a flattened canopy that spans 8-13m and provides welcome shelter to animals in the heat of the midday sun. The black-grey bark is rough, the leaves are small to minimise water loss and it has thorns that grow in pairs on the branches. Pale, clustered, aromatic flowers growing on old wood cover the acacia tree in early summer. Protein and carbohydrate-rich seed pods are produced by the acacia tree and are a welcome source of food to animals (kudu, impala, rhino, elephant) in the dry season.

Defence Mechanism
When a giraffe begins browsing on an acacia tree, the tree increases the levels of phenols in its remaining leaves, making them unpalatable. As the giraffe continues browsing on the tree, the leaves become more and more unpalatable and this prompts the giraffe to move on. At the same time, ethylene is emitted by the acacia tree, which stimulates other trees in the surrounding area (as far as 50m away) to increase their production of phenols. Consequently, giraffes only feed on one acacia tree in ten.

Trivia
♦The acacia tree is mentioned in the Bible in the Book of Exodus and Book of Isaiah, and is referred to as *Shitta*.
♦The biblical Ark of the Covenant was constructed from the acacia tree.

Baobab Tree
(Adansonia digitata)
Swahili: *Mbuyu tree*

The baobab tree is an ancient, slow-growing deciduous tree found at low altitudes in the hot, dry and arid regions of Africa, India and Australia.

The baobab has an enormous cylindrical trunk, which is between 7-15m in diameter. During the rainy season its girth increases to accommodate the 120,000 litres of water that it is capable of storing, shrinking back to its original size during the dry season. The fire-resistant, cork-like bark is 5-10cm thick and is a grey-brown colour. Damaged bark is quickly replaced by new bark allowing the tree to continue to grow and thrive.

The baobab is leafless for up to nine months of the year, during which time its thick, tapering, root-like branches are left exposed giving it the appearance of having been planted upside down, hence the nickname upside-down tree.

The leaves are divided into five to seven leaflets on a single stalk.

Large, pendulous, sweetly scented white flowers, between 17-20cm in diameter, open late afternoon from October to December. The flowers are pollinated by bats and bush babies during the night and die within 24 hours of opening. The dying flowers turn brown and fall to the ground, acquiring an unpleasant odour as they decay.

The fruit of the baobab is egg shaped. The outer woody shell is either a dark green or brown colour and is covered in tiny yellow-brown hairs. The white, powdery pulp inside the fruit surrounds black, kidney-shaped seeds.

A mature baobab can grow as high as 25-30m.

Uses of the Baobab Tree

Local inhabitants refer to the baobab as the "tree of life" as it provides food, water, shade and shelter to humans and animals alike.

Mature baobab trunks are hollow inside and have been used as pubs, storage barns, houses and prisons. Birds, small rodents, squirrels, bush babies, lizards, snakes, scorpions and insects all make their home in various parts of the tree.

The bark is used to make paper, cloth, nets, mats, baskets, snares, string and rope, and the roots are used to make cosmetics and tonics. The leaves are used as a vegetable and are a rich source of vitamin C, calcium, sugars and potassium. They may be eaten fresh, dried or boiled to make a spinach-like soup. The flowers provide nectar for fruit bats and bush babies and the pollen is used to make glue.

The fruit is a rich source of vitamin C and tartaric acid, and is used to make a refreshing drink that tastes like lemonade. The pith can be chewed to provide moisture or may be used medicinally to treat fevers. Wild animals such as baboons, monkeys, antelopes and elephants all eat the fallen fruit.

The seeds are either used to aid the fermentation of beer, as a thickener for soups or roasted to make a coffee-like beverage. An oil-like substance can be extracted from the seeds, which can be used as fuel or as a dye.

Trivia

◆The baobab has numerous nicknames:

-Dead rat tree. The fruit pods resemble rats hanging upside down by their tails.

-Cream of tartar tree.

-Monkey-bread tree.

-Lemonade tree.

◆The baobab only produces flowers after it is 20 years old.

◆Baobab trees can be 1,000 years old. Some are reported to be between 2,000-3,000 years old. Unlike other trees the baobab does not produce growth rings by which the age of the tree can be estimated. Radiocarbon dating is used to accurately calculate the age of the baobab.

◆Superstitious locals believe that picking the flowers of the baobab brings them bad luck, and could mean that they may be eaten by a lion. On the brighter side, soaking the seeds in

water and drinking it is believed to prevent attacks from crocodiles.

♦When the baobab dies, it rots from the inside outwards, eventually collapsing in a heap leaving only a mass of fibres behind.

♦Baobab oil is extracted from the seeds and is high in Vitamins A, D, E and F and has been a part of African skincare for centuries. The oil is said to have impressive moisturising properties.

Euphorbia Tree

Euphorbia trees are found in temperate regions of the world, as well as subtropical and tropical regions of the Americas and Africa. This succulent species originates from Africa and the Americas. They grow at low altitudes, in deciduous woodlands with well drained soil, and are tolerant of drought conditions.

The euphorbia tree is tall, upright, with multiple branches and has a cactus-like appearance. The main stem and branches are thick and fleshy, and are coloured dark green with pale green and white stripes. The short-lived leaves are small. It flowers in April and produces fruit in August that is eaten by birds.

The euphorbia tree produces a milky white sap called latex, which is poisonous and extremely caustic, blistering the skin and mouth and burning the delicate mucous membranes of the eyes, nose and mouth. In severe cases it can cause blindness.

Trivia

♦The euphorbia tree is known as the "milk bush", the "cathedral cactus" and the "candelabra tree".

♦The sap of the euphorbia trees has been used as a purgative.

♦Black rhinos are able to feed on the euphorbia tree with no ill effect.

♦Locals catch fish by using the sap of the euphorbia tree in ponds to paralyse them, after which they rise to the surface. They also use the sap to kill maggots in the open wounds of domestic livestock.

Sausage Tree
(Kigelia pinnata or *Kigelia africana)*
Swahili: *Mburu*

The sausage tree is a semi-deciduous tree that grows in the tropical regions of Africa, usually close to rivers and streams.

It grows upright for several years before developing branches that form a wide spreading canopy. The trunk is short and thick, and the grey bark shows signs of peeling with age. Underlying wood is a pale yellowy brown colour.

Lime green, leathery leaflets grow on a long stalk with a single leaf at the tip. In areas where there is rain throughout the year the sausage tree is evergreen, but in areas where there is a long dry season or prolonged drought, it will shed its leaves to conserve moisture.

Fragrantly scented, orangey-purple-red bell-shaped flowers grow in small clusters on long stems between July and October. The flowers open early evening and are pollinated by bats and insects.

Distinct, sausage-like fruit hang from rope-like stalks and fall to the ground from May onwards. A thin, grey skin covers the fibrous inner pulp that surrounds the wingless seeds. The fruit can be 30-60cm long and weigh between 5-10kg.

Sausage trees grow as high as 20m.

Uses of the Sausage Tree

The wood of the sausage tree is used to make oars and yokes.

The leaves are eaten by elephants and kudus and are used by locals to feed livestock.

Fallen flowers are eaten by wild animals - impala, kudu and nyala.

Unripe fruit is inedible and poisonous.

The fruit is eaten by bush pigs, porcupines, elephants, giraffes, hippopotamuses, baboons and monkeys. It is used in shampoos and skin preparations, and medicinally to treat warts, cuts, sores, rheumatism, syphilis and snake bites.

Baked fruit is an aid to fermenting beer. Boiled fruit produces a red dye.

Locals roast and eat the seeds as famine food.

Trivia

♦The sausage tree is nicknamed "the fat tail of the sheep".

♦Falling fruit can cause serious injury to people and substantial damage to vehicles.

♦The sausage tree is tolerant of drought conditions but susceptible to frost.

♦Fresh, unripe fruit is poisonous and has a purgative affect on the bowels.

The Serengeti
The place where the land runs on forever.....
Maasai: Endless plains

The Serengeti is situated in Northern Tanzania and is part of the Northern Safari Circuit of National Parks, the circuit of parks most frequently visited by tourists, (Arusha National Park, Kilimanjaro National Park, Manyara National Park, Mkomzi National Park, Ngorongoro Conservation Area and Tarangire National Park). The Serengeti is Tanzania's oldest national park and is considered to be the best. It is now a listed World Heritage site.

It covers an area of 14,750 sq km and has three distinct areas:
♦The Serengeti Plains, which is a vast treeless grassland.
♦The Western Corridor, which is a savannah.
♦The Northern Serengeti, which is open woodland and hills.
Only one river flows through the Serengeti, The Mara.

The Serengeti has the only active volcano in the area, Ol Doinyo Lengai.

It is strongly believed that little has changed in the Serengeti over the last one million years, the weather patterns, flora and fauna have more or less remained the same. It is regarded as one of the oldest, scientifically significant eco systems in existence on the planet today. It is famed for the largest remaining animal migration in the world, and is home to four globally threatened species, African wild dog, black rhino, cheetah and elephant.

The great migration was selected in 2013 as one of the seven natural wonders of the world.

History
Dr. Oscar Baumann, an Austrian explorer and cartographer, famous for exploring the interior of German East Africa, (Tanzania, Rwanda and Burundi), visited the area in 1892 and named it the Serengeti. He was the first European to enter Rwanda in 1892 and the first European to visit Lake Eyasi, Lake Manyara and the Ngorongoro Crater in Tanzania.

Stewart Edward White, an American game hunter, explorer, writer and novelist, visited the Serengeti in 1913. He later returned to the Serengeti in 1920 with a group of friends, and camped in the area named the Seronera, where he shot 50 lions.

In 1890 a combination of severe drought and the animal disease rinderpest wreaked havoc with the Serengeti's wildlife, and it is believed that it took until the 1970s for the wildebeest population to fully recover.

The British Colonial Administration made the Serengeti a partial game reserve in 1921, covering an area of 800 acres, and it became a full game reserve in 1929. Despite the fact that the Maasai had grazed their livestock in the Serengeti for over 200 years, it was decided in 1959 to evict them from the area in order to preserve the wildlife, and move them to the Ngorongoro Conservation area.

Human habitation is strictly forbidden in the Serengeti. Only the Tanzanian National Parks Authority and the Frankfurt Zoological Society are allowed permanent residency.

The Ngorongoro Crater

The world famous Ngorongoro Crater is located inside the Ngorongoro Conservation Area, which is administered by the Ngorongoro Conservation Area Authority. www.ncaa.go.tz

It is the world's largest unbroken and un-flooded caldera, and a UNESCO World Heritage Site. The crater was formed two to three million years ago when a volcano erupted and subsequently collapsed in on itself. It is believed that the original volcano was between 4,500-5,800m high. The crater is 19km in diameter and has walls that are 600m high, which actively discourages animals from migrating. It is home to 25,000-30,000 animals, and is reputed to be the most densely populated conservation area in Africa in terms of wildlife.

Dr. Oscar Baurmann, an Austrian Explorer, was the first European to visit the Ngorongoro Crater in 1892. Adolph and Friedrick Siedentopf farmed in the Ngorongoro Crater from 1899 until 1916.

The mineral rich floor of the crater supports a large open grass plain, which is home to a plethora of antelopes and the predators that hunt them. A large, shallow, seasonal alkaline lake is situated in the centre of the crater. This lake is known either as Makat (Maasai for salt), or Magadi, and is 18 Sq Km in size.

Gorigor Swamp attracts a variety of wildlife that enjoy playfully idling their time away in the cool waters, or others that momentarily pass by to quench their thirst.

Hippo Pool, as the name suggests, is home to the resident pod of hippos who spend their day wallowing in the cool waters and posing for photgraphs.

There is a forest on the crater floor called Lerai Forest. It has been used previously for rainmaking and fertility ceremonies. The ground is sacred and contains the graves of several Maasai elders. The Ngorongoro Crater is a site of particular cultural and spiritual significance to the Maasai, who are allowed to graze their cattle within the crater, but must enter and leave each day.

Tanzania's Volcanoes

There are nine volcanoes in Tanzania, Igwisi Hills, Izumbwe-Mpoli, Mount Kilimanjaro, Kyejo, Mount Meru, Nzozi, Ol Doinyo Lengai, Rungwe and SW Usangu Basin, with the most famous being Kilimanjaro. Three are worthy of special mention.

Mount Kilimanjaro
Mount Kilimanjaro, standing at 5,895m, is the highest free standing mountain in the world, the highest volcano outside the South American Andes and the highest mountain in Africa.

It is situated in north-east Tanzania, near the Kenyan border, and is part of Kilimanjaro National Park. It is a stratovolcano (composite volcano). Stratovolcanoes are steep sided, symmetrical conical volcanoes, and a crater is usually present at the summit. They are made up of multiple crusted layers (strata) of ash, lava, pumice and tephra. In its lifetime, spanning millions of years, a stratovolcano may have erupted many thousands of times. They are the most dangerous of all volcanoes and erupt violently with little or no warning. The lava does not travel far, is viscous and cools quickly.

There are three volcanic cones present on Mount Kilimanjaro. Shiro (4,005m) and Mawenzi (5,149m) are both extinct. Kibo, on which Uhuru summit (5,895m) stands, is the highest, largest and youngest cone. It is dormant, and may therefore erupt again. The last activity was recorded 200 years ago. Gas emitting fumeroles are present in the crater.

Mount Kilimanjaro has attracted, and continues to attract, people from all four corners of the Earth to attempt the climb to its summit. Approximately 30,000 people attempt to climb Mount Kilimanjaro every year. There are seven official routes to the summit: Lemosho, Shira, Machame, Umbwe, Marangu, Rongai and the Northern Circuit. The Mweka route is only used to descend the mountain. Many people fail in their bid to climb to the summit as a result of altitude sickness, and unfortunately some die.

The first three people to climb to the summit were two Germans in 1889, Hans Meyer and Ludwig Purtscheller, who were led by an 18 year old Tanzanian guide, Yohana Kinyala Lauwo (later called Mzee Lauwo). This event changed Yohana's life forever as he spent the next 70 years guiding people up and down the mountain. He died on 10 May 1996 when he was 125 years old.

Since 1912 Mount Kilimanjaro has lost 82% of its ice cap due to climate change. Its glaciers have receded rapidly, and it is predicted that it will be ice free by 2029. A sobering thought, as the indigenous people living on the slopes are reliant on the water from the glaciers of Kilimanjaro for their livelihood, to feed their livestock and irrigate crops.

Mount Meru
Mount Meru is a stratovolcano standing at 4,566m. It is the second highest mountain in Tanzania and is the ninth highest mountain in Africa. It located in north-east Tanzania, north of the city of Arusha and in the heart of Arusha National Park. It is 70km west of Mount Kilimanjaro, and on a clear day both mountains can be observed, and provide unique photographs if you can capture them both in one shot -

two iconic volcanoes almost side by side. The eastern side of Mount Meru was blown away and the summit collapsed in a violent eruption 8,000 years ago. The caldera is 3.5km wide, its diameter is 25km and it is regarded as one of the largest free-standing mountains on Earth. It is a stunningly beautiful mountain from whichever angle you look at it. It is classified as a dormant volcano and last erupted in 1910.

It is debatable as to when the summit of Mount Meru was first conquered. Records claim that Carl Uhlig, a German meteorologist and geographer, was the first person to conquer the summit in 1901, whereas other records claim that another German, Fritz Jaeger, was the first person to conquer the summit in 1904.

There is only one route up Mount Meru, the Momella route. An armed ranger is required when you start the initial ascent of the mountain because of the presence of potentially dangerous wildlife in Arusha National Park, (elephants and Cape buffalo in particular). The walk on the rim of the crater is reputed to be one of the most spectacular walks in Africa. Many people will climb Mount Meru in order to acclimatise to altitude before they attempt Mount Kilimanjaro. Mount Meru is more of a physically challenging climb than Mount Kilimanjaro and is not for the faint hearted, although Mount Kilimanjaro presents significantly greater challenges as regards the problems of climbing at altitude.

Ol Doinyo Lengai

Ol Doinyo Lengai is an active stratovolcano that stands 2,962m above sea level. It is situated in northern Tanzania, above the Serengeti, on the southern edge of Lake Natron, 112km from the city of Arusha and 112km from Olduvai.

Scientists discovered in the 1960s that Ol Doinyo Lengai is the only volcano on the planet that produces natrocarbonatite lava. The lava has a low silica content and is composed of 50% carbonate (carbonate is composed of sodium and potassium). The lava temperature is low at 600c (silica based lava temperature is 1,200c), consequently the lava only glows at night. The black-grey lava is very viscous and as it cools, minerals in the lava react with atmospheric moisture causing it to break down quickly and turn white. The black lava flows faster that a person can run. The last eruptions were in 2006-07 with ongoing activity still being recorded. The ash produced when Ol Doinyo Lengai erupts spreads for great distances, and is responsible for the nutritious grasslands that the wildebeest are reliant upon as they start on their annual migration.

Ol Doinyo Lengai is known as the Maasai mountain of the gods. It is said to be the home to Eng'ai, an ancient Maasai god. The Maasai believe that gods express their wrath by frequent eruptions and smoke. It is a place of pilgrimage and reverence. It is a place to go to pray for rain, more cattle and healthy children.

Tribes of Tanzania

The Detoga Tribe
Swahili:Mang'ati

The origins of the Detoga tribe date back 3,000 years. They originated from the Horn of Africa in Western Ethiopia and Southern Sudan, and gradually migrated southwards. They can be found living in and around Lake Eyasi, Lake Manyara and Mara Singida. Life is hard, as they live in semi arid areas where water is scarce and unclean.

The Detoga are of Nilotic origin and were originally nomadic pastoralists, but this has changed over the passage of time. They are now agro pastoralists, herding cattle, donkeys, goats and sheep, keeping chickens, and growing beans, corn, maize and millet on small plots of land. They are also recognised as highly skilled blacksmiths. Collecting scrap iron, they melt it down into ingots to make arrow-heads, blades for knives, jewellery and ornaments.

They are a proud people, are fierce warriors, and keep themselves to themselves. They are suspicious of strangers, viewing them as a threat. Family life is important, and they live in a small social circle with the man as the head of the household. They are polygamous, and the wives are ranked in the order in which they were married. A council of elders maintains social order and control by imposing fines and curses on the guilty.

The Detoga practice scarification, which is a form of body modification. Deep cuts are made on their backs and faces, and open wounds are left to heal naturally. Decorative facial scars are placed in a circular pattern around the eyes, and are used to identify which family they belong to.

Divination and witchcraft are regularly practiced, as is participation in primitive religious rituals. It is popular for the men to drink honey beer at rituals. They fear people who have dealt with the dead, and will not go near them or have contact with them for a long period time. Ordinary people are buried in the compound in which they live, whilst village elders are buried in a large conical mound. They believe that when a person dies they become a guardian spirit, and funeral ceremonies can last up to one year.

The Detoga live in traditional rectangular huts. The walls and the flat roof are constructed from upright tree branches that have intertwining branches, sticks and twigs. This may or may not be plastered and held together with a mixture of mud, straw, cow dung and cow urine. Self seeded plants may grow on the roof tops.

The Detoga wear colourful reddish brown clothing - the colour of the earth. A paste is made by mixing red sand with animal butter to tan hides. The women wear leather capes, and married women wear garments made from leather stripes. The women like to adorn themselves with jewellery. Colourful beads are used to make necklaces, pendants and earrings, and heavy earrings stretch the ear lobes. Bracelets are made of brass or copper, and have decorative patterns etched on.

Afterthought

Until recently the Detoga were isolated from the world, but they now face the same challenges to their continued existence as the Hadzabe tribe. They have resisted formal education, they have poor hygiene, a high infant mortality rate, poor nutrition and a high prevalence of infectious diseases. Tourists invade their private lives on a daily basis, the Masaai steal their cows, and the government takes the land from them. Their traditional way of life is under threat and is continually being eroded.

Trivia

♦The Detoga tribe believe that they are the oldest tribe in Africa. But so do a lot of other African tribes!

♦The Detoga tribe speak south Nilotic.

♦The Masaai are the traditional enemy of the Detoga tribe.

The Hadza/Hadzabe Tribe

The Hadzabe are indigenous, primitive, nomadic hunter-gatherers that can be found living in Hadzaland, 50km from Olduvai Gorge, between Lake Eyasi and the Rift Valley Highlands in Northern Tanzania. Olduvai Gorge is where the remains of Homo Habilis were discovered by Mary and Louis Leakey. Homo Habilis is one of the earliest members of the genus Homo, and lived at Olduvai Gorge 1.9 million years ago. The Hadzabe have one of the oldest lineages of contemporary humans, and now only about 1,000 (2018) individuals remain. Life for the Hadzabe has remained unchanged for thousands of years, and is a stark reminder of how early humans existed 12,000 years ago. However, recent incursions from tourists, and television crews, have inevitably begun to have an impact on the whole situation.

The Hadzabe are a gentle people who speak Hadzane - a distinct clicking language. They are egalitarian, believing in equality for all, regardless of age, sex and ability. They live in a society without rules, and there is no tribal or governing hierarchical body. There are no politics or religions, and no one is allowed to exercise continuing, personal authority over the tribe - decisions are made by mutual agreement. They enjoy high levels of freedom and self dependency, and have a strong belief in communal sharing. Everyone is engaged in child rearing.

They have never experienced serious disease, famine or war. There is no HIV or transferred sexual diseases. They are predominantly monogamous, and there are no inter-tribal marriages. They value traits such as hard work and physical attractiveness.

The average life expectancy is 33 years. Many die from malaria, sleeping sickness (tsetse fly) and injuries sustained whilst they are hunting.

The Hadzabe live in small bands of 20-30 individuals. The availability of food and water dictates when it is time to decamp and move on. The Hadzabe have few personal possessions and are able to carry them on their backs when they move to a new campsite. Illness, death or disagreements may make them decide to move camp. The shelter they live in is simple, and is constructed from branches and dried grass. In the dry season some of the Hadzabe sleep outdoors under the stars on large animal skins. Skulls of baboons may adorn the campsite, either nailed to the tree trunks or hung up in the bushes. Evidence of recent kills can also be observed, with body parts wedged securely between branches in bushes.

The Hadzabe live sustainably off the land. They do not grow crops and do not raise livestock. They leave no carbon footprint. Armed with hand made bows and arrows (poisoned or non poisoned), knives, and honey pouches to collect wild honey, the men go hunting early morning either individually or in a small group. The tip of the arrow is covered with poison from the desert rose shrub (Adenium Coetaneum). The poison is highly toxic and is used to kill large game. It contains cardiac glycosides that are toxic to the heart. Feeding themselves along the way on berries, drinking water from dirty puddles, climbing trees to retrieve a kill or an arrow, they move silently and swiftly through the bushy undergrowth as a highly co-ordinated team. They are on the move all the time and are alert to any dangers that the environment presents to them. They live in a woodland habitat with rocky outcrops, but this is the perfect habitat for Africa's most venomous snakes - black mamba, boomslang, puff adder and Egyptian spitting cobra.

The women and children forage daily, picking berries and fruit and digging up tubers with a digging stick. Grass baskets are used to carry the fruit back to camp.

Colonial settlers, the Tanzanian government and missionaries have tried to influence the Hadzabe and introduce them to farming and Christianity, but have failed. The tribe are now under pressure from tourism, safari companies and television documentary crews, and are fast becoming a tourist attraction. Visiting the Hadzabe is expensive. You pay large sums of money for the privilege of entering the area that the Hadzabe occupy, and then even more money to spend time with them on early morning hunting expeditions, (for the fit). Less fit tourists can join the women and children foraging for food, before ending the visit with a traditional dance.

Less than 300 (2018) Hadzabe now live the true traditional hunter-gatherer lifestyle.

Afterthought

In order to survive, hunter-gathers are constantly on the move searching for food. They need access to large swathes of land that support the wild life and plant life on which they are dependent. Ninety per cent of the ancestral lands that the Hadzabe originally inhabited have disappeared in the last 50 years.

Pastoralists have moved in, and have put additional pressure on the land. Farmers have cleared the land of trees to grow crops to feed their families. The pressure on wildlife is immense, their habitat is disappearing and there is nowhere to go. Climate change is now starting to affect the rainy season, and the timing of the rainy season is becoming unpredictable. The amount of water that falls is diminishing, lakes, rivers and streams are drying up, crops are failing and livestock are dying. Everything and everyone are affected. The pressure on the earth's dwindling, natural resources is enormous and the situation is currently on a downward spiral.

The Hadzabe now only hunt smaller mammals, (larger animals have disappeared due to loss of habitat), and they have to subsidise their diet with ugali. Coming into contact with westerners has compromised their health. They have been introduced to alcohol, and they have no immunity to common infectious diseases such as measles.

Like the wildlife that is rapidly disappearing, so is the Hadzabe culture.

Trivia
♦The Hadzabe tribe, the Tjimbe tribe (Namibia) and the Mbuti tribe (Congo), are the only three hunter-gatherer tribes currently in existence in Africa.

♦The Hadzabe tribe are the only people in Tanzania that are not taxed.

♦The Hadzabe tribe are not closely linked to any other tribe, either linguistically or by genetic heritage.

The Maasai Tribe

The Maasai are a primitive, semi-nomadic, pastoralist tribe of Nilotic-Hamitic origin that inhabit the semi-arid and arid lands of the Great Rift Valley in Kenya and Tanzania.

The Maasai are predominantly a warrior tribe whose lives revolve around their livestock - cattle in particular. They believe that when the Earth and sky were divided, the rain god Ngai gave the Maasai tribe cattle, and with it the right to steal from other neighbouring tribes. A man's wealth in Maasai society is measured by the number of cattle and children he possesses.

The Maasai believe that the ground is sacred and they do not dig up the earth to cultivate crops, search for water or bury their dead. They are particularly dependent upon cattle for providing meat, blood and milk for daily sustenance. Piercing the jugular vein (in the cow's neck) with an arrow allows blood to be collected in a calabash (bowl). Milk is then added to prevent the warm blood from coagulating. Moistened cow dung is used to seal the open wound over the jugular vein. If a cow is slaughtered the Maasai carefully cut up the animal and apportion the best cuts of meat to individual men based on their seniority. Whatever remains is given to the women.

Loss of land to national parks and game reserves has reduced the Maasai's access to essential water supplies, fresh pastures and salt licks, and they now face the ongoing problems associated with drought and famine. In order to survive they either buy food, grow their own crops or sadly have become dependent upon foreign aid.

Maasai Society

Maasai society is patriarchal. Women are inferior, subservient and live a life of cultural oppression. At birth they become a member of their father's family line. When a female Maasai reaches puberty, her father chooses her a husband - who is usually much older - in exchange for cattle or cash. She becomes one of many wives and will continue to produce children for as long as she is able. A woman is not allowed to divorce her husband, she has no inheritance rights and is not allowed to own land or cattle. If her husband dies she becomes the property of her husband's brothers.

Rising early in the morning, it is the woman's daily duty to milk the cows, sweep the huts inside and out, prepare and cook food for the men, repair the cracked hut walls as and when necessary, and walk whatever distance is necessary to collect firewood and water.

Maasai men are warriors and it is their duty to guard and protect their tribe, livestock and pastures. Taking the cattle, goats and sheep out each morning, they may trek many kilometres in their relentless search for fresh grass and water. When grass and water are plentiful the elders will sit and watch the *layonis* (young boys who are not yet circumcised) herding the cattle. When food is scarce the *morans* (warriors) take over from the layonis moving the cattle further afield. The elders then visit friends in nearby *manyattas* (a group of huts that is temporary settlement), drink beer or let the women tend to their needs while they sit and wait for the morans to return before sundown. Morans who remain behind will either go hunting, visit nearby manyattas or play with the *nditos* (young girls). When food is scarce due to drought conditions, or when the pastures are exhausted of food from over grazing, the Maasai are forced to move on necessitating the construction of a new manyatta.

Manyattas

Small manyattas consist of up to ten huts. Large manyattas consist of up to 250 huts. Manyattas may or may not have a perimeter hedge.

It is the man's responsibility to construct the circular perimeter hedge that surrounds the village mud huts. This keeps the livestock and Maasai safe inside, and keeps predators out during the night. The hedge stands six feet high and is made from sticks, tree branches and acacia thorn bushes. Up to four gates are present, which are opened early in the morning and closed at evening time.

It is the woman's responsibility to construct the mud huts, a task that can take up to seven months to complete. Traditional Maasai huts are constructed of upright tree branches with intertwining branches, sticks and twigs that are plastered and held together with mixture of mud, ash, grasses, cow dung and cow urine. This crude plaster is baked dry in the sun. Cracks appear regularly in the mud walls and the women and children are constantly repairing them. Ventilation holes are necessary to allow the smoke from cooking to escape, and these are located either in the roof or the outside walls. The presence of smoke deters disease-ridden mosquitoes or other pesky insects from entering the hut. The door is either made from wood or wickerwork, and in some instances a padlock may be present. The roof is dome-shaped and covered with layer upon layer of dried grass.

Each wife has her own mud hut, with a bed for her and her children. There is also a second bed in each hut for the husband, who will circulate round his wives. When the children are three to four years old they move into another hut. The beds are constructed of a wooden frame, straddled with an animal hide. Alternatively some Maasai sleep on the earthen floor.

Male Circumcision

The main Maasai celebrations are: birth, circumcision, the election of leaders and funerals.

Circumcision is the most important ritual conducted in Maasai society. This is when a boy becomes a man, entering the adult world of the morans or warrior class and earning the respect of the Maasai. Circumcision is known as *emurata* and takes place every seven years. Each seven-year period is given a name and boys who are circumcised together are known to each other as age mates. Within each age group there will be a nominated leader under which there are junior leaders. They hold these positions of authority throughout their lives.

Young boys who are not circumcised are known as layonis and are of low status, having a life of hard, manual labour. They are well disciplined and respectful of their elders, only speaking when spoken to. When they meet an elder they bow their heads in respect so that the elder can place his hand on their scalp. The layoni is well-informed and knowledgeable about Maasai beliefs, culture and traditions.

The process begins with the elders asking the boys if they are ready to be circumcised. If agreement is reached, preparations to make beer (*anaiho*) from honey, sugar and water commence. After fermenting for three days the roots of the aloe plant are added and the process of fermentation continues for another two weeks.

On the afternoon before the day of circumcision the warriors commence dancing and singing with the boys who are due to be circumcised and this continues on into the night.

On the morning of the circumcision the boys' heads are shaved and the morans take them out into the bush and wash them down with cold water. This process is known as *engare endolu*. The boys return to their homes in silence and are greeted at the entrance to the *boma* (livestock enclosure), by the witch doctor. The boys are circumcised one at time. The boys are then escorted to the tea house and put to bed, where they drink a cocktail of blood and milk to revive them. A dedicated moran is in attendance for the next 7-14 days while the boys recover. If a boy refuses to be circumcised, it will result in him being bullied, tormented and ridiculed for the rest of his life. They are not allowed to be circumcised in a hospital under modern medical conditions, neither are they allowed any form of pain relief. Many are quite ill after the procedure has taken place and need to resort to a course of antibiotics to clear up any infections.

The boys post-circumcision are known as *skolio* and will spend the next seven to twelve months in small groups, visiting each other's manyattas. They wear black cloth,

paint their faces black with white stripes and adorn their hair with feathers. Boys who were particularly brave during the circumcision process are allowed to wear head dresses made from ostrich or eagle feathers as a symbol of their bravery.

After this period another celebration takes place. The skolio becomes a junior moran and is allowed to grow his hair long, plaiting it into braids and smearing it with ochre and fat. He is also allowed to wear the traditional red cloth (*shuka*), which he drapes around his body. The morans from the preceding age group now become senior morans.

The boys progress after circumcision through a hierarchy of grades starting out initially as junior warriors, and progressing to senior warriors, junior elders and later senior elders. Senior elders are allowed to make the decisions that affect the whole tribe. In Maasai society each group lasts for about 15 years and each has unique responsibilities and codes of dress.

Female Circumcision

Female circumcision, or female genital mutilation as it is now commonly called, is illegal but still takes place in certain locations. It is believed that carrying out this procedure will reduce promiscuity and make child birth easier. Circumcision involves the partial or total removal of the female external genitalia. It is carried out by either an older woman or a female witch doctor, without anaesthetic. Female circumcision can lead to a lifetime of health problems and in some cases can be fatal.

When the circumcision is complete the two morans will hand the girl their spears as a signal that the process is finished and that she must now get up. The two morans then join in the dancing outside, and the girl must come out of the hut and hand the two spears back. She then returns to the hut to recover for a period of up to four months. Celebrations continue through the night. During the recovery period the newly circumcised girls are dressed in black and are referred to as *eskolio*. When they are fully recovered, which can take between seven to twelve months, they are referred to as *esingiki*, after which they can get married.

Maasai women are easily identified by their shaven heads, bright clothing and beads, and the removal of one of the bottom teeth.

Trivia

♦Long hair is a sign of beauty in a man and a shaven head is a sign of beauty in a woman.

♦Male and female Maasai pierce and stretch their earlobes. Long earlobes and cuts on the sides of the face of a woman are a sign of beauty. The tops and sides of the ears on both sexes may also be pierced and have metal rings inserted.

♦Milk obtained from the cows is separated into three lots: one is drunk as fresh milk, another is mixed with cow's blood and another is left to go sour.

♦Wood ash and cow's urine are used to sterilise the calabash in which cow's blood is collected.

♦The Maasai use dried cow dung as fuel for their fires.

♦A wonderful Maasai Cultural Museum is located at Meserani Snakepark, just outside Arusha, and is highly recommended for an insight into the Maasai culture. You are also welcome to hire one of the Masaai guides there to take you on a visit to a traditional Maasai home. www.meseranisnakepark.com

Going on Safari. Useful advice and guidance

We are experienced independent travellers, having gained a wealth of experience on our travels to Tanzania over the last 18 years. Spending several months each year in Tanzania has given us an insight into the many issues that going on safaris and game drives can present. We have experienced many adventures, some quite challenging, but all truly memorable, and have met some amazing people along the way who we now call our friends. We feel that our experiences now allow us to offer advice and guidance to those who wish to share the enjoyment and pleasure that the wildlife of Tanzania can offer.

The wildlife that you are going in search of while on safari are not restricted to the parks and reserves. The animals are free to move in and out of parks and reserves as they please in search of food, water and a mate, so always be on the lookout for photographic opportunities - and be mindful of personal safety!

Safari companies

If you have paid a safari company to take you on safari, insist that you have an experienced driver, that the vehicle has working seat belts and that the brakes have been checked very recently. If the driver is driving too fast and you feel uncomfortable, instruct the driver to slow down. There are an abundance of safari companies in Tanzania, and it is true to say that 'you get what you pay for'. We would strongly advise that you use

the best that you can afford, and if booking directly yourself then take the advice of other travellers, or publications such as Lonely Planet and Rough Guides. If you are in Arusha, the base for most safari companies, you can visit the Tanzania Tourist Board Tourist Information Centre, on Boma Road, and ask them to check that your safari company is not on their 'blacklist' of tour companies.

Entry requirements for Parks and Reserves

Parks and reserves have designated times when you are allowed to enter and leave. Generally, visitors are allowed in after 6.00 a.m. but must leave before 7.00 p.m. (check at the main gate where you enter). Passes for the parks and reserves are valid for 24 hours, but be aware that some passes become invalid once you exit through one of the gates, which means that you cannot return even if it is within your 24 hour period - you may have to pay for another pass, or pay a reduced fee to re-enter.

Check what the procedures are for buying an entrance pass as these change regularly, often with little advance notice.

When you have obtained a pass, keep it safe - you will be expected to show it to officials and rangers at any time within the park/reserve.

Maps and Navigation

A map of the park/reserve is essential for self-drive safaris. It also adds to the enjoyment of the visit if you are a passenger. Buy the map at your earliest opportunity, which may be the campsite shop, hotel/lodge shop or a recognised bookshop in the nearest town. Do not rely on buying a map at the main gate as they may have sold out, and the parks/reserves can be very difficult to navigate if you do not know where you are - it is so easy to get lost! The map should have details of the main tracks to be used in the dry and wet seasons, with supporting information/diagrams about the wildlife and flora.

Much has changed since we first started going on safari in 2003, when many of us had the original mobile 'phones that were used for texting and calls and not much else. There are now some excellent, free, off line GPS apps that you can download onto your smart phone, as well as more sophisticated ones that need to be paid for. MAPS.ME in particular is the one we favour, and not just because it is free! The map of Tanzania needs to be downloaded before you set off from home, whilst you have access to the internet, and it is also worth making yourself familiar with how the app functions and bookmarking places that you intend visiting. The app can plan your route, and gives you lots of invaluable information about the areas you are travelling through. Road signs in Tanzania are usually absent, so the app is useful for navigating your way through major cities and remote areas, safely getting you where you want to be. We were pleasantly surprised to discover that MAPS.ME has detailed maps of the parks we have visited, showing all of the major tracks and many of the minor ones. It is worth bookmarking places of interest as you travel round the park, and certainly book mark where you are staying in the park, just in case you get lost. The app also gives you your precise GPS setting, which you will need if you break down and someone is coming to your aid. The what3words app is also worth downloading onto your phone as back up, as this too gives you and the rescue services a precise location.

A power bank is a must for charging your 'phone and torch whilst travelling in Tanzania.

Self-drive safaris

Always listen to, and adhere to the advice of the guides and park/reserve rangers. If you are an independent traveller and you come across a guide or ranger, ask them where the animals have been sighted that day.

If you are driving a self-drive hire vehicle and you have hired a guide, make sure the guide sits in the front seat of the vehicle with you. The guide is there to spot the animals and is not the back seat passenger. Do not be precious about who hired the vehicle and who sits where. This is about getting the best out of the safari experience. It is also important that you engage with the guide. Ask questions.

You need to be patient, alert and vigilant at all times. You may have to wait a long time before you see anything, but when you do it is well worth the wait. Turn the vehicle's engine off and just enjoy the moment for as long as you want. Sheer bliss. An experienced safari enthusiast understands that it is all luck as to what you see on safari. It is nobody's fault if you do not see any of the wildlife on your wish list, so do not give the guide or yourself a hard time.

It is strictly forbidden to leave the main tracks and go off-road while in most parks and reserves. If you are caught doing so you may be asked to leave, and may even face a fine. If your driver does this in an effort to get closer to the wildlife, politely but firmly remind him of the rules.

Do not speed while in the park/reserve - ascertain what the limit is before entering. Speed limits are there in order to avoid harassing, stressing or harming the animals.

The terrain can be extremely treacherous, so treat it with respect. The roads are uneven and have numerous potholes, it is so easy to have an accident and overturn a vehicle. Be careful when driving through water, in muddy areas or across salt flats - you may get stuck and need towing out. This may cost! This is not an environment in which to have an accident or break down. You technically cannot get out of the vehicle while in a park/reserve, and if you do, you could be at high risk of being injured by the animals.

Make sure that you have your vehicle hire company's contact details on your mobile 'phone, and that the battery is fully charged. Make sure if you are relying on your own mobile 'phone that your network has a reliable connection in Tanzania. Alternatively, you can buy a SIM card in Tanzania very cheaply, and load on a bundle that includes internet and call time.

Your vehicle is like a hide, and in Tanzania the animals are generally extremely tolerant and dismissive of vehicles and you actually feel as though they cannot see you. This gives a false sense of security, and you must remain in your vehicle at all times, unless advised otherwise. Do not hang out of the windows of the vehicle to get closer to the animals or to get a better photographic opportunity. The animals can recognise the human form and can sprint into action with amazing speed.

In some parks/reserves you are allowed out at toilet spots, picnic spots or viewing points. One such picnic spot worth mentioning is the Ngoitokitok Spring Picnic Site in the Ngorongoro Crater. You are allowed out of the vehicle to toilet, stretch your legs and eat lunch. But beware, if you eat outside the safety of your vehicle you may be relieved of your lunch (and your fingers) by the birds of prey who regularly swoop down on unsuspecting tourists.

Do not be tempted to approach river banks or lakesides on foot, to dip your feet in the shallow waters or go for a swim to cool down. This is the natural habitat for crocodiles and hippos, you may not see them but they most certainly will see you.

Always carry plenty of bottled water with you. Firearms are strictly forbidden in parks/reserves. Drones are not permitted in Tanzania's national park and game reserves.

Respect the Environment
The main gate clearly displays the rules and regulations that you have to observe while in the park/reserve. They are also written on the back of the ticket/pass as a reminder. Like the Country Code that operates in U.K. national parks, you are asked to respect the environment by not smoking, not leaving any litter, food, cigarette ends behind, not lighting fires or removing any plant material, animals, soil or rocks.

Respect the Wildlife
The animals seen on safari are in their natural habitat - they are wild, highly dangerous and unpredictable. On sighting an animal, switch off the vehicle's engine so that you do not to disturb or influence their behaviour, and keep your distance. A minimum of 20m and maximum five vehicles is  recommended so as not to cause the animals any distress. Be considerate of other visitors in the park when travelling round the park and when observing the animals at close quarters. They too have paid a considerable amount of money to go on safari to see the wildlife.

When in close proximity to the animals avoid sudden movements that may startle and alarm them. Do not make any noises or gesticulate to gain their attention. The majority of the animals have excellent hearing, so keep noise to absolute minimum. Talk quietly among yourselves and in some instances use sign language as a form of communication. Turn off any mobile 'phones and any devices that have start up jingles.

If the animals are moving about, they have the right of way so do not obstruct them, allow them freedom of passage. It is particularly important not to get between a mother and her offspring. Females are very protective towards their offspring and are generally more nervous, agitated and aggressive.

It is amazing how close you can get to the animals, either in your vehicle or at picnic sites. Do not touch the animals as they will most likely strike back. Children should be kept in check and told not to shout, torment or tease the animals.

Feeding the animals is strictly forbidden, because they begin to associate humans with food and this can cause obvious problems - baboons in particular are notorious for this. Similarly, do not leave food or the remains of food around campsites, on verandas or window ledges, or inside the tent, as this encourages the animals to come into close contact with you. Leaving crumbs of food inside your tent attracts ants that are difficult to get rid of.

In tented lodges it is a good idea to take your own padlock and key to secure the zip. Baboons and vervet monkeys can easily unzip a tent and wreak havoc searching for food. In the vicinity of monkeys or baboons it is advisable to lock the doors of the vehicle (whether or not you are in it) as they are more than able to manipulate the door handle and get inside.

A powerful LED torch with a long range beam is extremely useful when camping, and is vital for checking the bush for wildlife if you need to go to the toilet in the middle of the night.

Walking Safaris

Walking safaris and trekking holidays are becoming increasing popular with tourists, and can either be pre-booked or booked when you arrive at your accommodation. Whatever you choose to do make sure you have the correct clothing and equipment with you, and that you are physically fit for such an undertaking. You are in a challenging, hostile, Inhospitable, and unforgiving environment, presenting many dangerous possibilities. If you are not physically fit and able to walk at a decent pace, you can ruin a walking safari both for yourself and anyone else in the group. You can also put yourself and other people at risk.

You will be under the guidance and supervision of a guide. You must listen and adhere to the advice of the guide at all times. Any deviation can put yourself or others in danger. Tanzania has an amazing and vast array of dangerous animals. Animals are hard to track and find, so be patient. Be patient with your guide. Walk quietly behind the guide through the bush and keep talking to an absolute minimum. Walking is usually in single file, and you must keep close to the person in front of you. Be observant and aware of your surroundings, use your senses - sight and hearing - all of the time.

As soon as you are walking in the bush, look around you, especially where there is dense vegetation, which is a prime place for the animals to rest in the midday sun when it is hot. Areas with restricted visibility should be avoided as should steep-sided valleys, gullies, river beds and deep, steep-sided dense reed beds where you can become trapped with no escape route.

Animals are only aggressive if threatened, startled or provoked. If you do come face to face with an animal or a snake in the bush do not move. This will take a lot of nerve, but animals and snakes do associate anything that moves as prey. Keep still until they have moved on. Smiling and showing teeth is a sign of aggression, direct eye contact is challenging, and sudden movement indicates attack. Animals are especially dangerous during the mating season, when they are physically mating or where young are present.

Be careful when observing predators stalking prey or when they are feeding. Do not approach wounded animals, if they are traumatised they will behave and respond accordingly.

Whatever safari you choose to go on it is one big adventure that not many people get to experience. Enjoy!

Responsible Tourism

Tourism is the world's largest industry and employs one in ten people. It relies heavily on human mobility as it brings in much needed cash into local economies, facilitating the largest transfer of money from rich to poor. Developing countries such as Tanzania need tourism. Most tourists who visit Tanzania do so for three reasons, to climb Mt. Kilimanjaro, to go on safari, and to visit the Island of Zanzibar. However, the biggest attractions are the safari opportunities offered by the iconic Serengeti and the Ngorongoro Crater.

Responsible tourism is becoming increasingly critical to us all, and no more so than in Tanzania. This whole subject warrants an entire book in itself, such is the importance to our planet and its inhabitants, but let us summarise some of the actions you can take should you be visiting Tanzania.

Game drives. There are regulations in place in all national parks and conservancies, aimed at preventing disturbance and harm to the wildlife. Unfortunately not all driver/guides adhere to these regulations, and this may well be due to the pressure to keep their clients happy. It is vital that you politely but firmly insist that your guide follows all regulations, and avoids harming the wildlife. This is particularly important regarding keeping to designated tracks and not driving off-road, keeping the required distance from wildlife, keeping to the stipulated speed limit and not exceeding the maximum number of vehicles at a wildlife sighting.

Night time game drives are becoming increasingly popular, and are now allowed in many private conservancies and sanctuaries. The attraction for the tourist is that you may see nocturnal wildlife not seen on daytime game drives, and there is also the possibility of seeing predators actively hunting. However, be mindful of the fact that nocturnal wildlife can be significantly disturbed and distressed when being chased by noisy vehicles with powerful searchlights interrupting their nocturnal hunting. There needs to be some consideration as to how unnatural, harmful and intrusive they can be.

Wildlife Conservancies. Unfortunately there are not as many conservancies in Tanzania as there are in many neighbouring countries. However, it is always worth exploring the possibility of visiting one, and many of them offer cultural and conservation experiences as well as wildlife projects.

Water. Water is essential for not only the survival of visitors, but also the people of Tanzania, and the conservation of water should always be a priority. If your hotel or lodge offers you the facility of an actual bath in your room, maybe you would consider only using a shower instead. It goes without saying that standing in a shower for an excessive amount of time is unnecessary.

Recycling. There is little or no recycling in Tanzania, so there are a number of actions that you should consider.

Take your own robust water bottle, and ask your guide if this can be filled from their safe water source, rather than using drinking water supplied to you in plastic bottles. Plastic bottles are becoming an increasing problem in Tanzania. You may wish to contact your travel company beforehand and ask them if they provide this facility - pressure from us may well persuade them to do this.

Anything that you have with you and would normally recycle back home should not be left in a trash bin in Tanzania, as it will not be recycled. If it is at all possible, take it back home with you and you can recycle it then - typical examples are used batteries and aerosol cans.

If you have any items of clothing that you do not intend to take home, do not throw them away. A really useful solution would be to give the clothing to general staff at your hotel or camp - they will be really appreciative of your gift.

Back home many of us have mobile 'phones and laptops that have been replaced by updated versions, and they are hidden away and forgotten in cupboards and drawers. Assuming that they still work, why not 'wipe them clean', and take them with you to Tanzania - there are endless opportunities to gift them to worthy recipients. You could ask your driver/guide to stop off at a government school, and you could donate the laptop to the school - make sure it has Windows and Microsoft Office loaded on, and that all your personal files have been removed (including the Recycle Bin.) It is worth checking that the school is a government school or a school run by a charity, as these schools really do struggle to obtain resources such as laptops. Your unwanted mobile 'phones can be given to workers at your hotel/lodge - they will be able to make personal use of them, or give them to family members.

Engaging with charitable projects. Most visitors to Tanzania are there to enjoy wildlife safaris, and the thought of engaging with a charity project never enters their heads - such work may be considered to be the domain of volunteers and 'do gooders'. However, you do not need to commit to anything onerous, why not just experience and share in some of the good work that is going on? The experience will be heart warming, and very probably heart wrenching, with huge emotional impacts.

Again, you can either do your own research, or ask your tour company to include something of specific interest to you in your itinerary. If your itinerary takes you past Meserani Snakepark, that iconic symbol of everything good in Tanzania, you could call

in and ask if you could be taken to any of the schools supported by The Meserani Project, or maybe even meet some of the families and individuals that have been supported by the project. It is here that you could donate unwanted laptops, mobile 'phones or unwanted clothing. Just ask for someone from the management of the park. The Meserani Project has its own section in this book.

Volunteering

Doing voluntary work in a developing country is popular amongst young people, and certainly generates the feel-good factor. There are many websites that offer opportunities to buy a 'package' that includes voluntary work in a school or project. Be aware that many of the packages that appear to be offered by charities or voluntary organisations are actually put together by commercial tour companies, and most if not all of what you pay goes to the company. We have been made aware of many negative experiences, and we would advise people to do their homework before making a financial commitment. Our best advice would be that you speak to previous participants. Several of our U.K. students who have travelled to Tanzania with us have returned at a later date, having booked a package where they believed they would be doing voluntary work for a charity working in schools. The packages they booked were for several months, and cost them several thousand pounds. After the initial induction they were almost abandoned, given very poor accommodation in unsafe areas, placed in schools with no support and no one available who can speak English, and literally 'left to get on with it'. Others have paid money to go and paint a school, only to discover that it had just been painted by a previous group of volunteers.

We do not want to advise against engaging in voluntary work, just be careful when doing your research. Check the full and exact details of what is being offered, the full costs, and most important of all ask to be put in touch with previous participants.

Gifts and donations. If you do wish to take gifts for people that you meet on your itinerary, please think carefully about what they should be. As mentioned previously, unwanted laptops, mobile 'phones and clothing are ideal gifts to donate to individuals that you meet, to schools and to charitable organisations such as The Meserani Project, but other suggestions could be:

Exercise books. Pens. Pencils. Mathematical sets. Shoes. Sports Shoes. These are all items that will be of practical use, will not be thrown away, and will therefore not be damaging the environment. Any items that could possibly be thrown away, and would be damaging to the environment should not be given as gifts.

Please avoid giving anything at all to children who are clearly begging - by offering items to child beggars you are teaching them that begging is a more profitable alternative to attending school!

Cultural experiences.

Engaging in cultural experiences and supporting the local community is a great way to 'give something back' to the country and people who have provided you with such amazing safari experiences. Activities can include village walks, low level mountain walking, bicycle safaris, visiting plantations, visiting local homes and villages, spending time with local artists and engaging with the indigenous people. The list is endless. It is extremely rewarding to engage with the local people and show a genuine interest in them and their way of life. We found it very humbling once when at the end of a guided bush walk the guide thanked us for talking to him. He explained that the majority of tourists do not asked questions about the wild life, they only want to take photographs and move on.

Support local people selling goods.

Do not purchase goods that exploit or threaten wildlife and their habitats. Bargaining is the expected norm, but please do it respectfully and be aware that language can lead to misunderstandings. We once witnessed an embarrassing incident in a campsite bar where a tourist insisted that a local woman in a small gift shop had given her a necklace as a gift. The lady came to ask for her money and the tourist flatly refused to pay, insisting it was a gift. The tourist just walked away feeling good about having 'won'.

Use of Electricity

Use electrical devices and the main supply sparingly, and do not leave lights on unnecessarily. The national electricity grid in Tanzania is erratic and can be turned off at any moment. Campsites may have their own generators, these are expensive to run and can easily be overloaded through tourists using devices such as hair driers.

The Mosquito
(Culicidae)
Swahili: Mbu

The mosquito is reputed to be the deadliest "animal" on the planet. Apart from transmitting the malaria parasite that is believed to kill up to one million people each year, it also transmits and infects its hosts with dengue fever, chikungunya, Zika fever, filariasis, West Nile virus and yellow fever. These are all deadly, harmful diseases which if untreated can be fatal.

Mosquitoes are widespread and are found throughout the tropics and temperate regions in close proximity to water.

The mosquito has a head, thorax and abdomen. There are six spindly legs and two wings that are attached to the thorax. It has two large compound eyes, two antennae and a long proboscis.

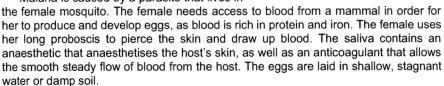

Malaria is caused by a parasite that lives in the female mosquito. The female needs access to blood from a mammal in order for her to produce and develop eggs, as blood is rich in protein and iron. The female uses her long proboscis to pierce the skin and draw up blood. The saliva contains an anaesthetic that anaesthetises the host's skin, as well as an anticoagulant that allows the smooth steady flow of blood from the host. The eggs are laid in shallow, stagnant water or damp soil.

The female mosquito lives up to three weeks. In her short life she lays up to 300 eggs, three times before she dies.

The male mosquito lives up to 10 days.

The signs and symptoms of malaria can start within seven days after having been bitten and infected, and include the following: high temperature, chills, sweating, headache, vomiting, diarrhoea, fatigue, muscular aches and pains. The parasite can lie dormant for up to one year after having been bitten. Seek medical advice immediately if you become unwell after you have visited an area where the disease is found. Untreated, malaria can be fatal.

A practice nurse and pharmacist will advise on the appropriate anti-malarial medication. Malaria medication should be kept on your person at all times. No malarial medication is 100% effective, so take the following precautions:

◆Reduce the amount of skin exposed to mosquitoes by covering up from dusk to dawn - wear long trousers that go below the ankle, socks that go above the ankle, shoes (not sandals) and long-sleeved tops with a high neckline.

◆Clothing should be loose fitting and made from fabric with a close, tight weave.

◆Some outdoor clothing can be bought that is impregnated with a mosquito repellent.

◆Use a good insect repellent containing 50% DEET and apply regularly between dusk and dawn when mosquitoes and other insects are most active. The guides or locals will inform you if mosquitoes or tsetse flies are present. DEET comes either as a lotion, roll-on or spray. Spray-on DEET is useful if you have to apply this quickly, but make sure you do not inhale the spray.

◆Permethrin spray containing DEET is also useful for clothes and inside tents/rented rooms, as are plug-in insect vaporisers.

◆Always use mosquito nets when provided, and make sure they are tucked underneath the bed.

♦Do not leave lights on unnecessarily as they attract mosquitoes and other insects.

♦Do not wear perfume, skin lotions or aftershave as these attract mosquitoes and other insects.

It is believed that global warming will dramatically increase the number of mosquitoes and their geographic range.

Malaria Trivia

♦There are over 3,000 species of mosquito, and they transmit more diseases than any other creature on earth.

♦Ninety per cent of all deaths from malaria occur in Africa.

♦Malaria is the world's second biggest killer after tuberculosis and HIV/AIDS.

♦Malaria has been with humanity for over 500,000 years, and it is believed to have been responsible for 50% of the deaths of people who have ever lived on the earth.

♦Animals do not get malaria.

♦It is said that mosquitoes have a preference for biting people who wear the colour blue, have just eaten a banana, have just drunk alcohol or have smelly feet. They are also more likely to be attracted to a pregnant woman in preference to a non-pregnant one.

♦It is a myth that taking vitamin B, eating garlic and the use of ultrasonic devices will protect you from malaria.

♦It is believed that Alexander the Great died from malaria in 323BC.

The Tsetse Fly
(*Glossina*)
Swaheli: *Mbung'o*

The Tsetse fly, a large biting fly found in sub Saharan Africa, is the major cause of poverty in the majority of the debt ridden, underdeveloped countries on this continent. The tsetse fly transmits the sleeping sickness parasite to animals and humans.

Sleeping sickness in domestic animals, on which the rural population are dependent for a living, has a devastating effect. They either die, or if they survive, they produce little milk, frequently abort the unborn calf and are unable to pull a plough. It is impossible for people to make a living in a tsetse fly infested location. Robbed of their livelihood, the local population are forced to move on. This results in overgrazing and overuse of land for food production.

The tsetse fly by default preserves vast tracts of land for wild life to thrive on, undisturbed. It is the best, unpaid game keeper in Africa.

The tsetse fly has a head, thorax and wide abdomen. It has two large separate eyes, two antennae and a long proboscis. The thorax is grey in colour. Six legs and two wings are attached to the large thorax. When resting, the wings are folded and rest on top of each other.

The tsetse fly lives in woodlands where there is dense vegetation, and on the banks of rivers and lakes. They shelter in dense thickets at the hottest time of the day. They are attracted to moving vehicles, and it is not just one individual tsetse fly that enters the vehicle, but a cluster. They are noisy, and fly fast and erratically around the inside of the vehicle. Their bite is painful, and can produce swelling around the affected part which can spread and last several days. You certainly know when you have been bitten by a tsetse fly.

The female mates once in her life, produces an egg every nine days and lives up to four months. The fertilised egg develops into a larva inside her body. She deposits the larva on the ground, where it burrows into the soil, emerging several weeks later as an adult tsetse fly.

Males live two to three weeks.

The tsetse fly infects its victim by biting and transmitting the trypanosomiasis parasite in its regurgitated saliva into subcutaneous tissue. Entering the blood stream, the parasite makes its way via the central nervous system towards the brain. Sleeping sickness needs to be diagnosed and treatment initiated promptly in the early stages of the disease. The initial symptoms of sleeping sickness are headache, muscular aches and pains and intermittent high fever. As the disease progresses distinct symptoms appear - sleep disturbance, changes in personality, mental impairment, seizures and coma. There is only one eventual outcome if left untreated - death.

There are currently no vaccines or prophylactics available to prevent sleeping sickness. The only thing you can do is to deter and prevent the tsetse fly from biting you. The same rules apply as those recommended for mosquito bites. Having been bitten on numerous occasions by tsetse flies we would question the effectiveness of insect repellents and our personal recommendations are:

♦Listen to, and follow the advice of the guide. The guide will be experienced and will know when you have entered a tsetse fly infected area. You may be advised to close the windows and roof hatch of the vehicle.

♦Wear clothing made from medium-weight fabric as the tsetse fly is able to bite through light-weight fabric.

♦Wear shoes that fully cover the foot. Ankle boots are a good idea.

♦Wear slouch socks that you can concertina round the ankle and provide further protection.

♦Tuck trousers into socks. Tsetse flies are very adept at flying up trousers legs. You will not know they are there until they have bitten you.

♦Do not wear skirts or shorts.

♦Wear long sleeved shirts with snug fitting cuffs.

♦Wearing a hoody is a good option.

♦Wear a long scarf that can be wrapped round the neck many times. This can also be wrapped around the head and face if necessary.

Trivia

♦The tsetse fly is also known as the poverty fly.

♦Tsetse flies are tough and very difficult to kill with a household fly swatter.

♦Male tsetse flies are attracted to humans, and females to animals.

Clothing

Going on safari is exciting, exhilarating and one enormous adventure. For many this will be a once in a lifetime holiday and for others who get the bug, the start of a lifelong relationship with Tanzania. Regardless of whether you are staying in a luxury safari lodge, a tented camp site or actually camping in the bush, your safari will be expensive - probably your most expensive holiday ever.

Having spent so much of your hard-earned cash on a safari, you would not want to risk anything going wrong, and choosing the correct clothing is something that warrants careful consideration. Climatic conditions, exposure to the elements, environmental hazards, the lack of facilities, personal safety, personal hygiene and cultural respect require some thought with regard to the type of clothing that can be worn in environments that will certainly be new and testing for you.

If you have booked your safari through a tour operator they will give you some advice on the type of clothing to be worn, but this is often cursory and superficial. It is worth thinking carefully about the type of clothing to be worn, as inappropriate clothing may well detract from what should be a pleasurable experience. Your clothes may need to be worn for several days without an opportunity to wash them, lack of facilities such as the availability of water (some lodges, guest houses and campsites will actually fine you for using water to wash clothes), the length of stay (which may not allow enough time for clothing to dry out), and luggage allowance (particularly on internal flights), may dictate the amount of clothing you can carry with you.

Do not wear expensive "fashionable" clothing when you are on safari as a combination of dust, perspiration, sun tan lotion, aftersun and insect repellents will soon discolour and spoil the fabric. If you intend to walk about in the cities, towns and villages do not wear new, expensive fashionable clothing or jewellery as this immediately draws attention to yourself - the perception is that you are a wealthy tourist on holiday. It is far better to wear old clothes that fully cover the arms and legs and allow you to blend in with the locals.

Clothes should be neutral (khaki coloured) and blend in with the background when you are on game drives or walking safaris. Brightly coloured clothing is easily detected by the animals that are out in the bush searching for prey. You put yourself and others at risk. A responsible safari guide can refuse to take you out in the bush if appropriately coloured clothing is not worn.

Avoid wearing blue in areas where tsetse flies are present, as it is believed they are attracted to this colour.

Cheap and functional safari type clothing can be bought on local market stalls, in some of the \of the larger high street stores and online. Outdoor pursuit shops that specialise in outdoor clothing are worth investigating, but do tend to be expensive unless items are on special offer. If you have planned your safari well in advance you should have time to shop around for the best deals.

The major outdoor clothing manufacturers invest huge amounts of time and money in researching and developing high tech, high performance fabrics designed to cope with every environment you can imagine. The more properties a fabric incorporates the more it will cost. Be quite clear exactly what function you want the fabrics and the clothes to fulfil. What is important to you? What would spoil the safari experience for you?

The properties the fabrics may have are:

♦Stain resistant and water repellent. It is impossible to keep clothes clean on a safari, unless you close all your vehicle windows and turn on the air-conditioning - in which case you will probably miss most of the animals! Once you open the windows and viewing hatch you will soon be covered in dust, so fabrics that are stain resistant are a good idea. Depending on the time of year you may experience torrential rain, or if you are up early in the morning or walking through rain forests then clothing can get wet from the dew on the plants. You may be some time and distance away from your accommodation and will not have the opportunity to change clothes.

♦Thermal insulation. Despite being close to the equator Tanzania can be surprisingly cool at altitude, when there is overhead cloud cover, at dusk, dawn and during the night, particularly during the long dry season from June to October.

♦High temperatures during the middle of the day will cause the body to perspire and the increased wetness of the skin will add to bodily discomfort. Clothing made from natural fibres are not advisable as they retain moisture, can be chilly and cause skin chafing. Fibres with high wicking properties that draw moisture away from the body will add to bodily comfort.

♦Odour-resistant fibres impregnated with silver are effective in retarding and destroying microbes responsible for bodily odours - a significant problem when water for washing and personal hygiene may be scarce.

♦Clothes with sun-protective fibres that afford protection from the sun's harmful rays should be considered. The sun is extremely fierce in Tanzania, and a combination

of altitude, cloud cover and low temperatures can be deceiving and lull you into a false sense of security. Do not underestimate how quickly the sun can burn and damage the skin.

♦Fast drying, minimum-iron fabrics allow more frequent changes of clothes.

♦Fibres impregnated with permanent insect repellents are highly effective against mosquitoes that spread malaria.

If you are buying new clothing, try them on before purchasing. You may be wearing them for several days so make sure they fit properly and are comfortable.

Clothing needs to:

♦Be lightweight and easily packed.

♦Be practical, comfortable and allow freedom of movement.

♦Have multiple zipped pockets for securing valuables (passports, cash and bank cards).

Suggested clothing

♦Safari jackets are recommended simply because of the number of pockets they have.

♦A warm fleece jacket is essential for the cold evenings.

♦A scarf to wrap round your head and neck to keep you warm on an evening or to protect you from the mosquitoes and tsetse flies.

♦Long trousers are a must for evenings and early mornings when the mosquitoes are most active, if they unzip and transform into shorts then even better as they can be used during the day time. Multiple pockets with zips are needed to secure valuables and are more difficult for pickpockets to access. Long trousers should be worn when bush walking as they offer some degree of protection from sharp thorns, grasses that are razor sharp and from snake bites. Eighty per cent of venomous snake bites are to the lower leg, almost all of which occur at the ankle level. Trousers should go over the ankle.

♦If you are in a tsetse fly infested area wear clothing made from medium weight fabric as the tsetse fly is able bite through light weight fabrics.

♦Shorts with multiple zipped pockets.

♦Long-sleeved tops are required from dusk until dawn when the mosquitoes are active. Tops with a zipped up neck and cuffs will further deter these unwelcome visitors. It is possible to buy shirts with sleeves that roll up and are held in place by a buttoned flap, or that completely unzip from the body of the shirt.

♦Socks that cover the ankles for use on an evening.

♦Wear slouch socks that you can concertina round the ankle. This provides additional protection if you are in a tsetse fly infested area. These should be worn all of the time.

♦Wear shoes that fully cover the foot. Ankle boots are a good idea. Tsetse flies can bite through socks. Their bite is extremely painful.

♦Trainers or sandals for inside your safari vehicle, in lodges and in campsites, but do not wear sandals in the evening or if you are walking in the bush. The ground can be littered with small seed heads with hooks on that embed themselves in your skin and are painful and difficult to remove.

♦A wide-brimmed hat or peaked cap to protect the eyes.

♦A good pair of sunglasses that block 100% ultraviolet light.

♦Thermals or pyjamas are necessary when camping in the long dry season when it is particularly cool at night.

Insider Tips

Although outside the scope of this book, it would be remiss of us not to share with you some of the personal experiences that have enhanced our safaris in Tanzania over the years.

Meserani Snakepark

Our number one recommendation - no trip to Tanzania would be the same without a visit to Meserani Snakepark. Originally a campsite set up on dry, arid scrubland just outside Arusha by a couple from South Africa, this has developed into a quite amazing compound offering so much for local and international visitors alike. Barry and Lynn Bale, (known to worldwide travellers as BJ and Ma), bought the land back in 1993 and through careful planting and much hard work they have developed it into what can only be described as a true oasis in the desert.

Within their compound there is:

♦A campsite, used mostly by independent travellers and overland truck groups. Without doubt it is the favourite campsite of any group that we take to East Africa, and a personal favourite of ours.

♦One of the most atmospheric bars in Tanzania, with memorabilia dating back to the 1990s.

♦A Maasai Culture Museum (an absolute must - the number of local schools who take their children there is testament to the quality of the experience).

♦The Meserani Snakepark Clinic. Recognised as the best place in Tanzania for snakebite treatment, this clinic offers free health care for the local inhabitants, and is funded entirely by profits from the bar at the campsite, and donations from supporters.

♦A comprehensive collection of reptiles (including Egyptian spitting cobras, black mambas and Nile crocodiles).

♦Snakes and crocodiles that you can actually handle yourself.

♦Camel rides, that can take you to a local Maasai village upon request.

However, what is so very special about BJ and Ma is the way that they have dedicated their lives to helping the local Maasai population - they provide free emergency healthcare in their medical centre (including expensive anti-snake venom), an orphanage, support for local schools, and they provide employment and self-help opportunities for many of the local population. BJ and Ma are indeed true saints and legends, and it was with great sadness in April 2020 when we heard that BJ had finally succumbed to a long battle with cancer - he quite simply was the most amazing man we have ever met in our worldwide travels.

www.meseranisnakepark.com

Cultural Tourism Programmes

Cultural Tourism Programmes (CTPs) are probably the best idea to hit Tanzania in recent years, and we strongly recommend that you take time to book some sort of itinerary with one of the many local organisations that exist throughout the traditional safari tourism areas.

The first CTP originated in 1995 and the basic idea was that when tourists had completed their safari and the safari companies had relieved them of their hard-earned cash, then the safari company would add on an activity provided by local people that involved cultural experiences and traditional activities. These activities were relatively inexpensive when compared with safari costs and the money paid went directly to the local people who provided the experience.

A typical example would be a half-day village walk and banana beer brewery visit, or an overnight stay in a Maasai village. Over the years these visits have become increasingly successful, not only through the income they generated for local people, but also because many tourists found that they enjoyed their 'cultural experience' more than the actual safari. As a result CTPs have been set up in more and more locations, and with an increased diversity of experiences offered.

Although we strongly recommend that any visitor to Tanzania books some type of activity with a Cultural Tourism Programme, we have to offer the obligatory word of caution with regard to the possibility of being ripped off - while it is sad that we have to warn of this, the underlying factor is that money is far too powerful in Tanzania and temptation is often difficult to avoid, even if you are a genuine and hard-working local inhabitant. However, the vast majority of CTPs are genuine, honest, excellent value for money and can provide you with truly meaningful and life-enhancing experiences.

If we were to recommend any activities in particular, then top of the list would be a four-day Crater Highlands Trek starting at Nainokanoka and finishing at Engerasero. En route you visit the Empakaai Crater, the slopes of Ol Doinyo Lengai (an active volcano) and one night is spent camping at the infamous Acacia Bush Camp - the most remote and desolate place on earth we have ever spent a night at. Your camping equipment and food are carried by donkeys and you are accompanied throughout by a Maasai donkey handler and an armed ranger. An easier option, but just as memorable, is a four-day hike through the lush and verdant West Usambara Mountains, starting and finishing at Lushoto. You are accompanied by a local guide, with accommodation and food being provided by local villagers. Our final recommendation, and the easiest in terms of physical effort, is a half-day walk through the sugar plantations of Mgaba in the South Pare Mountains. A local villager will take you for a leisurely stroll through the valley, where you will see life as it really is in this remote part of Tanzania, and you can even meet a real witchdoctor.

www.tanzaniaculturaltourism.com

Ndutu

Ndutu is part of the Ngorongoro Conservation area, but is often visited as part of a safari package to the Serengeti. Whilst the Ndutu area includes the Ngorongoro Crater, and is adjacent to the Serengeti, it is worth spending a few days here to enjoy the wildlife that can be found, but timing is crucial. If you visit Ndutu between December and March, you should be fortunate enough to witness an abundance of wildlife. It is at this time that the world famous migration is present in the Ndutu area, more particularly so in February when the wildebeest herds are calving. Although there is much less to see from April to December, the area is still

worth visiting as a peaceful and reclusive retreat from the mass tourism of the
Serengeti and Ngorongoro Crater.

West Usambara Mountains

Previously recommended in the section on
Cultural Tourism Programmes as a superb area
for easy-level trekking, the Usambara Mountains
are quite exceptional as a place just to visit and
experience a contrast in culture and climate.
Often quoted as the most friendly area of
Tanzania, it is also the most densely populated,
and because the mountain climate is so different
to that of the plains below, you will experience a
way of life that is seen by few visitors to Tanzania.
The town of Soni should be your first port of call,
and a stay at Maweni Farm is recommended.
Lushoto is the largest town in the Usambaras, and
it is here that the highly recommended Cultural
Tourism Programme is based. If you can handle
the surreal architecture of Irente View Cliff Lodge,
then you will certainly be impressed as you stand on the precipice of Irente Viewpoint
and watch the early morning mist rise up out of the Rift Valley.

Tarangire National Park

One of the national parks normally visited as
part of the 'Northern Circuit' of parks in Tanzania,
Tarangire is often missed out in the shorter safari
itineraries in favour of the Serengeti and the
Ngorongoro Crater. This is good news for those
who do seek out this delightful park because you
see more wildlife than Land Rovers, and not vice
versa as is too often the case in the more popular
parks. Tarangire has an abundant elephant
population, and is the ideal place to just sit and
watch how they behave. We are forever intrigued
by the way they interact with each other, and also
how they interact with their physical environment
- in Tarangire you have the chance to actually
witness it all on your own and not in a convoy of
four-wheel vehicles. Your travel company will
have selected your accommodation for you, but if you do have any say in the matter
then we would recommend Tarangire Safari Lodge - although expensive, it is probably

the cheapest lodge in the park, and
the views from the communal terrace
and from your static tent are worth
every penny.

DIY 'Self-Drive' Safaris

Organising a safari trip on your
own, which would involve hiring a self-
drive vehicle and being self-sufficient
inside a national park, is something
that we would not recommend unless
you are very experienced and
extremely confident. While it is

actually the only way that we ourselves now wish to travel in Tanzania, it presents many potential hazards, and unless you know exactly what you are doing, you are putting your personal safety under unnecessary risk. Make sure you are in possession of your passport and driving licence at all times, and be aware that speed cameras are increasingly used in Tanzania.

If you do ever embark on putting your own self-drive safari together, the most important piece of advice we can offer is that you hire a reliable four-wheel-drive vehicle, with a company that is capable of responding appropriately should you need assistance. We ourselves have always used Fortes Safaris, Arusha, and have had no complaints. We have only needed urgent assistance on a couple of occasions, and the response from Fortes certainly exceeded our expectations.

Kupenda Africa

If you do wish to avoid joining the mass tourism bandwagon and actually organise your own visit to East Africa, but would like the safety net of someone else taking on the responsibility of putting your itinerary together, then put yourself in the hands of Jason Smith of *Kupenda Africa*. Jason is from the U.K., and runs his own travel company based in Kenya, providing group, family and individual trips to Africa. He
specialises in Tanzania, and we cannot recommend him highly enough. When we take groups of students and adults on overland expeditions to Tanzania ourselves, we would not dream of using anyone else to cater for our specific requirements while we are there, whether it be the use of his overland truck, taking us on safari, or introducing us to further unique and meaningful experiences. Although Jason offers incredible value for money, the main incentive behind letting him look after you is his passion for the people of Tanzania - he will take you to places that the big companies do not bother with, and he will introduce you to experiences that will not necessarily increase his profit margin, but will make you fall in love with Tanzania - its landscape, its wildlife and its people. Take a look at his website, and feel free to get in touch with him to see what he can do for you.

www.kupendaafrica.com

South Pare Mountains

Previously recommended in the section on Cultural Tourism Programmes, the South Pare Mountains are much more remote and sparsely populated than the Usumbara Mountains, and as such they can offer something quite unique for the adventurous visitor. It is a forested area, with hidden villages and valleys, and you can visit wonderful homesteads perched on steep handmade terraces. The area is renowned for its history of witchcraft, and if you take advantage of the cultural tourism offerings, you can get an insight into this unusual practice.

Mbaga is the best place to use as a base for trekking and cultural visits, and if you are happy with basic but authentic accommodation, you can stay at Hilltop Tona Lodge.

Monduli Mountains

The Monduli Mountains are seldom visited, yet are only a thirty minute drive from the road that takes hundreds of tourists each day from Arusha to the Serengeti. The town of Monduli is a refreshing contrast from Arusha - calm, peaceful, civilised, green, and overlooked by the verdant Monduli mountain range. Because of the fertile soil, and the abundance of water, the town of Monduli is a centre for coffee production, and there are many coffee plantations on the slopes

of Monduli mountain. A guided walk around the coffee plantations is an easy and pleasant experience, and highly recommended. For the more hardy and adventurous you could book a guided trek on Monduli mountain itself, and there is every chance that you could see some wildlife - maybe even elephants. If your guide or travel company are not able to book you something in Monduli, call in at the Tourist Office on Boma Road, Arusha.

Guidebooks

Our constant companion when we first began to plan our visits to Tanzania, and the initial inspiration for many of our adventures, are the *Rough Guide* and *Lonely Planet* guidebooks.

After sharing our East African 'treasures' with you, some words of caution - all based on our own personal experiences.

Choosing a safari company

If you have booked a package deal with a tour company then the choice of safari company is beyond your control. However, if you find yourself in a position where you are booking a safari direct with a company, then it is a potential minefield. The ubiquitous warnings about tourists being ripped off by bogus companies and 'budget safaris' should be well heeded.

A whole section of this book could be devoted to providing advice on how to avoid being ripped off, but we would simply be regurgitating the advice offered in the *Rough Guide* and *Lonely Planet* guidebooks, so we are strongly recommending that you read one of these publications and follow its advice.

We ourselves once booked a Crater Highlands Trek through a company highly recommended in travel guides. The company had a superb website, and everything seemed in order right up to the day when we had arranged to hand over a substantial cash deposit to their representative in Arusha. We took the advice offered in the guidebooks and popped into the Tourist Office on Boma Road, Arusha, just to check the company out - were we glad that we did this! Our email contact with the company had been hijacked and we had actually been communicating with someone who had been systematically relieving tourists of their cash, and then disappearing into thin air. The Tourist Office were quite matter-of-fact about telling us, simply reinforcing to us how commonplace this problem is.

Park fees

On an organised safari arranged by your tour company your park fees are paid for you by the safari company, but if you have actually booked the safari yourself make sure that the guide does pay in full all park fees at the park entrance - it is not unknown for the guide to underpay and this could cause you immense problems if your paperwork is checked by park representatives while you are inside the park.

If you are on a self-drive safari then you would be wise to check out the small print on park fees on the relevant park website. Make sure you know what you are paying for, and if you are travelling with children or students, look carefully for the appropriate discounts. In Tanzania national parks, once you have paid your 24-hour fee you are allowed to leave the park (for cheaper overnight accommodation), and then return the next morning to complete your full 24 hours.

Personal safety
Some areas of Tanzania can be quite dangerous, for many different reasons. There are inherent dangers with regard to local crime, the environment and wild animals - you should actively seek the advice of your guide at all times.

Local transport
Using local transport is, in our opinion, the most hazardous component of any itinerary in Tanzania. Serious traffic accidents are commonplace and we witness them frequently. The ubiquitous *daladalas* (minibuses that ply local routes) have a very poor safety record, are poorly maintained and overloaded, and local authorities do not appear to regulate their use. The large coaches that connect the major towns, and drive at

breakneck speed irrespective of whatever is going on around them also have a poor safety record. If you do need to travel independently, then the shuttle buses that connect Nairobi to Arusha and Moshi are probably your best option. One of the most popular ones is Impala Shuttle - we use them every time we travel between Kenya and Tanzania and have never had any problems.

When to go
People usually travel to Tanzania to go on safari in the dry seasons, which are either December - March (short dry season) or July - October (long dry season). Avoid March - June (long rainy season) as the roads can become treacherous and impassable. The short dry season is very hot and can be uncomfortable, especially during the night when you need to be covered up to stop the mosquitoes biting you. The long dry season is much cooler and comfortable but can get quite cold in a tent during the night. However, when you go is entirely up to you and may be dictated by budget. A further point of consideration is that climate change is certainly affecting the weather in Tanzania, and seasons are becoming unpredictable.

Souvenirs
While on safari you will get the opportunity to visit the curio shops en route. Be aware that those visited as part of a safari package tend to be very expensive. You

may wish to negotiate with your guide to visit the local curio markets or street markets instead, engage in some serious bartering and have lots of fun. You will also be helping the local economy.

Tipping

Your guides, drivers and cooks will be paid a wage by the safari company, but this is more often than not very low. The safari company will usually tell you that you are expected to pay the driver/guide something in the region of $8-10 per guest per day for a group guide, $15-20 for a private guide, $5-10 for a safari chef and $1-2 for general staff. This may come as a shock, particularly if you are on a lengthy trip, and you may not have budgeted appropriately. However, if you are in a large group, then you would need to discuss these amounts amongst yourselves. The problem is that because these people are generally paid such low wages by the safari companies, and work is usually seasonal, they really do rely heavily on tips to supplement their income. Your response to this predicament is a matter of your own choice, but if you do feel obliged to pay a tip, reject any pressure to give more than would be sensible and adequate.

Money

Only buy new US Dollars - notes more than 10 years old may not be accepted in Tanzania because of fraud/counterfeit money.

Do not be tempted to exchange currency with locals, particularly those who harass you as you cross the border. Despite the favourable exchange rates you may be buying counterfeit money, and being in possession of this could land you in jail.

At the time of publication, all contact details and other information above was known to be correct, but may change with time.

The Meserani Project

We are donating all proceeds from the sale of this book to The Meserani Project - indeed, this project was a major inspirational factor when the idea behind writing our first book on African wildlife first crossed our minds.

The Meserani Project is a registered charity, but is still regarded as a 'homegrown' project, set up by a secondary school in the heart of Middlesbrough, an urban town in the industrialised north-east of England, and now run by a small number of volunteers from Teesside and North Yorkshire.

It all began in August 2004 when a group of pupils from Acklam Grange School became involved in some of the most impoverished schools in Tanzania and Kenya as part of a three-week overland camping expedition. Emotions overspilled when the pupils visited Lesiraa Primary School, in the Meserani district of Tanzania, and were confronted with wooden shacks that were literally falling apart, a complete lack of sanitation and a desperate shortage of even the most basic of educational resources such as pens and exercise books. What affected the pupils most however, were the wonderful and natural smiles that greeted us from every child - despite their desperate situation. The pupils felt that they could not simply walk away and turn their back on Lesiraa School, so vowed to set up a project when they returned to school in Middlesbrough, dedicated to making some sort of change at Lesiraa. The Lesiraa Project was created, and following further school trips involving Acklam Grange pupils, it evolved into The Meserani Project and was registered with the U.K. Charities Commission in 2009. The rest, as they say, is history.

The most noteworthy achievements to date as regards practical resources that have been provided are:

14 classrooms in four primary schools, 31 water tanks for 6 schools, a dormitory for a girls' boarding school, solar power for two schools and a clinic, water harvesting systems for a primary school and a clinic, renovated four teachers' homes at a primary school, beds for 116 pupils at two secondary boarding schools, 80 desks and chairs for a boys' secondary school, 70 desks and chairs for a primary school, laptops and projectors for a Vocational Training Centre, laptops and projectors for an Adult Learning Centre, whiteboards for three secondary schools and a Vocational Training

Centre, 300 trees in two primary schools, a photocopier and printer for a girls' secondary school, a generator and TV/video player for three secondary schools.

Apart from all these practical/resource achievements, the main focus of the project now is our involvement in sponsoring young people in the remote Meserani district of Tanzania to go through secondary school, further education and university. Without such sponsorship, these young people would have received no education beyond primary school. The statistics at the time of publication are:

268 young people have been sponsored throughout various stages of their education. 261 pupils have attended one of seven secondary schools that we have links with. 84 students have started their two years of A' Level studies. 13 students have started their two year Vocational Training Courses. 15 students have started Certificate and Diploma Courses at College or University. 24 students have started their three year Degree courses at university.

A further development of the project is to host groups of school pupils, groups of adults, families and teachers, who spend time in Tanzania supporting the work of The Meserani Project as volunteers, and at their own expense.

Because the project is run at their own expense by a group of six trustees from Teesside and North Yorkshire, and there are no administrative costs at all, every penny that is raised is spent directly on the project in Tanzania - nothing at all is syphoned off as necessary expenses. By purchasing our book, you have contributed to the work of the project, and we thank you for that.

www.meseraniproject.co.uk

Glossary

Altitude	Height above sea level.
Antlers	Bony protuberances that have a branch like structure on the front of the skull, and are shed annually.
Aorta	Main major artery that carries blood away from the heart.
Asphyxiation	To lose consciousness due to lack of oxygen.
Arboreal	Tree dwelling. Spends the majority of life living in the trees, only coming to the ground on rare occasions.
Arid	Dry, desert environment with little or no rain.
Biome	An extremely large ecosystem.
Browser	Animals that feed mainly on leaves, but will eat twigs from low lying branches of trees and bushes.
Bulk grazers	Animals that are not selective about which grasses they eat.
Buoyancy	The ability to float or rise in water.
Caldera	Collapsed volcano.
Canid	Mammal belonging to the dog family.
Carcass	The dead body of an animal.
Carnivore	Meat-eating animal or bird.
Carrion	Dead, rotting flesh.
Caste system	A complex organisation made up of different social classes, who all perform different duties to the mutual benefit of the whole group.
Climate	Average weather conditions.
Cloven-hoofed or even-toed ungulate	A hoof that splits into two or four toes (antelope, hippopotamus, giraffe, warthog).
Cognitive	Ability to acquire knowledge and reason.
Cold-blooded	Cold-blooded creatures are unable to generate their own body heat. Their body temperature is regulated by the temperature of the surrounding environment.
Conservation dependent	Dependent on conservation efforts to prevent it from becoming threatened with extinction.
Contagious	A transmissible disease that is passed on by contact.
Crepuscular	Primarily active at dusk and dawn.
Cud	Partly digested food that an animal regurgitates back into its mouth to continue chewing.
Deforestation	A forested area that has been cleared by humans causing permanent damage to the ecosystem.
Degradation	Deterioration of the environment. Depletion of resources. Destruction of ecosystems.
Desert	Annual rainfall is less than 25cm. Deserts may be hot or cold.
Desertification	When the climate of a dry region becomes even drier. The vegetation dies and is eaten by grazing animals, leaving the soil vulnerable to the effects of erosion.
Diurnal	Active during the day and resting at night.
Dorsal	On the back.
Dorsum	Back of the body.
Drought	Shortage of water.
Ecosystem	A community of plants, animals and people that interact with the climate and soil.
Endangered	At serious risk of extinction.
Equid	Member of the horse family.

Estivate	A period of dormancy similar to hibernation, but takes place when temperatures are high and conditions are dry.
Eviscerate	To disembowel - removal of internal organs/entrails.
Extinct volcano	A volcano that has erupted in the past but will not erupt again.
Faeces	Dung, excrement.
Family	An extended family that consists of the breeding pair, the latest litter, previous litter and adolescents.
Fauna	Animals that live within an ecosystem.
Female philopatry	A social system where the female remains in the group or home range in which they were born.
Fledge	To leave the nest.
Forage	Search for food.
Frugivore	An animal that thrives on raw fruit, roots, shoots and seeds.
Gazelle	A small antelope renowned for its beauty, elegance, gracefulness, agility and speed.
Gestation	The process of foetal development in the womb.
Grazer	Grazers feed only on grass on the ground.
Habituated	Accustomed to/used to.
Haemorrhaging	Prolific, intense bleeding.
Harem	A group of mammals that consists of one dominant male and a harem of females. The size of the harem varies from species to species.
Herbivore	Plant eater.
Hierarchy	A system where there is a graded order.
Horns	A permanent bony protuberance.
Hydrophobia	Fear of water.
IUCN	International Union for the Conservation of Nature
Infanticide	The act of killing the young/offspring.
Infectious	A disease that is passed on without contact.
Infrasonic	Sound that is extremely low pitched and cannot be detected by the human ear.
Insectivore	A plant or animal that eats insects.
Iteroparous	Offspring are produced by more than one female and are incubated in one clutch.
Invertebrate	Does not possess a backbone.
Involuntarily	Automatically, spontaneously, unconsciously.
Keratin	Fibrous substance found in hair, nails, feathers and hooves.
Laterite	Soil that is highly weathered. The soil bakes in the sun and forms a hardened crust.
Latrine	Toilet.
Nocturnal	Active at twilight and throughout the night.
Nomadic	Migratory, moving from place to place.
Matriarch	Dominant female, usually the oldest and largest.
Midden	Dung heap. Informs intruders that the area is already occupied by an animal of the same species. An intruder entering the area is not welcome and may encounter aggressive behaviour. Occasionally they are tolerated if they remain subordinate and are not perceived as a threat.
Mixed feeders	Animals that graze and browse, feeding on a variety of vegetation.
Molar	A tooth, usually place at the back of the mouth, used for grinding and crushing food.

Monogamous	Only has one partner at a time. May form a breeding pair and may mate for life.
Montane Forest	Forest found at high altitude
Musth	State of heightened sexual excitement in large, male mammals, particularly elephants.
Myocarditis	Inflamed heart muscle.
Natal	Of or relating to birth.
Nilotic	Relating to the Nile River or inhabitants of the Nile region.
Nomad	A person who moves from place to place with no fixed abode.
Odd-toed ungulate	Odd toed ungulates have one or three toes.
Oestrus	Sexually receptive and fertile (female).
Old World	Refers to the Earth's eastern hemisphere and includes the continents of Africa, Asia, Australia and Europe.
Oligarchy	A complex social group dominated by one or more dominant males.
Omnivore	An animal that eats and digests vegetable and animal matter.
Orifice	Opening.
Ossified	Has changed into bone.
Oviparous	Eggs that are produced by the mother that hatch outside the body.
Ovoviviparous	A snake that produces soft eggs that break open at birth.
Parasite (Complete)	An animal or plant that lives in or on another animal or plant (host), and is totally dependent upon it for nutrients.
Parasite (Semi)	An animal or plant that lives in or on another animal or plant (host), and is partly dependent on it for nutrients.
Patriarchal	Male-dominated social structure.
Plain	A large area of flattened land.
Plasma	Clear fluid found in blood, which carries the platelets and red and white blood cells.
Platelet	A particle of blood necessary for clotting.
Polyandrous	Females having more than one male to mate with at one time.
Polygamous	Has more than one partner at the same time.
Polygon	Many sided figure.
Predator	An animal that kills and eats other animals.
Precipitation	Water that falls from the sky either as rain, snow, hail or sleet.
Prehensile	Has the ability to grasp an object.
Primate	A mammal with flexible hands and feet and a highly developed brain.
Raptor	A bird of prey.
Regurgitated	Partly digested food that is coughed up, usually to feed the young.
Ruminant	A mammal that chews its cud (goat, deer, cattle, giraffe, camel).
Rutting	Mating period (mammals).
Savanna(h)	Open grassland with scattered bushes or trees.
Scavenger	Feeds on the remains of plants or animals.
Scute	Horny or bony external plate or scale.
Selective grazers	Animals that eat specific grasses or plant matter.
Silicide	The death of an individual caused by close relatives.
Sibling	Brother or sister.
Solitary animals	Adult animals that remain alone, and only meet up to

	mate during the breeding season. Examples are snake, serval cat, leopard, black and white rhino and the caracal.
Species	Type of animal or plant. A population that can breed freely in and amongst themselves
Stereoscopic vision	The field of vision of each eye overlaps and enables the individual to judge distances.
Sub Sharan Africa	Area of the continent of Africa that lies below the Sahara.
Sub species	A population within a species that may have become geographically isolated, and takes on new unique characteristics. It is genetically similar to the species so it can still interbreed
Symbiotic	Two different species that benefit from living together.
Retractable	Ability to withdraw inwards.
Talon	The sharply hooked claw of a bird.
Tap root	The main root of a plant that goes downwards with offshoots that grow sideways.
Temperate climates	Do not experience great extremes in temperature.
Temporary associations	Animals that are not bonded to each other, usually leaderless and non-territorial.
Terrestrial	An animal that spends the majority of its life living on the land.
Territory	An area of land occupied by an animal or group of animals that do not share the resources with other animal of the same species.
Tropics	That part of the Earth that lies between the Tropic of Capricorn (23.5° south of the Equator) and the Tropic of Cancer (23.5° north of the Equator).
Ungulates	Mammals that have developed hooves to aid walking and running, instead of claws. Ungulates are terrestrial herbivores that graze on grass, seeds, leaves, fruit and herbs.
Vertebrate	Possesses a back bone.
Viviparous	Gives birth to live young.
Weaned	Has the ability to live on food, other than the mother's milk.
Xerophytic	Drought-resistant plant.

Acknowledgements

Putting this book together has been hard work; it has taken an incredible amount of time and has been one of the biggest challenge of our lives, but because it has involved our interaction with the people and animals of Tanzania it has been great fun as well. While researching and writing this book numerous people have helped us along the way by providing advice, information and guidance, and we would like to take this opportunity to acknowledge their contributions.

We are indebted to Chris Packham for taking time out of his busy schedule as a BBC Wildlife Presenter to write the foreword to the book.

The following people have either read and commented on our work, advised us, inspired us, or have sourced information for us:

Our dear friends BJ (deceased) and Ma - owners of Meserani Snake Park, Arusha, Tanzania, who have inspired and supported us throughout our journey whilst writing this book, encouraging us to push the boundaries, out in the bush, engaging with the wildlife and indigenous tribes.

Grace Kagwiria (deceased) and Jason Smith - owners of Kupenda Africa Travel Company, who introduced us to Africa and its people, and taught us the benefits of venturing off the beaten track for new and different wildlife and cultural experiences.

Griff Hosker - author, who gave us his time and instilled in us the confidence to go it alone publishing this book.

Loti Naparana - Senior Guide and Herpetologist at Meserani Snake Park, who has provided advice and factual support on the many minor, but important details about the wildlife of Tanzania.

Mike Riley - Sound Recordist, for introducing us to Chris Packham.

Zoe Wildsmith - Director, The Content Creation Company, who has given us her time, practical advice and support.

Plus of course, the numerous local guides whom we have had the pleasure of meeting on our travels out in the bush.

The Authors

Diane and Peter's first trip to Tanzania was in 2003 and happened by pure chance. They had intended to go to the U.S.A. for a very special holiday to celebrate their silver wedding, but then 9/11 happened and their plans changed. The U.S.A. was off the agenda and the decision to go on safari somewhere in Africa was agreed. A wonderful three weeks of safari experiences ensued, even though it was a 'package' holiday, with tour guides who looked after them, but made sure they did not see the real Africa and its people. At this time Diane and Peter did not know that this trip was to change their lives.

They now spend much of their time not only in Tanzania, but also other countries in Africa that provide genuine wildlife experiences. Tanzania is certainly the focus of their interest, and they have set up a project supporting education in a remote area of Tanzania, a project that is now a U.K. registered charity. They are both experienced at bush camping in the wild, and have trekked in many remote areas, sometimes using donkeys to transport their camping equipment on the longer expeditions.

Frustration with the usual travel guides motivated Diane to start writing her own wildlife guide. It was intended to be a factual, easy to read book, awash with colour, and one that would stimulate the reader's interest in African wildlife and the challenges they encounter. She has spent countless hours researching articles, contacting the wildlife experts for clarification on facts and data and pouring through all the wildlife photographs taken in Tanzania. Hopefully she has produced a book that engages the reader, that fires up their passion for wildlife, and encourages them to do something meaningful about protecting and conserving these defenceless animals and the environment. All photographs in this book have been taken by Diane and Peter, and are therefore a true reflection of what you may see on safari. Diane's ardent passion and enthusiasm for the wildlife of Tanzania has further expressed itself through the illustrations she has done for this book.

Peter independently leads and supports groups of students and adults, and independent visitors from the U.K., the U.S.A. and Russia on expeditions in the areas covered by the book, and has received several regional, national and international awards for the charity work he has undertaken in Tanzania.

Diane and Peter run a UK registered charity, The Meserani Project, which has supported deprived schools and children in Meserani, a remote area of Tanzania, since 2005. At the time of print the project has built and equipped fourteen classrooms at four primary schools, sponsored many pupils from these schools to go through secondary education, further education and university, provided buildings and resources to three secondary schools, and is currently supporting the building of a new secondary school in Meserani. All profits from the sale of this book will go directly to this charity.

Made in the USA
Monee, IL
19 May 2024